Bearing Witness

Abstraction is memory's most ardent enemy. It kills because it encourages distance, and often indifference. We must remind ourselves that the Holocaust was not six million. It was one, plus one, plus one. . . . Only in understanding that civilized people must defend the one, by one, by one . . . can the Holocaust, the incomprehensible, be given meaning.

—Judith Miller

Bearing Witness

TEACHING ABOUT THE HOLOCAUST

Beth Aviv Greenbaum

Boynton/Cook Publishers
HEINEMANN
Portsmouth, NH

Boynton /Cook Publishers, Inc.
A subsidiary of Reed Elsevier Inc.
361 Hanover Street
Portsmouth, NH 03801–3912
www.boyntoncook.com

Offices and agents throughout the world

© 2001 by Beth Aviv Greenbaum

The author and publisher wish to thank those who have generously given permission to reprint borrowed material:

"Things That Are Worse than Death" from *The Dead and the Living* by Sharon Olds. Copyright © 1983 by Sharon Olds. Reprinted by permission of Alfred A. Knopf, a Division of Random House, Inc.

"On Trail" and "Shema" from *Collected Poems* by Primo Levi translated by Ruth Feldman and Brian Swann. English translation copyright © 1988 by Ruth Feldman and Brian Swann. Reprinted by permission of Faber & Faber, Inc., an affiliate of Farrar, Straus and Giroux, LLC.

"O, the chimneys" from *O The Chimneys* by Nelly Sachs. Translation copyright © 1967, renewed 1995 by Farrar, Straus and Giroux, Inc. Reprinted by permission of Farrar, Straus and Giroux, LLC.

Library of Congress Cataloging-in-Publication Data
Greenbaum, Beth.
    Bearing witness: teaching about the Holocaust / Beth Greenbaum.
        p. cm.
    Includes bibliographical references (p. 183) and index.
    ISBN 0-86709-510-5
    1. Holocaust, Jewish (1939–1945)—Study and teaching. I. Title.

    D804.33 .G74 2001
    940.53'18'07—dc21   2001025901

Editor: William Varner
Production service: Lisa Garboski, bookworks
Production coordinator: Elizabeth Valway
Cover design: Joni Doherty
Cover photo: "Women and children on the ramp, immediately after their disembarkation from the train. On the right is one of the veteran inmates allocated to help the new comers." Copyright © 2001 Yad Vashem The Holocaust Martyrs' and Heroes' Remembrance Authority.
Manufacturing: Louise Richardson

Printed in the United States of America on acid-free paper
05 04 03 02 01   VP   1 2 3 4 5

For Eli

Contents

FOREWORD		ix
ACKNOWLEDGMENTS		xiii
INTRODUCTION: A FINGERNAIL'S WORTH		xv
1	In the Beginning	1
2	Poetry of Witness	7
3	Hate: Racism, Prejudice, Anti-Semitism, and Dehumanization	21
4	Taking a Stand	38
5	The Ghettos	53
6	Resisting	73
7	The Master Race	86
8	The Camps, Part I: Night	100
9	The Camps, Part II: Survival in Auschwitz	112
10	The Camps, Part III: The Women	134

11   On Forgiving   150

12   Aftermath   157

APPENDIXES   173
GLOSSARY   181
WORKS CITED   183
INDEX   189

Foreword

In the world of the slave labor and death camps, at a time in history when most prior assumptions had to be discarded, conventional laws were abrogated, truth was perverted, and precepts of a civilized society were turned upside down. Those who were condemned to live and suffer under that heinous oppression clung to one searing desire. It centered on the overriding hope that somehow, whether they survived or not, word of these unspeakable events would make its way through barbed wire and out of sight of the watchtowers to reach what remained of civilization on the outside. As we now know, there was at least fragmentary knowledge by that outside world during the years of the Holocaust, and that what there was, elicited only feeble action and, in most cases, a total absence of it. The victims were to find out that the only constant they could rely on was the brutality of their tormentors, in the course of days that seemed more as though a permanent night had settled in. All of that only if they were "lucky" enough to stay alive for the moment.

By and large, the world stood by in inaction, if not indifference, while the machinery of death was allowed to grind on relentlessly. To the victims it seemed inconceivable that this barbarism was devised and implemented by the countrymen of some of the world's greatest poets, writers, and composers of whom they were so immensely proud. It made a mockery of the enlightenment that their *Kultur* had contributed to the world.

Since those tragic events, we have learned in ever-increasing volume much of what transpired then, although I fear that what I have called "the unfathomable, giving rise to the ineffable," may always prevent us from gaining a complete understanding of that bestial regression into the dark ages.

Nevertheless, it is balm on old wounds to see what Beth Greenbaum has done in her classroom to bring the reality and immensity of those events to her students. *Bearing Witness* is as comprehensive a curriculum for teaching the Holocaust as we have ever come across. Availing herself of every medium, from the written word, to film, to plays, to poems, she has compiled the starkest, the most powerful and relevant material that was recorded during and after those nightmare years. It ranges from firsthand accounts and works by eminent writers and filmmakers that have become classics of that canon, to the most wrenching recollections by "ordinary" men and women to have reached us from the abyss.

What is most striking about Beth Greenbaum's method of teaching is that she is not content to merely present the facts to her students, but manages to engage them until they literally walk in the shoes of the victims, and to some extent in those of the perpetrators. Lengthy discussions follow the presentation of the material, and by challenging her students to face the moral dilemmas the victims were confronted with almost daily, she brings as much reality to the events as is possible from this distance in time and location. The effectiveness of her teaching is evidenced in the countless perceptive reactions on the part of her students, be it in their verbal analyses or in the essays they are compelled to write. It seems that no one leaves her course without an entirely different perspective on that world that was than when they began those sessions. In one instance, she is able to drive home the immensity of that loss and waste of human potential by pointing out that of the 900 victims Oskar Schindler and his wife, Emilie, saved, there are today 6000 people alive due to that isolated act of compassion alone. How many scientists, thinkers, physicians, and others were among the millions who perished and who could have contributed to the welfare of humanity?

The author asks many probing questions in unsparing detail that defy facile answers, thereby greatly heightening the awareness of her students. There are lengthy analyses of books, plays, and films and an exhaustive list of those sources, as well as relevant Web sites that all contribute to a better understanding of what transpired during that era of torment. She is careful not to provide simple answers to the complexity of history and points out that it is one thing to denounce such acts of inhumanity, but quite another to oppose them, making clear that "neutrality always aids the aggressor." In that connection, she is realistic about our possible inability of preventing genocide in the future.

Beth Greenbaum skillfully brings better understanding of the Holocaust by linking those events to issues her students may be facing in their own lives. The course explains much of what preceded the Holocaust, as well as the shattering reality of its aftermath. Above all, Ms. Greenbaum expects her students to discern and analyze the symptoms of hatred and bigotry that ultimately can lead to genocide. After all, that is our only hope of preventing a recurrence of such gratuitous acts of cruelty. At the same time, apprehending it will provide a moral compass for any endeavor we, along with her students, may pursue in life. A study of this epoch will show them the universality of such a threat to human existence.

The book is meant to present a range of themes, locales, and time periods that will give a comprehensive overview to the reader. The focus is on six major works of Holocaust literature: *The Diary of Anne Frank* and *Night,* by Elie Wiesel; *Survival in Auschwitz,* by Primo Levi; Arthur Miller's stage play, *Incident at Vichy;* Art Spiegelman's graphic depiction of his parents' experiences during those years, Incident at Vichy, *Maus I;* and finally, *The Sunflower,* by Simon Wiesenthal. Each deals with a different aspect of the Holocaust experience and leads to a host of searching questions during the discussions that follow in which students take on the voices of victims, of bystanders, and of perpetrators. In the course of it, they are exposed to a complete spectrum of human response, from the basest man can inflict, to the noblest he or she can achieve. It shows, for example, how, under those surreal circumstances, suicide might be considered a form of resistance and an escape from a "fate worse than death."

Although her own course extends over a full semester, Ms. Greenbaum suggests a variety of alternate Holocaust curricula, containing material that fits the time constraints others may encounter. The book is an invaluable contribution to the preservation of those annals, especially significant because of the limited time left to survivors to refute the words of those who would deny the Holocaust. It was with great foresight that General Dwight D. Eisenhower, after inspecting the horror of the camps our troops liberated in April 1945, wrote these words, engraved on the face of the United States Holocaust Museum, in Washington, DC:

> The things I saw beggar description. . . . The visual evidence and verbal testimony of starvation, cruelty and bestiality were overpowering. I made this visit deliberately, in order to be in a position to give first-hand evidence of these things, if ever in the future there develops a tendency to charge these allegations merely to "propaganda."

Beth Greenbaum has given expression and fulfillment to the most ardent wish of all those who prayed that the world should know what was being perpetrated on them, at a time when it was nearly futile to pray for survival. In doing so, she is paying tribute to the memory of the martyrs and doing full justice to the admonition "Zachor," or "Always Remember."

Gerda Weissmann Klein
Kurt Klein

Acknowledgments

I wish to acknowledge first and foremost, my students at Groves High School, without whom this book would not be possible. I thank them for their generosity in conversation and writing. I gratefully thank my colleague, Lindy Bruton, who taught Holocaust Literature at Groves before I did and who passed on to me her library of books and videos as well as the anthology of narratives, poetry, and short stories she'd compiled. I thank the Birmingham Public Schools for their vision and compassion in making Holocaust Literature a semester-long English course. I thank the Holocaust Memorial Center in West Bloomfield with doors open to its library and collections and speakers. And I want to thank all the writers and filmmakers whose words have helped me make some sense of the effect of the Third Reich's horrid policies. I thank Bill Varner for his vision for this book and for guiding me through its writing. And I thank my husband who supports wholeheartedly my endeavors and encouraged me to work part time so I could write.

Introduction:
A Fingernail's Worth

Heritage Ablaze (watercolor by Alyssa Schefman)   This painting,
Heritage Ablaze, symbolized the effect of the Holocaust from one generation to the next. The ring was a gift to my grandmother from her
older sister who perished in the Holocaust. It is the only physical arti-
fact that my grandmother had of her sister. My grandmother cherished
this ring and passed it to my mother, who in turn passed it along to
me. The unusual stone in the ring changes color in certain lights or
atmospheres. I like to think that my great aunt's spirit shines through
the ring.   Alyssa Schefman

Anne Frank's diary introduced me to what happened to Jews during World War II. In the 1950s and early 1960s, it had no name. Only an unspeakable horror, a sense that had I been a child growing up in Germany or Holland—or anywhere in Europe for that matter—I, too, would have had to hide.

In fourth grade I wrote a paper titled, "If Hitler Won the War." The paper was about how, if Hitler had been victorious, he would have enslaved America and killed its Jews. Even at nine years old I imagined the horror of Hitler's power. When William Shirer's *The Rise and Fall of the Third Reich* came out, I read the pages that described what happened to the Jews. Of 1,245 pages, only 48 were about the camps. If it could happen then, it could happen again.

Though I was a Jewish girl growing up in an assimilated city and school, the meager literature available about what was then referred to as "the concentration camps" frightened me and made me feel grateful that I lived in America, a place where that could not happen.

I first heard the term *Shoah* and its English equivalent, "Holocaust" in Israel in l972. In Hebrew, *Shoah* means conflagration, fire, holocaust. I had arrived just before *Yom HaShoah,* or Day of the Holocaust, a day that began with the sounding of sirens throughout the country, a minute of silence when all cars, trucks, buses, workers, pedestrians, tractors stopped. Israel was founded upon the ashes of the Holocaust.

I read Elie Wiesel's *Night* and I learned what Anne Frank could not tell because Anne did not survive long enough to write *that* book; Wiesel told what it was like to live in Auschwitz; he shed some light on what it must have been like for my mother-in-law who had also lived in Auschwitz. And then I understood something more about her son, who cried out in his sleep because he dreamed of men in jackboots chasing him.

I asked my husband's Aunt Este, who was visiting from Israel, if she was willing to tell us what happened to her—and to my children's grandmother—during the war. She answered, "I could talk and talk for weeks without stopping and tell you only a fingernail's worth."

We sat in the backyard on a hot summer's day and Este told us how she had gotten false papers just the day before her village in Hungary was evacuated; how returning with the papers, she saw German soldiers ransacking the house; how Este returned to stay with her parents and was deported with her parents. (Her younger sister, my mother-in-law, was taken with another transport.)

Este told us how she was lucky, and how her older sister was not. At Auschwitz, the men were separated from the women. When Este, her mother, and her older sisters and were waiting in line to be "selected," a prisoner said to Este, "Give the baby to its mother. You're too young to die." Este handed her nephew to her sister and they were sent to the "left," to the gas and crematoria; Este was sent to the right. When she tried to join her sister and nephew and mother, a guard hit her over her head. She fell, and when she came to, her family was gone and she entered Auschwitz—to the "right."

There was so much more that she couldn't tell. And so I read—and tried to discover what happened to my ex-husband's aunt and mother—and to millions of other Jews who lived in Europe when civilization lost its bearings. Over the years I have read the literature of what has come to be known as "The Holocaust." I read to understand, to know what had happened. If there were any ulterior motive, it was to understand my young husband and his mother, and after we were divorced, to understand the darkness he had lived in and slept in. I had no intention of teaching Holocaust literature. The topic was entirely too painful to take for a whole semester at a time.

Seven years ago, however, John, the English department chair at Groves High School, found me sitting at a table overlooking a fishing harbor off the coast of Maine. I was watching lobstermen standing in their skiffs, paddling back to shore after hours on the ocean checking their traps for lobsters. The light played on the pastel boats and water. John had phoned to see if I would be willing to transfer from Seaholm High School where I was currently teaching, to come over to Groves High School—a mile down the road—to teach Holocaust Literature. Both schools are in the same public school district.

"No, I can't. It's too painful," I said. I didn't want to teach Holocaust Literature because I didn't want to be forced to teach the material of pain. I wasn't sure I wanted a semester entering and descending into the inferno, and focusing on and teaching horrors I would not be able to put out of my mind. I looked out at the calm waters, the boats bobbing by their buoys, the sunlight settling on the cubist houses on the opposite shore of the harbor, and felt relieved. Someone else could do it.

Three years later for personal reasons I transferred to Groves and was immediately assigned a section of Holocaust Literature, which I reluctantly accepted.

To me, the material is sacred. I am teaching about the annihilation of six million people, about what led to the deaths of someone's parents and siblings and aunts and uncles and cousins and children, of whole towns. When a student puts her head on her desk or looks out the window, I wonder if the material hurts too much, if it is a natural response to try to block and deny. And I wonder if, perhaps, the student is treating the material as another boring high school subject.

At Groves the response to taking a course in Holocaust Literature is overwhelming. The principal and the faculty see the course as an opportunity not only to teach history and literature, but also to teach the dire consequences of intolerance and hatred. Our school caters to a diverse population, and all facets of the student body enroll in Holocaust Literature: honors students and LRC (learning disabled) students; Chaldeans and Jews; Christians and atheists; Muslims and Hindus; Asian Americans and African Americans; Mayflower Caucasians, as well as East Indian, Middle Eastern, and Russian immigrants. In fact, Holocaust Literature is one of our most popular English electives; almost half the senior class of 300 students chooses to take a semester of Holocaust Literature.

A course like this exposes students to a literature that bears witness. As I read the texts with my students I try to keep in mind how the texts form perceptions of the Holocaust. How do we as teachers choose these texts and films? What do we want to know?

Daniel Schwarz says in *Imagining the Holocaust,*

> As the historical period of the Shoah recedes, imaginative literature will help keep those events alive. Do we not know more about the War of the Roses and the history of Britain from Shakespeare than from Holinshed's chronicles? If ever a past needs a human shape, it is the Holocaust; yet, as we shall see, putting a human shape on inhuman behavior challenges our ability to imagine evil and to represent it linguistically." (6)

How Does Holocaust Literature Fit into the Curriculum?

In 1969 when I was a freshman at the University of Michigan, my roommate raved about a new course: Afro-American History. I enrolled and was among the few white students. But if I wanted to study Jewish history or literature, I had to devise my own ways of studying it through existing classes. There were no courses that offered an opportunity to study specifically Jewish or Holocaust literature. In fact, there was no such thing then. Ethnic studies of the 1970s and 1980s (African American, Asian American, and Native American literature and history) made possible Jewish and Holocaust studies.

Today, at least twenty-four states mandate or recommend the teaching of the Holocaust in their public schools. The lessons promote tolerance and diversity as well as an exposure to the corrosive effects of hate. Often, mandating the teaching of the Holocaust is part of a larger initiative for civic and moral education in the schools (Novick, 259).

The first state to mandate Holocaust education was Florida. Governor Lawton Chiles said as he signed the law in 1994,

> The souls of those who perished in the Holocaust still cry out for justice, not through retribution, but through education and enlightenment—the truest enemies of tyranny and brutality. . . . Sadly, many students in our

schools have demonstrated an alarming and dangerous lack of knowledge about the millions of Jews and others who were slaughtered during the Nazi's reign. That must change—because the price of ignorance is simply too high. The bill I sign . . . acknowledges that the path to true enlightenment must include the darkened hallways of places like Auschwitz and Dachau. It is not an easy lesson—but one that must be learned anew. (Task Force)

The Florida law suggests that teaching the history of the Holocaust will lead to "an investigation of human behavior; an understanding of the ramifications of prejudice, racism and stereotyping; and an examination of what it means to be a responsible and respectful person for the purposes of encouraging tolerance of diversity in a pluralistic society and for nurturing and protecting democratic values and institutions . . ." (Task Force). Truly a big agenda.

Studying the Holocaust allows the survival of the texts—and therefore, the extinguished voices. In ways, Holocaust Literature resurrects the damned, the people whose voices were all but extinguished. Ironically, in the Jewish concept of death, we live on in the memories of the living. Perhaps through Holocaust studies we pay the greatest honor to the dead: we make them live.

A course in Holocaust Literature exposes, takes students into a Dante-esque descent into the hell created by human acts. In fact, by the third week of class, students often begin reporting Holocaust nightmares. They dream themselves into the camps and ghettos. The material invades their subconscious thoughts. They dream of being chased. Of being confined. Of starving. The readings and videos get to them.

One student wrote in her journal that while sunbathing in her yard on an unusually warm February day, she told her friend that she could no longer put on her mascara first thing in the morning because she knew it would run when she cried in her first period Holocaust class.

Studying the Holocaust is like putting the Holocaust into psychological treatment. We examine our worst nightmares. What do they signify? Where do they come from? How did they get into our psyche? What connects to them? What do we know that is like them? We strive to understand the underpinnings, the dark secrets that made the literature of the Holocaust. This enormous body of information cries for examination, begs us to make sense of it, to make meaning and find meaning in its facts and stories.

The course forces students to see—and perhaps experience—more than they would like. Ultimately, it forces students to learn that we are responsible for our decisions. To act or not to act. To see or not to see. Can we force students to see, to act? We may teach them about the role the bystander played—how by not taking a stand genocide was allowed to happen. Yet we deceive ourselves and our students if we think by teaching them to say "Never again" they will stop genocide and racism. We *have* let it happen again. And again. Since the Holocaust in the middle of the twentieth century, we have witnessed genocide in Cambodia, Rwanda, and Kosovo.

Philip Gourevitch, author of *We Wish to Inform You That Tomorrow We Will Be Killed with Our Families: Stories from Rwanda,* said in a National Public Radio interview with Terry Gross,

> We are all somewhat less safe than we'd like to imagine, not because we're all in immediate danger of being hacked up by our neighbors, but for fifty years, since the genocide convention was passed, and certainly, the way that the Holocaust which is sort of the defining genocide of modern consciousness has been remembered, there's an increasing tendency to interpose, "Never again," and "the world must oppose" on a somewhat facile level, which is to say we all stand opposed to genocide after it happens, but what Rwanda also shows is that the idea that we would act out of a sense of a common humanity to defend people before such a slaughter simply doesn't hold up.
>
> The world doesn't care to act in these situations—it holds back. . . . Denouncing evil and acting against that evil is not the same. . . . These are very complex political things that are taking place, and if one doesn't look at them as such and seek to unravel them, one is at a greater risk of falling prey to them. (Fresh Air)

Gourevitch's comments strongly suggest a need to study and unravel these atrocious events. He cautions us, however, not to expect we will learn too quickly to end them; despite our studying and our knowledge of the past, we have not yet been able to tame the murderous rages of men. We may like to preach "Never again," but how can we, when in the face of our lecturing in the last decade of the twentieth century we have witnessed genocide after genocide? Then what are our lessons? To educate ourselves not so that it won't happen again, but to be aware, to be able to make informed decisions in the world, to discuss the issues, to care. If our caring helps, even a little, we have done something.

Teaching Holocaust Literature

Teaching Holocaust Literature is not like teaching Shakespeare or Virginia Woolf. I cannot can stand in front of the room and say, I love this stuff. This is one of my favorite blah blah blah. No. This literature informs, allows us to know and to understand—in increments. The murder of the Jews of Europe was such a cataclysmic event that to understand it means examining the diverse strings of the braid, the various strands and weaves to see how they twist together.

There are so many different agendas regarding the teaching of Holocaust: to teach morality, to teach history, to teach stories so we don't forget. A teacher's job is to explore and expose. Above all, we need to let the literature speak for itself. A teacher's job is not to tell what to believe, but to help students find their way through the material, to help them form their own judgments and thoughts. "When we write—and read—about the Holocaust, we do so to arouse ourselves, to awaken our conscience, to keep our obligations to those who were lost, those who survived, and those of future generations" (Schwarz 3).

The United States Holocaust Memorial Museum provides guidelines for teaching the Holocaust on their website: *ushmm.org/education/guidelines .html.* The site offers very good methodological considerations, including not only a concise definition of the Holocaust, but also suggestions as to how to handle the material, such as avoiding comparisons of pain, avoiding simple answers to complex history, making careful distinctions about sources of information, striving for precision of language, avoiding stereotypes, translating statistics into people, and being sensitive to appropriate written and audio-visual content.

Their suggestions about incorporating the Holocaust into existing courses weigh in heavily on using the Holocaust to teach morality. "Because so many of the stories intersect with issues in students' own lives, Holocaust Literature can inspire a commitment to reject indifference to human suffering, and can instruct them about relevant social issues such as the effects of intolerance and elitism" (*ushmm.org*).

Holocaust Literature casts light into one of the darkest shadows in human history; it is good literature, worth reading not only because of the lessons it teaches, but because it reaches into the depths of human experience. The literature enlightens and engenders class discussion. The literature allows students to see and understand the effects of legalized intolerance, of legalized hatred.

In *Maus II*, Art Spiegelman's alter-ego, Artie, is asked by reporters after the success of *Maus I* to "Tell our viewers what message you want them to get from your book." Artie, who sits behind his drawing board in a flood of discarded paper, surrounded by cameras and microphones, asks, "A message? I dunno . . . I–I never thought of reducing it to a message. I mean, I wasn't trying to CONVINCE anybody of anything. I just wanted . . ." and he never gets to finish his sentence as more questions are hammered at him (42). A message? Can we reduce Holocaust literature to a message? There is so much to absorb.

Holocaust Literature invites students to see, to inform their thinking and believing. It asks students to grapple and come to terms—to think and to understand. I want students' answers to come from them as they surmise—as Keats on his peak in Darien—what all this means.

I want my students to appreciate the literature as it unfolds. I want them to grasp the immensity of the event and the range of human response as we move through and study together the literature of the Holocaust. We study Holocaust and read its literature to make sense of the senseless, to honor the survivors by honoring the memory of the lives of the victims and survivors.

How This Book Is Organized

Each chapter is designed to introduce a specific theme or period through readings, videos, discussions, and journal responses. The focus is on six major works of literature:

- *The Diary of Anne Frank*
- *Night*
- *Survival in Auschwitz*
- *Incident at Vichy*
- *Maus I*
- *The Sunflower*

These works are supported by additional readings and videos. Books and videos cited may be easily found at local libraries, video stores, Amazon.com, Borders.com, bn.com. or by typing the title into an Internet search engine. Because of the heavy video content and because there is so much need for discussion and debriefing, most of the assigned writing is done in journals for homework—though students tell me they appreciate my reserving class time for writing.

Journal assignments two or three times a week provide a way to process the material, to push the students to think, and to engender an honest, candid reaction to the material. Once a week students refine, polish, and type up a journal entry. This process forces them to assess their own writing and submit for a grade the piece which they most like, which they would most like to share with the teacher—and perhaps the class. This process also encourages students to revise into essay form writing that begins more informally. The entire journal is submitted for a grade twice per marking period.

The journal entries offer opportunities for narrative, descriptive, analytical, critical, and creative writing in response to literature, discussion and the issues raised. Several suggestions for more formal papers are also provided; in fact, most of the journal suggestions could lend themselves to more formal papers.

While the study of Holocaust Literature embodies respect for tolerance, multiculturalism, and human rights, it also provides an opportunity for students to think honestly and genuinely as they bear witness to the awesome truth of the Holocaust.

We study Holocaust Literature in order to try to understand a most grievous act of inhumanity. We study Holocaust Literature to learn to bear witness, to see what man is capable of doing—as aggressor and persecutor, as the victim and survivor, as bystander and rescuer. We study Holocaust Literature to try to understand a time when the mores of civilized society were legally annulled. We study Holocaust Literature to descend into the inferno—as Dante would have us do—and to come out of that hell of inhumanity with greater understanding of what it means to be human—what it means to seek—and offer—redemption.

Bearing Witness

1

In the Beginning

Studio portrait of two Jewish
children, Rajal and Szlojme
Dresner.   Szlama Kleiner, courtesy
of USHMM Photo Archives

The first day of the semester. The first day of class. I want my students to think
about why they're here. This isn't a traditional English class. I want them to
narrow the distance between themselves and the material. I want the material
to affect them like a prayer. The writings and films and speakers are nearly sacred. They have come to us from fire and ash. I don't have this feeling about
other literature. And my students may not have this feeling about Holocaust
literature, yet. But I want them to. I want them to respect what we are about
to read and view.

    I wonder if students should be exposed to this level of pain. I find I can
handle the material more easily if I can treat it like other "Englishy" material,
that is, to have students look at how the literature works, what images and
metaphors they notice, what motivates and moves the main characters or protagonists. The normal questions we ask about literature. Yet, this literature is
not normal. It is literature of *extremus,* literature that shows mankind at its
worst, most evil. Men and women perpetrate and are subjected to the most

1

heinous crimes we can imagine. I fear students will become numb, inured to the pain. I fear students will use the Holocaust as a measure for the pain others have suffered. I fear that suffering in other genocides or other literatures may lose its impact if compared and held up against the horrors of the Holocaust.

On the other hand, Holocaust Literature is literature that shows man at his most noble—men and women who broke laws to help and took risks to save other human beings. It is about the weakness and strength—and humanity—of those who endured and survived. It is about the living and the dead. It is about honoring both those who survived and those who did not survive by reading about and knowing about what happened during a time when the world chose to close its eyes. It is about denying the Holocaust deniers. It is about studying evidence and truth—it is about educating ourselves.

Before discussing anything with my students, I ask them to write a journal entry. I want them to think about why they are here, what they hope to learn, and why they want to take this course, uninfluenced by their teacher. After taking attendance the first day of class, I ask the students to write the first of many journal responses:

Why are you taking this course? What do you hope to learn? Discover? Think about? What do you know about the Holocaust? Where did you learn it? What literature of the Holocaust have you already read?

I believe the "answers are in the pen," that sometimes it is best to write before discussing so that students may process and organize their thoughts. Most students sign up for Holocaust Literature with vague ideas based on prior readings, the course's reputation, or just a hole in their schedules. I let them write for ten to fifteen minutes, then we discuss what they've written.

Students say they want to know the facts. They want to know about the atrocities. They want to know about the participants. They want to know the causes, how economics and the Depression lead to Hitler's rise in power. They want to know about and understand suffering. They are curious about the psychology of those who *made* it happen and those who *let* it happen. They want to understand evil. They want to know what it means to be human in this horrible context.

Students want to understand how to make a difference today, and wonder if that is even possible. Many say they do believe they can make a difference in the world. Some have already participated in the multicultural retreat the school offers, benefiting from four days of intimate discussions and Outward Bound-type activities that help our students appreciate and honor their diversity. Several students suggest that if we understand what happened then, maybe we can understand and protect the human rights of others now.

More than one student has a grandparent who was in the camps. Abbi tells us how her grandfather lied when she asked him why he had a blue-black number tattooed into the skin of his arm. He told her that he got it in "jail." Abbi explains that she was confused and angry that he did not tell her the truth immediately; she also admits that perhaps he was afraid of the pain he might cause her if he told her the truth. Julia O., a recent immigrant from the Ukraine, tells us her grandmother and many relatives were in Auschwitz.

Another student, Sandi, tells how while visiting her grandfather's home-town of Vienna, her grandfather began spewing anti-German rhetoric. She and her family jumped on him: "You're racist. How can you of all people speak with stereotypes and prejudice?" She wanted her grandfather to main-tain "politically correct" behavior in the midst of the city that allowed his family to perish. Her comments prompt Calvin to say *his* father hates all Muslims. "Why?" we ask, and he tells us how at seven years old, his father was forced to watch Iraqi Muslims hang his Christian father. Calvin's family is today part of the burgeoning Chaldean community in Detroit. Students' mouths drop as they try to comprehend how one can hate—and how hate has hurt so severely their classmates' families.

Nick wants to know what makes a person do "that" to another? Nick, a white, seventeen-year-old Christian, has been to the multicultural retreat, and he becomes our voice of conscience. "How could people do it?" he asks. "How could the Germans do it?"

"It was the times," some say. "The Depression." They've learned from their history classes that many were lured to the Nazi Party's promise of jobs. It was easy to accept the Nazi racial laws. It was easy to scapegoat.

"What's scapegoating?" a student asks.

Many have not heard the term before. I try to explain: It comes from Biblical times when a goat carried peoples' sins out to the wilderness. Leviti-cus XVI tells us that on Yom Kippur, the Jewish Day of Atonement, the priest would sacrifice one goat to God and the second goat would carry all the con-fessed sins to *Azazel*—Hell, or the spirit of evil. The priest would lay his hands upon the scapegoat as people confessed, then he would send the scapegoat into the wilderness (Porton). Now, if we cast blame on someone who doesn't deserve that blame, it's called *scapegoating*.

And Aaron shall lay both his hands upon the head of the live goat, and con-fess over him all the iniquities of the children of Israel, and all their trans-gressions in all their sins, putting them upon the head of the goat, and shall send him away by the hand of a fit man into the wilderness. And the goat shall bear upon him all their iniquities unto a land not inhabited and he shall let go the goat in the wilderness. (Leviticus XVI, 21–22)

"But how could the Germans be so mean?" another student asks. An innocent question.

I probe. "What do you think?"

Students shake their heads. They cannot understand the will to murder millions of people, let alone even one person.

Someone suggests that people were just following orders. They feared for their own lives if they did not do as they were told. I bring up Daniel Jonah Goldhagen's controversial book, *Hitler's Willing Executioners,* and its premise that ordinary German citizens willingly went along with Hitler's orders to exterminate the Jews. Goldhagen suggests ordinary people did not have to participate in the killings if they did not want to. Most were just fulfilling an urge to murder Jews after centuries of anti-Semitism.

Our discussion of the possibility that people willingly participate in hate crimes brings into our discussion the gruesome death of Matthew Shepherd, who was beaten and left for dead on a Wyoming roadside because he was gay. We discuss the shootings in Columbine, Colorado, how two boys could actually point their guns at classmates and shoot them while laughing. What happened to their moral censors? How could they so disregard human life? Where does the urge and ability to kill come from?

Their questions lead us to a discussion of Stanley Milgram's experiment at Yale University in the 1950s in which participants in the experiment were asked to administer increasing volts of electricity to "learners" who made mistakes. Most administered the full amount of voltage allowed. (See Chapter 7 or *www.muskingum.edu/~psychology/psycweb/history/Milgram .htm#Theory.*) Milgram's experiment suggests that ordinary men, as well as the lunatic, sadistic fringe of society, were willing to participate in the German order to kill. His findings portray what Hannah Arendt maintains in her 1963 book, *Eichmann in Jerusalem,* that evil is banal and that ordinary citizens carried out monstrous deeds by simply following orders (Furman). Arendt suggests that it does not take much for an ordinary person to forsake his conscience.

I am amazed at the depth and breadth of discussion, at the connections students make. In a way, that is what teaching is about: the leap-frogging associations we make from events to books to movies to personal experience to academic studies.

When students submit their one- to two-page typed journal excerpts, many describe their feelings upon beginning the study of Holocaust Literature. I appreciate their candor, their sense of discovery as they reach into themselves to reflect on what it means to take this class.

Robyn, who has been through many years of a Hebrew school education, explores the personal nature of studying the Holocaust, of moving beyond numerical accounting to human experience:

> I feel too ignorant about the Holocaust. I've learned about it at Hebrew school and public school, but never really *learned.* There seems a difference between hearing "six million dead" and actually knowing what happened to *people.* To be appeased by numbers seems to give victory to Hitler; what Hitler attempted to do was to snuff out the *person* in the Jew and make him into simply a figure. Numbers are for math class, not for human beings. It seems vital to go beyond the mere facts of the Holocaust to actual understanding.

Trisha, a devout Catholic who constantly questions the morality of choices people make (she was in my American Literature class and Composition class the year before), writes:

> . . . By taking this class, I am searching for some kind of answer to the question of why this happened in the first place, and the awful idea of whether or not it could happen again. But unfortunately, I don't think that I will ever really understand in one semester why this happened. To kill that many people and be able to have that much power over the world just amazes me. The psychology behind Hitler and his ideas is so complex that till this day we still haven't gotten to the root of what drove him to commit such a horrible crime. So in the end, I hope to learn about the Holocaust, but I fear that I will never really be able to understand it.

I am gratified that she seeks no answers. That she realizes that even as we study this material in depth, she will never really be able to understand it. Even Elie Wiesel, a spokesman and writer of the Holocaust, whom I have heard called "the Holocaust incarnate," says he will never understand.

Helen, another Jewish student, personalizes the Holocaust and imagines herself a victim:

> I've seen the footage of mountains of burning bodies, and heard the eerie crackle behind the recording of Hitler's brain-washing voice, and the effect it has on me never dulls. I still get shivers when I think about how my family could have been involved in the tragic events that took place. I'm always interested to learn more about the Holocaust, after all, they say if you don't know your history, you're bound to repeat it.

And Nick, a blond-haired, blue-eyed Christian, writes about a personal experience:

> ... My barber that I went to for many years was a survivor of the Holocaust. He used to speak to kids, and I remember one day he told me the story of how his family was asked to take a shower and they were gassed. At the time I heard this I couldn't believe that someone could have done that. I always saw the numbers on his arm and every time it reminded me of what he told me.

In writing, each of these students expresses some of the how and why of their presence in the class. They are, I hope, becoming grounded, finding a base from which their learning will build. At the end of the semester, I will ask them to ponder the same question: What does the Holocaust mean to you? I will see—and they will see—if the experience of studying the Holocaust has changed how they see and understand.

2

Poetry of Witness

Polish survivor Jadwiga Dzido shows her scarred leg to the court, while expert witness Dr. Alexander explains the nature of the medical experiment performed on her in the Ravensbrueck concentration camp.   National Archives, courtesy of USHMM Photo Archives

I saw with my own eyes . . .

—SIAMANTO

To introduce the profound and enduring suffering caused by genocide, aware that I cannot in good faith teach about *all* horrible acts committed by mankind, I tell students I am inept, unable to do justice to all the evil perpetrated in the name of statehood or religion. However, we will look closely at a few poems that come to us from the pain of others. I call it the poetry of witness, as it tends to be written by an observer—or one who imagines what it must have been like to observe. Four poems we look at include Siamanto's "The Dance," Sharon Olds' "Things That Are Worse Than Death," Carolyn Forché's "The Colonel," and Willa Schneberg's "The Locket."

Students note that in these poems the speakers almost always say, "You will not believe what I have to say . . ." and "I saw this with my own eyes."

These simple truths, uttered by survivors and witnesses, take us into truly un-believable and powerful experiences. Even the speakers do not trust that the listener will believe. They must make it clear that what the reader is about to hear happened, really, and that they saw it with their own eyes. In Elie Wiesel's *Night* and Primo Levi's *Survival in Auschwitz*, both writers express fear that when they return from the camps no one will want to hear or believe what they have to tell. I ask as we embark on a literature that is primarily memoir, What leads someone to bear witness?

In his poem, "The Dance," about the Armenian genocide (*www.hyeetch.nareg.com.au/genocide/story4_p1.html*), Siamanto writes,

> In a field of cinders where Armenians
> were still dying,
> a German woman, trying not to cry
> told me the horror she witnessed:

> "This incomprehensible thing I'm telling you about,
> I saw with my own eyes.
> From my window of hell
> I clenched my teeth
> and watched . . ."

The German woman describes how she envied her wounded neighbor who died without seeing "twenty graceful brides" danced to their deaths while a crowd roars, brandishes their swords, and looks on. Someone "anoints" the "brides" with kerosene, and the crowd watches them burn. The speaker asks, "How can I dig out my eyes, how can I dig, tell me?"

I want my students to notice several things. First, I want them to see how difficult it is to bear witness, how painful it is to see—and then to tell what has been seen. I want them to empathize with the speaker, to hear, to listen. I want them to be aware that what they witness through poems and stories and films may seem unbelievable—though it is indeed real.

I also want them to learn to read a poem—to hear what the poet/speaker is saying. Often students balk at reading poems. They tell me they have a hard time finding the so-called hidden meanings. I ask them, "Where do the meanings hide?" They pause—and soon realize the meaning is in the words, in the images, in the metaphors, even in the sounds and line breaks. And so we look closely at what the poem says and how it is written.

About "The Dance," students want to talk about the horror of bearing witness, the horror of what the German woman saw, as well as the horror of what the Turks did to the Armenians. But this year, they also want to talk about the crowd—the other witnesses, the bystanders who became participants. "How could they just watch?" Alyssa asks as she flicks her long, brown hair from her face. "What do you think happened to the people who saw?"

The discussion jumps off into a totally unexpected topic: the pleasure of being a voyeur of violence! David recalls an arrest he witnessed last summer in Rehoboth, Virginia, how the cops pulled a boy off his bike, beat him up, and how a crowd gathered and shouted encouragement to the police. Others cite watching car races just to see the crashes, hockey games for the fights, rubbernecking at traffic accidents, watching gladiators, football. They get a charge, they admit, from scary or violent movies and television shows. I mention "reality" television—and we talk about what draws an audience to want to witness that which shocks and surprises. "We like violence," they say. "It's fun to watch."

How easy it is to tap into our baser feelings of anger and violence and disdain. Our discussion, I hope, leads to an understanding of how so many could participate as witnesses and bystanders to the horror of the Nazi years—and how those who witness feel compelled to live to tell.

What Do You Notice?

We also discuss "Things That Are Worse than Death," a poem by Sharon Olds from her book, *The Dead and the Living*.

"THINGS THAT ARE WORSE THAN DEATH"

(*for Margaret Randall*)

You are speaking of Chile,
of the woman who was arrested
with her husband and their five-year-old son.
You tell how the guards tortured the woman, the man, the child,
in front of each other,
"as they like to do."
Things that are worse than death.
I can see myself taking my son's ash-blond hair in my fingers,
tilting back his head before he knows what is happening,
slitting his throat, slitting my own throat
to save us that. Things that are worse than death:
this new idea enters my life.
The guard enters my life, the sewage of his body,
"as they like to do." The eyes of the five-year-old boy, Dago,
watching them with his mother. The eyes of his mother
watching them with Dago. And in my living room as a child,

the word, Dago. And nothing I experienced was worse than death,
life was beautiful as our blood on the stone floor
to save us that—my son's eyes on me,
my eyes on my son—the ram-boar on our bodies
making us look at our old enemy and bow in welcome,
gracious and eternal death
who permits departure.

I ask students what they notice in the poem. I want them to notice the little things as well as the big. I want them to notice how the poet constructs the poem, how she merges the political with the personal. They tell me the speaker speaks of witnessing a woman, her husband, and their five-year-old son tortured in front of each other, "as they like to do." They tell me the speaker imagines herself tilting her son's head back to slit his throat, then slitting her own throat—to save them from being forced to witness each other's torture, to save them from "things that are worse than death."

The discussions provoked by the poem are astounding. Students have a hard time grappling with the idea of a mother being able to, needing to, kill her own child. The concept of something worse than death—the torture, the pain—is hard for seventeen and eighteen year olds to grapple with.

Students notice the need to escape from the pain of witnessing, through "gracious and eternal" death, an old enemy who "permits departure." They draw parallels to Siamanto's witness who wants to dig out her eyes, even to Oedipus who gouges out his eyes when he has seen too much. The pain of seeing. And knowing. They notice the choice the mother has to make—to spare her son the pain of witnessing and torture by killing him herself.

We draw, as Laura, my student teacher suggests, a *line of contention*. "Could you kill your own child to protect him?" Laura asks. All hands rise. Many say they could not watch their own child tortured and live. Another brings up Toni Morrison's *Beloved* in which a mother murders her daughter so she will not have to live as a slave. Then someone asks, "Would dying be giving up?" Natalie, a thoughtful young woman with long, blond hair, suggests that though none of them can even begin to imagine the situation and the incredibly painful emotions that would drive certain decisions, perhaps it is better to go on living and suffering in order to bear witness.

I ask students to consider what it means to bear witness as they write in their journals. What does it mean to see things you thought you'd never see? Things you don't want to see? How can a writer tell what she's witnessed—or heard?

Natalie describes the effect of passing on what one has heard. She is sensitive to what it means to tell, how without these voices of witnesses we could not possibly know or change:

Siamanto has educated us (to say the least) because of his experience. Not that what he saw was a positive experience, but because he passed along the German woman's story, we can begin to see the terror. We are affected by it and changed by it. Without the witnesses of the Holocaust, we would not be able to see what truly happened.

Julia P. internalizes and feels deeply what Old's expresses. I am impressed by her sensitive reading:

> The image of a woman slitting her son's throat "before he knows what is happening" just made me cringe. I would never ever want to see someone I'm close to suffer. I'd never like to see anyone suffer, period. . . . I believe that what Sharon Olds writes about *is* worse than death. Much worse. That image, those sounds, live with you forever. You cannot forget what you have witnessed and that knowledge will always be in your mind, which is disturbing me even as I write because images are flashing in front of my eyes.

Scott F. approaches the assignment from a different perspective. He wants to be a writer. He thinks about why he might write such a poem; he understands that poems are not just written to tell a story, but also to avenge a wrong. He understands the pen as a weapon:

> If I were a writer, I would do it to do more than just tell a story. If I wrote a poem about something terrible that was done to me, or a relative or a friend for that matter, I would write for revenge. . . . I think that might be why these poems were written—to avenge the tortures of innocent people, because there is really no other way to do so.

The Pen as Weapon

"The Colonel" by Carolyn Forché takes us behind the scenes in El Salvador where Forche went to study poetry and Spanish. She is a guest at a colonel's house where she witnesses his great wealth in the midst of war and poverty. It is, she says, a poem "trouvé," a poem found, recorded as she saw it in paragraph form. The poem in its entirety may be found in her book, *The Country Between Us,* or on Carolyn Forche's website (*www.previewport.com/Home/forche-y3.htm*).

Forché begins her poem, "What you have heard is true." Like the other poets we look at, she opens her poem with a plea to understand that what we are about to hear, as unbelievable as it may seem, she has seen with her own eyes. Then she tells us about dining with a colonel in El Salvador during the military takeover in the 1970s.

We discuss the poetics of the poem. Students ask, "How can a poem be a paragraph?" I ask them to consider various poetic devices: What images do we see? What metaphors? The moon swings bare on its black cord as if it is being hanged; there are broken bottles embedded in the walls around the house that "scoop the kneecaps from a man's legs or cut his hands to lace." The colonel's daughter files her nails surrounded by daily papers, pet dogs, and a pistol that lies on the sofa cushion. The contradictions amaze. Rack of lamb, good wine, a gold bell on the table to call the maid—and a bag of ears that when dropped into a glass of water swell and come alive. These ears, once swept to the floor, hear—they catch the scrap of the colonel's voice and they press themselves to the ground, perhaps to hear even more? I wonder aloud how Forché's magical realism affects our understanding of the poem.

"The Locket" by Willa Schneberg is about the death of Dr. Haing Ngor who survived Pol Pot's Cambodia and Killing Fields by pretending to be a taxi driver. (If there is time, I show *The Killing Fields* to expose students to another genocide, so they may see and empathize with the subject of Schneberg's poem, Dr. Haing Ngor.) The poem tells about his death by mugging in L.A. when he would not give up the locket that belonged to his wife:

"THE LOCKET"

Dr. Haing Ngor survived the Pol Pot Time by pretending to be a taxi driver. He won an Academy Award for playing Dith Pran in the film The Killing Fields. *He was murdered in Los Angeles on February 25, 1996.*

I
If what they say is true
about the locket,
Haing Ngor died for love.
He was found slumped over his Mercedes,
not unlike the one he owned in Phnom Penh
before Pol Pot had his way with the country;
Ngor would not let the thugs take the gold locket
with the only picture that remained of his wife,
the one he stole back from the Khmer Rouge puppet
who snuck into his shack looking for his wife's jewelry
after Huoy had *crossed the sea.*

II
He would have suffered the vise's spikes on his forehead again
and the endless pinging of water on his temple

if he could have stopped them
from ripping off his neck
the talisman of his wife
he always wore
behind his clothes, next to his skin.
Huoy died in childbirth too malnourished to feed the fetus.
Haing's doctor's hands could do nothing but cradle her
as she stopped fighting the hunger,
his black bag empty.
If Haing Ngor had performed a miracle
and the baby slid out of her tired body,
Angka bullets would have shoved
the tears of the two still alive
back into their eyes
before kicking them into the earth's moist belly.

III
Afterwards, he buried her in two silk outfits,
so she would have a change of clothes in paradise.
Then he did something only widows are supposed to do:
He shaved his head and wailed
like a wife for her dead husband.

(Willa Schneberg's "The Locket" was published in the January/February 2000 issue of *The American Poetry Review.* She worked with the United Nations Transitional Authority in Cambodia from 1992 to 1993.)

Schneberg, like Forché, begins her poem with a prelude, "If what they say is true . . ." Again, she must trust what she has heard—and relay it to us. The speaker of this poem must tell, she must bear witness not to what she herself saw, but what she has heard about someone she cares about. She imagines what it must have been like for her friend in Cambodia, how "he would have suffered the vise's spikes on his forehead again / and the endless pinging of water on his temple." Through Schneberg's poem, we, ourselves, are forced to imagine the Pol Pot Time and to feel the loss of a single man.

For a journal assignment, I ask students to choose one of the poems and write about what happens. I want them to begin by thinking not of the author or poet as the one who acts or speaks in the poem. They should begin to see that the poet is not always the speaker. So I ask,

- Who is speaking?
- What does the speaker observe?

- What kind of witness is the speaker?
- How many levels removed is the speaker from the subject?
- Why do you think the speaker is often *not* the one who experienced the event?
- Why do you think the speaker needs to tell this particular story?

How Do We Bear Witness?

In order to help students understand what it means to speak as a witness, I offer them the option of writing a poem about an event they have "witnessed" in person—in the news, on television, or heard from a friend or relative. I read some of my poems to them, risking exposure. Only two of my poems have been published, in *Bittersweet Legacy* (University Press of America, 2001). I wrote "What's Really True" after reading a newspaper article about a man, a Holocaust survivor's child, who aimed his gun at a black fifteen year old who was leaning against his black Jaguar in a parking garage. The man reminded me in some ways of my former husband. Reading my poems makes my voice quiver. I have tremendous stage fright as I share with my students my attempts at poetry. I hope in sharing what I've written, my students will have more confidence writing and sharing their work.

"WHAT'S REALLY TRUE"

In a parking garage in Birmingham
on a day so hot the boy sought shade,
a white man ordered "Lie on the ground
or I'll shoot," and he pressed his rifle's butt

into his shoulder and aimed
at the boy he believed
was stealing his other car,
a black Jaguar. Suburban racism,

the papers said. Turns out
the white man's a child
of Holocaust survivors, he's married,
has a son, pays his dues

to the ADL and ACLU.
By day he's a neurosurgeon—severs
bad flesh from good, then scrubs his hands
and sterilizes his greens.

By night he turns in his wife's arms
to dream again—black boots,
raised rifles, running, being chased,
groveling for grace.

"Don't you hear the bombers,
the tanks?" "You're dreaming,"
she whispers, "You hear traffic
on Woodward, the three a.m. train."

Even with his arms around his wife in their bed
every fence is electric, every kid a thief,
every cement floor a place to press his cheek
to feel the gravely cold in all the heat.

I take a deep breath and read another poem, inspired by a photograph on the front page of *The New York Times* of a woman killed in a bus bombing in Tel Aviv. At the time, my daughter was in Tel Aviv riding the public buses. I was moved by the woman—she could have been me.

"BUS #20"

Ramat Gan, Israel, July 24, 1995

In the photograph in *The New York Times*
is a woman dressed like me. She lies
on the street, dark cloth over her face draped

like blue folds painted in Madonna's veil.
She wears a white blouse, a watch, a long
dotted skirt, and tennis shoes. Her toes point

to the charred bus where an old man leans back
as if sleeping among empty seats and broken glass.
That woman who wears the kind of clothes I wear

was likely on her way to work or to shop,
to buy the food her family likes to eat.
I don't think she was very religious.

Her bare arms are by her side, one hand tucked
beneath her thigh, the other open
as if to catch hot sun, cold rain, some air.

I'm shaking by the time I finish reading. I look around the room, hoping for encouraging reactions. Then I ask students to think about what they might like to write a poem about. What have they read in the newspapers?

Seen on television? This particular semester, my questions thud. No one even knew about the earthquake in India. I take a breath—and ask again if there's anything they've witnessed either from the news or from their lives? And slowly, students start to respond. "Columbine," one says. The memory is still fresh. Two years ago two high school students in Columbine, Colorado, killed their classmates and then themselves. Our memories of the horror are fresh. Even at our school, just after the shootings our many doors to the outside were locked and police cruised our parking lots. Another student ventures into the silence and mentions the crash of the Oklahoma State basketball team's plane. Another describes witnessing the death of a water polo player on the deck of the school pool. Another describes watching a friend get hit by a speeding car. Calvin says he could write about his father witnessing *his* father's hanging in Iraq. Laura describes how her mother, a teacher in Detroit, gave a second-grade student a D for her homework—the child came to school the next day with an iron burn on her cheek. Jen tells about her mother, a teacher in Southfield, whose student died in an apartment fire he probably set.

With these experiences of witnessing out on the proverbial table, I lead my students through a series of writing exercises:

- Take a picture of the scene in your mind. Describe what's there. Don't leave out any details!
- What's actually happening in the picture? Any action? What do you smell? Taste? Touch? Hear?
- Is anyone speaking? What are they saying? Write the monologue or dialogue.
- Look through the things you've written. Underline good images. What are they *like?* Can you use metaphors to describe what things are like?
- Does this scene remind you of anything *you've* personally experienced?
- What do you know now that you didn't know before?
- Now, underline the good lines and chunks of writing. Pull them out and write a poem. If you prefer, revise the writing into an essay.

My students write for twenty minutes, a half hour. They don't want to stop. I feed them one new direction every five minutes or so as I notice them dropping their pens, finishing the last chunk of writing. I tell them to write more, to say more about what they've already said. I want them to find the detail that reveals, that tells.

I'm impressed by the writing that comes in the following week. Some students choose to write directly and critically about the professional poems. Others try their own inventions. Most of the first draft poems need to be revised, need in particular work on cutting dead wood, compressing language, using line breaks to advantage, and letting the vivid images speak for themselves without editorializing. I give everyone As (for effort and encouragement—this is *not* a creative writing class!) and ask for revisions.

Becky, who witnessed the death of a young friend, writes:

"SPEED"

Becky Thurau

She laughs and smiles as she flies
down the sidewalk on her new pink bike
like a bird just learning to use its wings.

She looks back at me as the speeding
black Buick approaches the corner.
I saw her last smile.

Screeching brakes—loud bombs
going off over and over in my head.
I scream; her bike's in the ditch beside me,

her body's mangled in between
the yellow stitching of the concrete,
face up, one arm behind her head.

Her hair changes from golden blond
to deep red flooding the pool around her
like a puddle when it pours.

"Get up," I whisper.
I begin to weep.
I want to turn away.

But my eyes are stuck;
even when I close them
I can still see her ripped clothes

hanging from her lifeless body.
My mom comes running and grabs me
in her arms. Before her trembling hands

cover my poisoned eyes, I see
one white shoe splattered with blood
at the side of the road.

Laura, whose mother told her about her abused student, had difficulty finding the voice in her poem, but the images she finds are stark:

"THE STUDENT"

Laura Nanes

My Mom said her little cheek was blistered;
the iron left its mark like a gravestone.
Out of love? No.
More bruises
black and blue
blister and blood.
Her dad even poured alcohol on her naked body
evaporating away her dignity;
she stood for an hour
tasting vomit.
Homework isn't done; she can't stop shaking.
The second-grader brought home a report card,
"D" in homework
(meaning dumb, delinquency, death?);
her father went to school to blame the teacher, my Mom.
He towered over her like a volcano ready to erupt.
Mom prayed for someone to come help,
she expects protection.
Her student doesn't.
Teachers run to Mom's aid;
she changes the "D" to "B" (for breath?).
I've never missed a homework assignment.

Jen, whose mother also teaches, writes:

"TRAGEDY"

Jen Prince

I can picture it,
That small first-grade troublemaker named Brandon
Like children of the Holocaust,
He had his own chamber of death.
The fire in his bedroom rapidly spread
Destroying everything in its path.
He screamed, his little brother cried,
But the smoke made it difficult to breathe
And the deafening roar of the fire smothered the sounds

Of the two boys that died that evening
In the seeming safety of their own home.
Brandon could not cry enough tears to put out the fire
He had started with his own two hands.

And Katie, who watched a fellow water polo player die before her eyes, writes:

"WHY?"

Katie Rollo

Everyone was in shock,
Nobody knew quite what to do.
While a water polo game was being played,
Off to the side one girl was dying.

She fell in slow motion,
lay on the ground convulsing.
Parents in the stands screamed
"Call 911," "Stop the game."
Her coaches and a nurse ran to help,
encouraging her to keep breathing,
a simple thing.

In the stands people stood wide-eyed in horror,
The pool became still.
The only sounds came from the coach,
"It's okay Kim, just keep breathing."

Then it was frantic,
the rest is a blur,
a doctor, and
everyone was led out
taking one last glimpse
saying one last prayer.

Her body lay trembling,
her face white as a ghost,
And her eyes with a look of terror.

Why her? Why was it Kim?
Why weren't her parents there that day she died?
Why weren't they beside her
as she took her last breath,
her last look at the world?

I ask students who wrote poems to read their poems to the class. It is gratifying for me to see their work appreciated by their classmates. We don't critique the poems, rather we look at what works, what the poet says, what the poet has witnessed. We are beginning to understand, I hope, what it means to tell, what it means to bear witness.

3

Hate

Racism, Prejudice, Anti-Semitism, and Dehumanization

Shattered storefront of a Jewish-owned shop destroyed during Kristallnacht (the "Night of Broken Glass"). Berlin, Germany, November 10, 1938. National Archives, courtesy of USHMM Photo Archives

The hottest places in Hell are reserved for those who, in time of moral crisis, maintain their neutrality.

— DANTE

How do we teach students to recognize hate? To understand tolerance?

The stated purpose of the United States Holocaust Memorial Museum in Washington, D.C., is to teach tolerance. The Los Angeles Holocaust museum is named the Museum of Tolerance. The stated goals of most Holocaust curricula are to teach tolerance. Yet, before we can teach tolerance we need to teach an understanding of hate—of what leads to intolerant acts.

On the Museum of Tolerance's website, Mark Weitzman, who provides teacher guidelines for teaching Holocaust Literature, writes:

> Teaching the Holocaust is a challenge of awesome proportions. Few if any events in recent history have had its impact or implications. Perhaps the most important lesson of the Holocaust is to move away from the perception that it is important only to Jews. Jews were victims, but the crimes were committed by persons raised in European cultures that were in great measure shaped by Christianity. This teaches us that any society can descend to that level unless safeguards are put into place; and, one of the most important places to begin is in the classroom. The Holocaust must be brought into the classroom so that students can learn to analyze the hatred and bigotry that can lead to genocide. Any remembrance or teaching of the Holocaust, whether secular or religious, must aim at preventing its recurrence.

Defining Genocide

To help students understand the Holocaust in the context of other genocides, I ask students to think about genocide historically and in modern history. Within only this century we have witnessed killing fields in Armenia, Cambodia, the Balkans, and Rwanda, to name only a few. How do we define genocide? In Elie Wiesel's view, "Genocide is the intent and the desire to annihilate a people" (*Newsweek,* 4/12/99).

How do we objectively look at the Holocaust in the context of other genocides? How do we define genocide? Does our studying the Holocaust diminish other abuses of human rights? We must be careful that it does not. I ask students to define genocide and to research and describe one historical or recent genocide (besides the Holocaust). I ask them to include dates, the population affected, the motivation of the persecutors, the action/programs of the persecutors, and their effect on the victims.

Following their research—mostly on the Internet—students express amazement that our modern society has permitted its members to destroy life so easily. One student asks why there isn't much media coverage of these genocides. Stephanie S. suggests that these genocides' numbers can't compare to the numbers of those killed in the Holocaust. I wonder if that is the reason. The Jewish Holocaust was not covered in the media as it happened; in fact, it took years before it was even defined as a genocide (a combination of a Greek root *geno* for human and the Latin root *cide* for killing) or for Holocaust to be written with a capital H.

R.J., a student, suggests that we got involved in Kosovo because the victims were westernized, they were more like us. Leigh agrees, "We were more

Figure 3–1. *Cover of the anti-Semitic German children's book, 'Der Giftpilz' (The Poisonous Mushroom). Courtesy of USHMM Photo Archives.*

involved with that war. Why?" Helen says, "Maybe it has to do with *where* the genocide takes place," suggesting that if the genocide occurs in underdeveloped countries, we in America are not as interested in getting involved because they are not like us. Helen has a point. Janet, a student of Asian descent, suggests that perhaps we went into Kosovo because we have learned more . . . perhaps the media paid more attention . . . perhaps President Clinton and Secretary of State Albright simply cared more. Other students suggest that *we* have to care more, *we* have to notice; after all, Hitler felt entitled to act in Germany and Europe as he did because, as he said, "Who, after all, speaks today of the annihilation of the Armenians?"

Elie Wiesel argues that we must not remain silent. "Surely when human lives are involved, indifference is not an answer. Not to choose is also a choice, said the French philosopher Albert Camus. Neutrality helps the aggressor, not his victims" (*Newsweek*). In *Messengers of God,* Wiesel writes about Job's suffering:

> When the Pharaoh wondered how to resolve his own Jewish question [freeing the Jewish slaves], Yethro (an advisor) declared himself in favor of granting Moses' request—to let his people go—while Balaam (another advisor) opposed it. When consulted in turn, Job (another advisor to Pharaoh) refused to take a stand, preferring to remain neutral, silent—neither for nor against. And it was for this neutrality, this silence, the Midrash tells us, that he incurred his later sufferings. In times of crisis, of danger, no one has the right to choose caution, abstention; when the life and death of a human community are at stake, neutrality becomes criminal. (Messengers, 213)

It is a heavy burden to my students to feel responsible for speaking out, for not remaining silent. I admit to my students that I often choose not to watch television news; it is too painful. Kate objects: "The media is the only way to the outside world of hell that our sheltered souls will never see and never be able to experience." "Shouldn't we stay informed?" another student asks. We all agree the answer is yes, but it is difficult to stay on top of the news, on top of events—and then to act. And how do we act? students ask. What can we do?

Students suggest writing letters to editors, writing checks to help, going overseas as part of relief missions, trying to inform others so they can care, joining Amnesty International. Yet, in effect, we feel impotent. We feel unable to do much. We discuss those who have made a difference: Ginetta Sagon, who started Amnesty International to support human rights everywhere after she herself was a prisoner during World War II. We discuss Elie Wiesel's speaking out and bearing witness. We discuss the simple act of voting for representatives who reflect our points of view. We discuss the possibility of education and teach-ins. We pat ourselves on the back for taking a small step in the direction of understanding by taking this class and together studying one horrendous act of genocide.

I suggest several books and videos for further reading. I give extra-credit for book and movie reviews. Books and films worth reading and watching include:

> Peter's Balakian's *Black Dog of Fate* (the Armenian genocide through his grandmother's experiences).
> Nicholas Cage's *Eleni* (about his Armenian mother's harrowing escape).

Thea Halo's *Not Even My Name: From a Death March in Turkey to a New Home in America, a Young Girl's True Story of Genocide & Survival.*

Philip Gourevitch's *We Regret to Inform You That Tomorrow We Will Be Killed with Our Families: Stories from Rwanda* (essays originally written for the *New Yorker* magazine about the Rwandan war and genocide).

The Killing Fields (a film about the Cambodian genocide, starring Sam Waterston, Dr. Haing Ngor ("The Locket"), and Athol Fugard).

Rwanda and Genocide in the Twentieth Century (see *www.pbs.org/wgbh/pages/frontline/shows/rwanda/reports/dsetexhe.html*).

The Beginnings of Anti-Semitism

In 1542, nineteen years after instructing Christians to "deal kindly with the Jews and to instruct them in the Scriptures," Luther wrote an essay on the "Jewish Question." This pamphlet, "Gegen die Juden und ihre Lügen" (Against Jews and Their Lies), went through two editions during the four remaining years of Luther's life. I pass out Martin Luther's virulently anti-Semitic tracts, but I don't tell my students who wrote them. I want them to try to determine the author of this blasphemous diatribe:

> What then shall we Christians do with this damned rejected race of Jews? Since they live among us and we know about their lying and blasphemy and cursing, we cannot tolerate them if we do not wish to share in their lies, curses, and blasphemy. . . .
>
> First, their synagogues . . . should be set on fire, and whatever does not burn up should be covered or spread over with dirt so that no one may ever be able to see a cinder or stone of it. . . .
>
> Secondly, their homes should likewise be broken down and destroyed . . . they ought to be put under one roof or in a stable, like gypsies, in order that they may realize that they are not masters in our land, as they boast, but miserable captives.
>
> Thirdly, they should be deprived of their prayer books and Talmuds in which such idolatry, lies, cursing, and blasphemy are taught.
>
> Fourthly, their rabbis must be forbidden under threat of death to teach anymore.
>
> Fifthly, passport and traveling privileges should be absolutely forbidden to the Jews.
>
> Sixthly, they ought to be stopped from usury.
>
> Seventhly, let the young and strong Jews and Jewesses be given the flail, the ax, the hoe, the spade, the distaff, and spindle, and let them earn their bread by the sweat of their noses . . .

To sum up dear princes and nobles who have Jews in your domains, if this advice of mine does not suit you, then find a better one so that you and we may be free of this insufferable devilish burden—the Jews. (Eban, 199–200).

After reading these edicts out loud, Jessica pronounces: "It feels foul in my mouth to say those words." Eric thinks these words were issued by the Nazi Party in the 1930s. These students are not used to proclaiming vitriolic hate. I tell them these are not Nazi laws, but rather proclamations against the Jews from the sixteenth century. I want them to realize that the anti-Jewish laws devised by the Nazis were not new, that anti-Semitism festered in Europe for hundreds of years.

We notice that Luther's desire to impose hateful laws against the Jews and ultimately make Germany *Judenrein* (Jew free) unfortunately parallels and forms a precedent for the laws devised by the German state during the 1930s and 1940s. These laws, called the Nuremberg Laws, imposed strict sanctions on Jewish citizenship and life. The Nuremberg Laws may be found at the following sites:

- *motlc.wiesenthal.com/pages/t055/t05556.html* (Nuremberg Laws)
- *www.myschoolonline.com/site/0,1876,0-141838-38-35597,00.html* (New Jersey Learning Network Site lists several sites with links that explain the Nuremberg Laws)
- *www.skirball.org/attract/nuren/nurn.html* (links to photographs of original documents)
- *www.mtsu.edu/~baustin/nurmlaw3.html* (list of laws)

In class we contrast and compare the Nuremberg Laws to Martin Luther's edicts. It is easy to find similarities—and to see how twentieth century anti-Semitic laws grew out of sixteenth century edicts. We also discuss how the Nuremberg Laws compare to Jim Crow Laws in the American South: blacks were prevented from using "white" bathrooms and drinking fountains; blacks had to sit at the back of the bus; polling laws and the grandfather clause prevented black citizens from exercising their right to vote.

To further emphasize the endemic anti-Semitism in Europe, I show *Heritage: Civilization and the Jews #4: The Crucible of Europe from the 9th to the 16th Centuries* narrated by Abba Eban, the former Prime Minister of Israel. The film shows a thriving Jewish culture—in the Golden Age of Spain as well as in Europe—to give some sense of what is lost as the racist laws of the 1930s and 1940s clamp down and then attempt to eliminate Jews from the face of the earth.

Students come to understand that what happened in twentieth century Germany was not new. Crusades, pogroms, edicts to remove Jews from where they live, blame for poisoning wells during the Black Death all occurred during the past five hundred years. According to Raul Hilberg,

> . . . Since the fourth century after Christ there have been three anti-Jewish policies: conversion, expulsion, and annihilation. The second appeared as an alternative to the first, and the third emerged as an alternative to the second.
>
> The destruction of the European Jews between 1933 and 1945 appears to us now as an unprecedented event in history. Indeed, in its dimensions and total configuration, nothing like it had ever happened before. As a result of an organized undertaking, five million people were killed in the short space of a few years. The operation was over before anyone could grasp its enormity, let alone its implications for the future.
>
> Yet, if we analyze this singularly massive upheaval, we discover that most of what happened in those twelve years had already happened before. The Nazi destruction process did not come out of a void; it was the culmination of a cyclical trend. We have observed the trend in the three successive goals of anti-Jewish administrators. The missionaries of Christianity had said in effect: You have no right to live among us as Jews. The secular rulers who followed had proclaimed: You have no right to live among us. The Nazis at last decreed: You have no right to live. (Hilberg, 7–8).

Students seem surprised that the anti-Semitism of the Nazi period did not simply spring up, as they have learned in history classes, due to the Depression in Europe and the need for a scapegoat. They are not aware of the long-standing hatred and prejudice toward Jews. They begin to see how easy it was for the German government to persuade its people to follow its lead in ostracizing and condemning those who were different: First the mentally and physically handicapped (social Darwinism at its worst persuaded that some were not good enough to reproduce and so they were sterilized—which led to an even more drastic move; they were euthanized—see The History Place: *www.historyplace.com/worldwar2/holocaust/h-euthanasia.htm*), then the Gypsies, then the Jews. And in the fall of 2000, we once again see hate crimes directed against Jews: synagogues burned in Paris, a twenty-year-old Jew stabbed in London, a rabbi shot at in Chicago. Yet my students are silent. It's easier to speak of anti-Semitic acts sixty years ago than to directly address what is going on today. What can we do? I ask. Most shake their heads. We agree that at least we can stay informed and inform others.

In her journal Robyn reflects on the pain she experienced watching the Abba Eban film:

> I wanted to put my head down and cry. . . . I don't think I'm going to like having this class first hour. Seventh hour would be nice; I go home and then I could cry. Or pray. Or laugh. Or whatever odd emotional thing I feel I need to do. Even fourth or fifth hour, right before lunch, would be decent. There's still that free alone time afterwards. . . . It just seems so morbid to feel one of the greatest sufferings of a people in history—and then have to go on with life, just pretend what I learned doesn't affect me at all. I have to go to AP English and talk about how bad Tess Durbeyfield's (sic) life is because her dear Angel left her. Oh boohoo. *Shut up and stop whining, Tess, you idiotic twit. You have no idea of suffering; you have no conception of pain; you know nothing at all.* All the great tragedies—*Oedipus, Hamlet,* even *Tess of the D'Ubervilles*—next to the Holocaust are nothing. Tess is Pippi Long-stocking next to Auschwitz.

Robyn brings up an important question. How do we understand other tragedies in the face of the Holocaust? The Holocaust subsumes other genocides and atrocities. Isn't there a danger that in studying the Holocaust we denigrate the horror of other tragedies? Robert Novick in *The Holocaust in American Life* writes,

> The principal lesson of the Holocaust, it is frequently said, is not that it provides a set of maxims, or a rule book for conduct, but rather that it sensitizes us to oppression and atrocity. In principle it might, and I don't doubt that sometimes it does. But making it the benchmark of oppression and atrocity works in precisely the opposite direction, trivializing crimes of lesser magnitude. (14)

Life for Jews Before the War

Before the coming of the Nuremburg Laws, Jewish communities thrived in Europe, especially Poland. A whole Yiddish culture sprang up. To help students appreciate that there was indeed a life before the World War II, I introduce a story by Yiddish writer, I. L. Peretz. I want my students to see the vibrant, living culture that existed. I want them to see something of what was lost. I also want them to notice the concerns of these turn-of-the-century Jews, what mattered to them. "The Three Gifts" by I. L. Peretz, was originally published in 1904. The story may be found in the *I. L. Peretz Reader* or on the tape recorded by KCRW for National Public Radio and the National Yiddish Book Center.

The story reveals unspeakable human violence and faith. It is a biting condemnation of all who find entertainment in watching the suffering of others. Peretz lines up good and bad in a world where most can't tell it apart. In the story, a soul of a man who just died must find three gifts to appease the angels in order to get into heaven. The first gift he brings is dirt from the Holy Land—bloodied by a man murdered by thieves who believe jewels rather than dirt are in his little sack; the second gift is a gift of a needle—used by a young woman who has pinned her skirt to her bare skin—to protect her modesty as she is dragged behind a horse to her death for the outrageous act of appearing in public on a Christian holiday; and the third gift is a skullcap retrieved as a man runs through a gauntlet to his death.

Students at first are puzzled by the story. What kind of gifts are these? Al proposes that they are all good deeds, great acts of devotion to God in the face of persecution. Yet Steve questions why acts of generosity or charity aren't honored rather than faith in God. We discuss the various gifts—how they reflect the beliefs of a medieval culture of faith.

"How are Jews portrayed in this story?" I ask. As a humble, holy people, they say.

"And how is the non-Jew portrayed?" I ask. This question forces students to see how Peretz reveals the gentile, the Christian—and it is not a pretty picture. The Christians in this story are anti-Semitic. They believe the Jew contaminates their society. They rob and steal from Jews. They kill Jews for trespassing in their Christian world. And yet, I point out, this is how *the Jews* believe the Christians see *them*. It is, after all, written from the Jewish point of view. Nick quickly interjects, "There's no excuse for anti-Semitism."

For journals I ask my students to write about how nineteenth century Jews see themselves within a Christian world. I want them to understand not only how anti-Semitism was experienced, but also how the joy of holiness infected everyday lives.

There Once Was a Town is a PBS video documentary narrated by Ed Asner about Eishyshok (pronounced Esh-e-shook), a shtetl (village) in the Ukraine where Jews lived and thrived for over 900 years. Hundreds of photographs taken in Eishyshok before the war hang in a multi-story, permanent exhibit at the United States Holocaust Memorial Museum. A chapter from Yaffa Eliach's book, *There Once Was a Town: A 900-Year Chronicle of the Shtetl of Eishyshok,* is reproduced at *www.twbookmark.com/books/78/0316232521/chapter_excerpt381.html.* (This video was particularly interesting to my students because the mother and grandfather of one of their classmates were featured in the film.) Eishyshok was invaded by German Nazis in June of 1941. Einsatzgruppen (killing squads) massacred over 3000 of the town's 3500

Jewish citizens (see Chapter 7). The story of the massacre is told by one who survived by crawling out of the pit of the dead; the story of the vibrant town's schools, weddings, religious life, and market life is also told.

To enhance their understanding of just who some of these millions of people were, I ask students to visit the Simon Wiesenthal Center website (*motlc.wiesenthal.org/exhibits/faces/*) to see the exhibit, "And I Still See Their Faces," photographs of Polish Jews before the war. In a journal entry, I ask them to describe in detail at least one photograph—or describe the effect of seeing so many photographs at once of Jews whose lives were extinguished.

Symbol of Hate: The Swastika

To help students understand the effect of symbols, in particular, the swastika, I draw a swastika on the board. They walk into class aghast that there would be such a sign on our chalkboard, but they also know this is a Holocaust class, and wait to see what we're going to do with it. (More interesting are the reactions of the unsuspecting students in the following class who are quite alarmed that there would be a swastika on a board in their school!) Without discussion, I ask students to write their immediate reactions in their journals. What happens to you when you see this symbol? What do you know about this symbol?

My goal for this exercise is to not only get students to identify their own reactions to racist symbols, but also to demystify it, to take its power away by identifying it with Hindu culture as a symbol of prosperity and well-being, as well as with Native American art.

I do not want to discuss the swastika before students formulate their own thoughts. I don't even want to tell a student who asks how to spell it. I want them to discover for themselves how they feel, to reconstruct memories of how they have experienced reacting to this abhorrent—yet misunderstood—symbol.

My own reaction, I tell the class, is visceral. I feel horror if I see a tattoo or a flag or a patch. I feel anger. It's a racist sign, like the Confederate flag. I can hardly draw it. Its pacifist meaning has been usurped by racists.

Nick says, "The minute I see it, I see hatred. It makes me feel my eyes have seen wrong. I wish it would be erased. I feel the same way when I see the Confederate flag."

Abbi says, "It angers me. There're still people who feel that way in judgment of people. I think it's a Hindu symbol of peace that's been twisted."

Julia P., an African American student, describes what she saw in the parking lot at a recent rock concert: "On a van was a big Confederate flag. It's like saying, 'We're white, we're better'."

Megan describes the swastika she saw on the actor in *American History X:* "I really can't explain it, but all I could think about was how could people have so much hatred? How can people hate someone just because of their race or religion?"

We talk about a swastika tiled into the floor of a local elementary school. It was laid in the 1920s as a Native American symbol, before Hitler usurped the symbol. Now, several groups want the tiled swastika tiled over or removed. Educate, instead of covering up, most students say. Robyn says, "You're giving the Nazis a lot of power if you give them the right to corrupt the meaning of the swastika." We talk about the hypnotic effect of the symbol on the Nazi flag, which leads to a discussion of the controversy over the Confederate flag flying over the capitol in South Carolina. At the time, the NAACP was boycotting tourism in South Carolina until the flag was removed. I am pleased with the connections my students make, once again, leap-frogging through ideas to reach a new understanding of the political power of symbols.

In their journals they continue our discussion.

Nitasha sees how even her own perception of the swastika goes against the grain of her religion:

> The swastika can be seen as a symbol of good and prosperity. The Hindus believe in the good of this symbol. They think of it as a symbol that will bring them good in their lives. Being a Hindu myself, I do believe in the good side of the swastika. However, that was not the first thing that came to my mind when I saw it. The first thought that entered my mind was the evil aspect of it, and what the Germans turned it into.

Jane, who left Russia with her family to escape religious persecution, considers what it means to look at something she doesn't want to see, to bear witness:

> I glance at the board, shivers start running up and down my spine, my heart starts beating faster and faster, I look down at my arms and the hairs are standing up as if I just saw death. . . . I need to look away, to forget what the swastika looks like, to forget what happened. I can't do that though, I need to remember, to tell the future generations to keep the memories alive, no matter how hurtful they are.

In her journal, Marissa describes an unpleasant experience remembered from ninth grade, just before she transferred to Groves:

> I was sitting in my algebra class and I saw a swastika engraved into my desktop. I tried to erase it, but it had been deeply carved. I was horrified that prejudice and hatred of this magnitude existed at my own school. I'm

also reminded of a boy who used to stop people in the halls at my middle school and ask them if they were Jewish. If we replied yes, then we were cruelly teased by him and his friends. These experiences opened my eyes. I realized this type of ignorance and hatred still exists and is prevalent in my community.

Jackie, an athletic as well as a thoughtful student, writes,

I can remember a time when I really felt fear. I was on my way to a soccer tournament in Midland, Michigan. Out in that area there's not much to see but farmlands and highways. On the side of the highway was a billboard. It was painted white, but was so old that it had a yellowish tint to it and was chipping away. I'll never forget the message and picture it displayed. "All those for anti-Semitism, yell 'Heil Hitler'." Next to this message was a swastika and Nazi with his hand in the air.

This was the most terrifying billboard I have ever seen. What scared me the most was that it was in an area where many Michigan Militia live. It also disturbed me because how could something so terrible still be going on, even after 50 years? Just when you think a tragedy has ended you see something like this and realize that it will never be over.

In their reflections these students, Jewish and non-Jewish, face a symbol that has intrusive and horrifying meaning; they have witnessed and felt someone else's rage expressed in the interlocking black lines of the Nazi swastika. And they have a glimmer of what it means to be the object of hate.

Now, after a sense of what came before, after considering our reactions to the Nazi symbol, we look at the words of Adolf Hitler. Hitler wrote *Mein Kampf* (My Struggle) from his prison cell. It was first published in 1924.

We discuss pages 168–169 from Ralph Manheim's translation of *Mein Kampf*. In this passage Hitler equates Jews with Marxism and the betrayers of the German working class: Marxism's goal is "the destruction of all non-Jewish national states. . . . But now the time had come to take steps against the whole treacherous brotherhood of these Jewish poisoners of the people. . . ." In these two pages Hitler refers to Jews as a "venomous plague," "betrayers of the German working class," a "whole treacherous brotherhood," "poisoners of the people," "vermin," "treacherous murderers," a "viper," and "perjuring criminals" who should be "taken off the nation's neck." Ultimately, he calls for the ruthless "extermination of this pestilence." All in two pages. One may open the book to any page and find similar rantings.

It is important for students to recognize not only the hate Hitler spews, but also the metaphoric language he uses. If Jews are equated with vermin, vipers, a venomous plague, and a pestilence, it becomes easy to call for their "extermination."

Students' reactions to *Mein Kampf* are surprising. When I pass around my copy many do not want to touch it. They pass it around like it is a hot potato. They are aghast that it is so easy to obtain a book that to them feels "sinful and dirty." Robyn says she would not want to take the fat red book out of the library, she wouldn't want to be seen with it. No one in class wants to read further in the book. "It's too filled with hatred," "I feel like I would be tainted," they claim. Even Laura, my student teacher, says that when she was looking up information on the swastika at the University of Michigan library, she didn't want anyone to see what was on her computer or what she was printing!

Should hate literature be censored?

Helen comments, "It would probably be bad to ban the printing and reading of Hitler's book. We would just be doing exactly what he did when he burned mountains of Jewish literature during the Holocaust. Also, it's good to keep some of the evil lingering and reminding us so that we never forget what happened and so that we don't allow such terrible event to repeat in the future."

Scott F. says, "When *Mein Kampf* was passed around the room the other day, everyone seemed disgusted and didn't want to touch it or even look at it. I know exactly what they were feeling. It's a very weird feeling to hold something that caused so much trouble, was so evil, *is* evil, in your own hands. There it is—bright red—staring at you. Laughing at you. It's such a terrible thing, and you can't do anything about it, or do anything to it to get revenge. I wanted to throw it on the floor, jump on it, tear it to shreds, scream obscenities at it, spit on it, and burn it."

Note: *Mein Kampf,* in its entirety, may be found on a hate site for Stormfront, if you can get past the hate mongering, and the opening which states, "Support Stormfront and Stand Up for Your White Heritage" (*www.stormfront.org/books/mein_kampf/index.html*). Excerpts may be found at The History Place (*www.historyplace.com/worldwar2/riseofhitler/kampf.htm*).

I show one of two videos at this point, either *The People's Century: "The Master Race"* or *Heritage: Civilization and the Jews: Out of the Ashes* so students may see the implementation of the Nuremberg Laws and the confinement and persecution of the Jews during the 1930s and 1940s. Surprising to my students is the official racism inflicted upon white people. *The Master Race* portrays how propaganda developed and infiltrated German society, how the belief in a master race took hold. *Out of the Ashes,* narrated by Abba Eban, also shows the coming of the racial laws, Kristallnacht (the Night of Broken Glass when synagogues and Jewish businesses had their windows smashed) and the internment of Jews in camps.

Always when I show videos, I ask students to take notes. Often I collect them to see how thorough they are, and I grade them by how much ink is on the page. I want my students to pay attention. I warn them that watching the documentaries is infinitely more interesting—given the voices, the visuals, and the presentation—than my lectures would be! Taking notes helps keep them awake. And for those who would drop their heads to their desks and doze off as soon as the lights go off, I offer the option of standing at the back of the room.

After the movie there is silence. How to discuss? How to make my students notice what's important? No one volunteers, so I ask this semester's class who have already had quite a bit of exposure to the Holocaust, "What's new for you? What surprised you?" And I go around the room asking each student to speak. They comment on the euthanasia of the mentally ill, the children's book that portrays Jews as poisonous mushrooms that should be picked and eliminated, the incredible racism, the effect of the Nuremberg Laws, the horror of the camps. Calvin, whose grandfather was hanged in Iraq, says he didn't know it was that bad for the Jews.

Students may see more propaganda instruments (including the children's book in the film *The Master Race* at the United States Holocaust Memorial Museum's website: *www.ushmm.org/outreach/propag.htm.*)

In groups, I ask students to define *hate* and *hate crimes.* I ask them, "What is hate? Why do we hate? What hate crimes have you witnessed on the news? Why are hate crimes committed? Is hate ever justified?"

To learn more about historical events that led to the Holocaust, I ask students to go the United States Holocaust Memorial Museum's site map (*www.ushmm.org/outreach/tc.htm*). The site contains historical information, timelines, maps, biography, and a glossary. Topics I suggest for research to complement the films we've seen in class are "The Nuremberg Race Laws" and the "Night of Broken Glass." In journals, I ask them to describe what they find on the site.

About the Holocaust Museum's website Trisha writes:

Today I spent some time exploring the Holocaust Memorial Museum website. At first I was a little cynical about the whole website thing. The idea that someone or an organization could possibly think that a Web page could even get close to capturing the essence of the Holocaust really just made me mad. People spend years researching and putting together one book on the

Holocaust, so I was convinced that the website wouldn't be well done. To my surprise I was very impressed. Its main goal seemed to be to inform students about the Holocaust. I haven't really read anything that was just informative. We have read a lot of "feelings" stuff. Literature that gets across a horrible story firsthand. But this website held more information than I have ever really seen before.

Another big assignment I give is to assess hate on the Web. This assignment causes some anxiety and consternation as students look at, often for the first time, the vitriolic hate of the Ku Klux Klan, White Stormfront, and various other hate groups.

Students are appalled and disgusted by the "despicable stuff" they saw. It was a dose of reality, of seeing just how deeply hate still runs. Many report turning from their computers and almost shielding their eyes as they

---

Hate on the Web

Assess at least five sites that foster and engender hate or that work to counter hate. To assess a site, find it on the Web, read through the alleged "facts" and details and descriptions, describe what you've found, and determine if the information is true, false, propaganda, informative, and/or inflammatory. What is the purpose of the sight? Who is it meant to appeal to? What reaction does the site elicit? Write about 200 words (about a page, double-spaced; or a half page, single-spaced) on each site. You might want to start at *www.adl.org* or *www.nytimes.com/learning/general/featured_articles/990318Thursday.html* at the New York Times Learning Network: "Rising Tide: Sites Born of Hate: Racist Pages Grow in Number and Sophistication and May Lure the Unwary." Another good site is *www.hatewatch.org,* originally a Harvard Law School Library Web page that was eventually incorporated in Massachusetts to actively monitor hate groups on the Web; it also contains links to current hate sites.

Hatewatch.org defines a hate site as, "an organization or individual that advocates violence against or unreasonable hostility toward those persons or organizations identified by their race, religion, national origin, sexual orientation, gender or disability. Also including organizations or individuals that disseminate historically inaccurate information with regards to these persons or organizations for the purpose of vilification."

read. They have not before been exposed to such virulent and visceral hate. Sites that particularly roused their ire included *www.jewwatch.com, www .whitesonly.net, www.hitlerisgod.com, www.kukluxklan.net, www.holywar.net, www.AmericanSkinheads.com,* and *www.godhatesfags.com.*

One question we discuss: Should hate sites be censored? This question leads to a discussion of first amendment rights—including the right of the American Nazi Party to march with their flags in Skokie, Illinois, a predominantly Jewish suburb of Chicago—supported by the Anti-Defamation League, the American Civil Liberties Union, and HateWatch.com.

About visiting the sites, Charlie says,

> The most offensive site I encountered was called "88 Skins for Genocide" (*www.swasticas.com*). To be honest, I don't think I would have even visited it if I hadn't already been semi-desensitized by the first few sites I visited. The whole site was covered in swastikas and pictures of Hitler. They proudly proclaim, "All non-whites should leave now or else! Blacks, Jews, Mexicans, Orientals, homosexuals, communists, liberals you have been warned, the rope is waiting. Our day is coming, your days are numbered."

Dan says,

> The "Jokes" section (*www.AmericanSkinheads.com*) is terribly disturbing, though not quite as disturbing as the notion that there are people in existence who will read the jokes, laugh at them, and be puzzled by how anyone could create such fabulous material. At *www.holywar.com* there is a charming graphic of a big red Cross stamping and crushing a gold Star of David.

Jamie says,

> The more sites I went to the more I felt sick to my stomach and just wanted to get out of there. I felt bad going to these sites because they tally how many visitors they have had and I don't want them thinking I went there because I was interested and believed in what they were saying.

Omar says,

> I visited sites spouting hatred toward gays, Jews, African Americans, as well as other racial minorities. These sites are eye opening, a representation of the existing prejudice among people. Seeing such blatant racism and bigotry in people becomes both disappointing and scary for me, being a minority.

And Dana says,

> I was nauseous. It really makes you think of how this kind of mentality can exist in us. I think without a doubt, this was the most eye-opening assign-

ment I have done in years. I think it is good to know what is really out in our world.

All who wrote about the websites came away with a profound appreciation of not only the meaning of our first amendment, allowing such vitriol to be spewed in public, but also how dangerous and abhorrent expressions of hate and prejudice can be. These are mostly sheltered students, sheltered in the sense that they don't experience much of the ugly side of hate in a school that eschews prejudice and honors diversity, who found their research on the Web to be an enlightening experience, as well as, for some, a call to action.

A powerful video I show in connection with their study of the hate sites is the HBO video *Hate.com: Extremists on the Internet,* which addresses the issue of hate on the Web (*www.hbo.com/hate/home.shtml*). The website describes the film, suggests ten ways to fight hate, and more interestingly, answers six questions about the legal aspects of laws regarding hate crimes and censorship. The video documents hate crimes committed by "lone wolves" inspired by website hate.

Another video I show, *Facing Hate with Elie Wiesel and Bill Moyers* opens with Wiesel accepting his Nobel Peace Prize in Oslo in 1986 with these words: "We must speak, we must take sides." Then the PBS documentary shifts to a conversation between Elie Wiesel and Bill Moyers. We see photographs of Wiesel's lost family and his lost family home in Transylvania. Wiesel discusses the meaning of the word hate ("its 'an ugly word'") and how Germans didn't hate Jews because "we weren't human beings." Wiesel states after about 20 minutes of the interview that his anger is with Roosevelt and Churchill, leaders of the free world, because they knew and they didn't tell the Jews what was happening.

A class discussion about what *should* the United States have done ensues. Why was Wiesel most angry at those who could have helped him rather than those who persecuted him? Should Roosevelt have warned the Jews before they were rounded up? Even at risk of betraying the fact that the United States was able to break the Nazi's secret codes? What moral obligations do we as a nation have? What moral obligations do we as individuals have?

4

Taking a Stand

A group of children who were sheltered in Le Chambon-sur-Lignon, a town in Southern France. August 1942.   Mert Bland, courtesy of USHMM Photo Archives.

The only thing necessary for evil to triumph is for good men to do nothing.

—EDMUND BURKE

Sometimes we must interfere. When human lives are endangered, when human dignity is in jeopardy, national borders and sensitivities become irrelevant. Whenever men or women are persecuted because of their race, religion, or political views, that place must—at that moment—become the center of the universe.

—ELIE WIESEL

Every day we read in the newspapers about human rights abuses. Today it is about children in Sri Lanka, conscripted into rebel forces, who were forced to take a cyanide capsule when captured. Yesterday, poor women in Eastern Europe forced into prostitution and a world of violence, xenophobia, disease, and misery. In the last few years we have read about killing squads in Kosovo, Rwanda, and East Timor. A whole course could be based on the daily media's reporting stories of abuse. There is no dearth of material—or horror.

How much do we want to know? When do we take a stand? When do we risk our own lives to be heard? When should we speak out against the abuse of human rights? The answers are not easy. While my students and I want to raise our voices for all who suffer, how do we do that? We feel like reeds in the wind. Who will listen? Who will hear? Who will do something? And yet. And yet if we are silent, we know that no one will hear. If we are silent, we know that nothing will be done.

Embedded in much of the literature of the Holocaust is a plea for someone to hear, someone to hear the cries, someone to at least bear witness to what happened. The major Holocaust museums and learning centers promote the idea that the message we must take from the literature is to not remain silent:

> The consequence of indifference toward persecution of others is always some measure of suffering which should make us realize all the more keenly that we are responsible for one another. Silence and neutrality breed destruction and suffering.
>
> By examining the historical, sociological, and ethical factors involved in the Holocaust, perhaps we can muster the strength to take political and social action in order to avert discrimination and prejudice. (Holocaust Memorial Center)

From the didactic to the more artistic, implicit within the literature of the Holocaust is a call to respond when human rights are denied. I introduce two poems that express what we used to say in the 1960s: If you're not part of the solution, you're part of the problem.

> First they came for the Communists,
>   and I didn't speak up, because I wasn't a Communist.
> Then they came for the Jews,
>   and I didn't speak up, because I wasn't a Jew
> Then they came for the Catholics,
>   and I didn't speak up, because I was a Protestant.
> Then they came for me,
>   and by that time there was no one left to speak up for me.
>
> *Reverend Martin Niemoeller, 1945*

Reverend Niemoeller spoke these words after he was released from eight years in Nazi prisons. Niemoeller was a German U-boat captain in World War I, before he became a pastor. He supported the Nazis when they first came to power, but broke with them in the early 1930s. He was arrested in 1938 for treason and spent the war years in prison.

"The Hangman" by Maurice Ogden expresses the same thoughts as Niemoeller's words. The poem is written in rhyming, syncopated verse about a hangman who comes to town "Smelling of gold and blood and flame" who puts up a scaffold as wide as the courthouse door. Then, as he takes his victims, first an alien, then a political dissident, then a Jew and a black, the scaffold grows—"fed by the blood beneath the chute / The gallows-tree had taken root." No one protests. And finally, the last person in town is hanged. The hangman asks,

> "For who has served me more faithfully
> Than you with your coward's hope?" said he,
> "And where are the others that might have stood
> Side by your side in the common good?"

(The entire poem may be found at the North Carolina Council on the Holocaust's website: *www.dhhs.state.nc.us/holocaustcouncil/HANGMAN.HTM.*)

It is easy for students to see the moral message. They like the ease with which the hangman's story unfolds. They "get it" quickly. I like to point out that this is a *didactic* poem. Most don't recognize the word. I ask them to compare the effect of the poem with the effect of the poems by Siamanto, Olds, Forché, and Schneberg. The point is made—they begin to understand the difference between verse written to teach a lesson and poetry that cries from the heart. Yet, they are also anxious to discuss the implications of a world in which no one speaks out for the persecuted and abused.

During our discussion, I mention that I have a friend who often makes racist comments. "Do you correct him?" Nick asks. I sadly shake my head. "Why? Why don't you stop him from making racist remarks?" He wants me to take a stand. I tell him I have. My comments have made no difference. I can't change him—and I choose to remain his friend rather than correct him all the time. This is a difficult idea for Nick: Letting racist comments slide. He, and the rest of our students, have been well trained to respond assertively to racist, homophobic, and anti-Semitic remarks and jokes. I praise him for his sense of justice—and I try to show the dilemma I face with a friend or a relative who slurs others. Should I take a stand, I ask, when I can truly change someone's thinking as well as when it is useless and I will lose a friend? Do we have to temper our outrage and urge to speak out with sensitivity for the situation? Nick is not completely satisfied.

These poems and our discussions prompt several journal responses about remaining silent in the face of tyranny and injustice. I ask students to apply their interpretations to situations they may have experienced or observed. Another journal option I offer to students is to respond to indifference, to seeing and choosing not to see, to hearing and choosing not to hear. I ask them to consider Elie Wiesel's words from his 1986 Nobel address and his Nobel lecture:

> . . . There is so much injustice and suffering crying out for our attention: victims of hunger, of racism and political persecution—in Chile, for instance, or in Ethiopia—writers and poets, prisoners in so many lands governed by the Left and by the Right.
>
> Human rights are being violated on every continent. . . . Human suffering anywhere concerns men and women everywhere.
>
> . . . To this day, I don't understand how the enemy drove ten thousand Jews to Babi Yar day after day between Rosh Hashanah (the New Year) and Yom Kippur (the Day of Atonement). Babi Yar is not *outside* Kiev, Babi Yar is *in* Kiev—and they were all machine-gunned. They went through the streets, people saw them marching, heard the machine guns. What happened to the people? Did they become deaf, blind, mute? I cannot understand their indifference. Nor can I understand and I say so with pain in my heart, the silence of people who were good people. Roosevelt was a good man and Churchill was a great man. They had the courage to fight the mighty Hitler and his powerful armies. But when it came to saving Jews, somehow the principles of humanity no longer applied. (Kingdom, 233–241)

From our discussions of standing up and speaking out in the face of evil, we segue into Louis Malle's film, *Au Revoir les Enfants*, (*Good-bye My Children*), in which we witness a good priest who risks his life to save four Jewish children. This lush film, in French with English subtitles, portrays the young alter-ego of Malle as a boy in a Catholic school in 1944. Julien Quentin befriends a Jewish boy, Jean Bonnet, who is hiding from the Nazis. Bonnet's family is in Marseilles and it becomes clear, as his mother's letters stop, that she has been deported. The film introduces the fear of living without getting caught. "Are you afraid?" Quentin asks Bonnet when they are lost after dark in the woods, and Bonnet answers, "All the time."

In the end, the priest and the children are captured by the Nazis and the French collaborators. Students are disappointed that the good and the just do not prevail. It is their introduction to the bad that happens to good people. It is their introduction to those who fought to defend the Nazis' victims and who fell victim themselves. It is their introduction to the risks one takes when choosing *not* to be a bystander.

Tal, who is from Israel, suggests that the priest in sheltering the children was a true Zadik, a Hebrew word that means a righteous person. "He understood that it's unjust to punish any person or child for being Jewish (or any other religion, race, or ethnic background). He probably felt that turning these helpless, innocent children in would be a far worse crime (or even sin, for that matter) than keeping them hidden."

For a journal response, I ask students to think about why Louis Malle wants us to see, to know what he remembers. How, I ask, does Quentin reveal his developing relationship with Jean Bonnet? Why? Consider the scene in the French restaurant; the Germans who come to the Catholic priests for confession; the two boys playing the piano together; the ride back to the school with German soldiers; Quentin's quick glance to Bonnet when the Nazi is there to arrest "the Jew." What do we learn about the Holocaust through remembered scraps and glances? I want students to notice the small gestures that tell so much.

For another journal response, I ask, "Why does the priest risk his life to hide four Jews? Consider what Hillel, a great Jerusalem rabbi of the first century B.C.E., said, "If you save one life, you save the world." (These words are said in *Schindler's List* at the end of the movie as Oskar Schindler is thanked by the Jews he saved.) I want students to consider how even though we may not be able to save everyone, the effect of saving even one life is enormous — the one saved gains a world; in each life *is* a world.

The first chapter of *Lucien's Story* (*www.nytimes.com/books/first/k/ kroh-lucien.html*) supports the viewing of *Au Revoir les Enfants* and gives a sense of what a child feels as his mother and then he were arrested.

[The first chapter of *Lucien's Story* may be found on the Internet (as well as other first chapters of recently published books) by going to *nytime.com,* then clicking on "Books," then clicking on "First Chapters," then "K" for Kroh (the author's name) under "Previous Nonfiction Chapters," then scanning down the alphabetical list for Aleksandra Kroh.]

Lucien's Story is beautifully written and translated. We see an eleven-year-old boy on the eve of his and his mother's arrest. Students recognize the confidence young Lucien has in the laws that govern France. He cannot imagine that the French system of justice will not protect him and his mother. Thus, we see through the eyes of a child the breakdown of civil protection and civil rights. We also witness the profound doubt that "this could not happen to me . . ."

Students may also want to consult the 1,902-page *French Children of the Holocaust* edited by Serge Klarsfeld and published in 1996 by New York University Press. The book is a compilation of over 2,500 photographs of French children who were deported. The photographs catch these children posing in lederhosen and rubber boots, with stuffed animals and pretty dresses, and in snapshots pasted to ID cards. In all, records show that 11,402 children were deported, of whom perhaps 300 survived (*The New York Times,* 5/12/96).

Another video (re-released in February 2001), which portrays French collaboration during the war, is Marcel Ophuls' *The Sorrow and the Pity.* A classroom of students may not have patience for watching all four-and-a-half hours of Ophuls' opus on French compliance and resistance during the German occupation, but it may be worthwhile to suggest it as an extra-credit project. The film was made famous by Woody Allen in *Annie Hall* as he and Annie see the documentary more than once. Most surprising is the revelation that France was not forced to send its Jewish children to Germany, but elected to do so anyway.

In an op-ed piece in the *The New York Times* during Maurice Papon's trial as a French collaborator charged with organizing the arrest of nearly 1,600 Jews during World War II and arranging for their transport to a transit camp in Drancy, a Paris suburb, Robert O. Paxton writes:

> The Vichy Government helped the Nazis. In 1940 the Nazis wanted only to dump German Jews into unoccupied France. Yet the Vichy Government went further and registered its Jews, excluded them from jobs and forced many foreign Jews into camps. By 1942, when the Nazis began their extermination program, the French Jews were vulnerable. . . . New archival research proved that Vichy, France was the only western European country under Nazi occupation that enacted its own measures against Jews.

In Marge Piercy's poem, "The Housing Project at Drancy," the speaker tries to locate just where the deportation center at Drancy was located. Drancy was the place where French Jews were held until they were deported to Auschwitz. "The world as microwave oven, burning from within. / We arrive. Drancy looks like Inkster, Gary, the farther reaches of Newark." No one will give the speaker directions to the place where the deportation center stood. "Why do you want to know?" the Frenchmen ask when she inquires where the camp was. Finally there, she finds that "Crimes ignored sink into the soil like PCBs /and enter the bones of children." A chilling conclusion. The pain that doesn't go away is like metallic sludge. This poem offers students a different perspective, that of someone fifty years later trying to imagine what it was like— as they are forced to do with each piece of literature, each video they view.

To introduce what happened in Vichy, France, during the war we watch a short video (available through the Jewish Museum in New York City) titled *Assignment: Rescue.* It is about the heroic efforts of Varian Fry, an American who chose—rather naively at first—to live in Marseilles and try to save European artists threatened by the deportation of Jews. He saved the likes of Marc Chagall, Jacqueline and André Breton, André Masson, and Heinrich Mann by offering them American visas so they could make their way over the Pyrenees or by ship to Spain, and then to the United States.

There is a companion book written by Varian Fry, also titled *Assignment: Rescue,* that offers a more in-depth look at the rescue process and makes for fast, easy, and interesting reading.

For a journal response, I give students a quotation by Bertolt Brecht, playwright and author of *The Jewish Wife:* "I know, of course, it's simply luck that I've survived so many friends. But last night in a dream I heard those friends say of me: 'Survival of the fittest' and I hated myself." I ask students to explain what Brecht means. Why does he hate himself because in a dream friends accuse him of surviving because he was most fit?

Students may discuss survivor's guilt, the fact that it was indeed "luck" that saved those who survived, that because of a craft or art one survived at the expense of one who may have been just as good a person.

In an effort to help students understand the difficult choices Varian Fry faced, my student teacher, Laura Hamburger, and I designed a simulation exercise for our students. We wanted them to put themselves in the so-called shoes of someone who had the power to make decisions about who would escape and who would stay, who might live and who might die. Our experiment had some surprising results.

Note: A word about simulation exercises with regard to Holocaust studies: In general, it is advisable to stay away from simulations. Simulations, according to teacher guidelines at the United States Holocaust Memorial Museum, encourage simplification of very complex issues. How can one understand hunger? How can one understand what it was like to go through a selection? We demean the process of understanding if we minimize and reduce horror to games.

If they are not attempting to recreate situations from the Holocaust, simulation activities can be used effectively, especially when they have been designed to explore varying aspects of human behavior such as fear, scapegoating, conflict resolution, and difficult decision-making (*www.ushmm.org/ education/guidelines.html*).

There are many unexpected results from this exercise. First, we hoped students would come to understand the difficulty of choosing who may live

You Choose

You are representing the United States in an effort to save Jews from the onslaught in Europe. People are lining up for visas to get out of war-torn France—away from the threat of deportation. You have only five visas to give out. Five people will receive from you the paperwork necessary to escape to safety. The question is: Who will get these visas? How will you choose? Provide rationale for your decisions.

Process:

1. Pick five people from the following applicants.

2. Join a group of four or five and reach consensus on the five people you wish to save.

3. Discuss as a class.

Judy:	15 years old, comes from a wealthy family, class president
Eric:	17 years old, very athletic, great soccer player, middle-class upbringing
Anna:	18 years old, comes from an orthodox Jewish family, never "formally" educated
Fred:	15 years old, excels at chess, building model airplanes, and chemistry
Emma:	18 years old, extremely beautiful and healthy, pregnant (first trimester)
Martin:	16 years old, works at his father's bakery to help make "ends meet," learning disability, loves to write
Margo:	15 years old, no family, works at a tailor shop, designs beautiful clothes in her free time, average student
Lily:	17 years old, sings in the school choir, star of the school play
Jake:	16 years old, has a tendency to find himself in trouble, kicked out of school, very artistic
Chloe:	15 years old, involved in student council, plays tennis, raised her younger brother
Robert:	16 years old, straight A student, specializes in writing plays, alcoholic parents

and who may die. We also expected them to grapple with issues of elitism versus equality, that is, was it fair, as was Varian Fry's mission, to choose only artists and intellectuals? What we didn't expect was students to balk at the assignment.

Nick: "I felt like Hitler. The whole time I didn't want to do it, I didn't want to choose who would live and who would die, but it was an assignment. It's proof of how the Holocaust succeeded. When you said pick five, I did it. You're the teacher. I'm a student. Imagine if a gun is held to your head! How is the Holocaust possible? Here's how it's possible: You're raised to respect a higher power—and look, you told us to do it and we did it."

We also didn't expect that out of three classes, none of the students would choose Anna, the Orthodox girl who was never "formally" educated. (In a fourth class, only one student picked Anna—so that her heritage and religious faith could be passed on.) Did this show our prejudice? And every class chose Emma who was pregnant. That was easy—they got to pick "two for the price of one."

Rationale for "selection" (even the word bothered some students, as they associated the word *selection* with Dr. Mengele's selection of concentration camp inmates for the gas chambers) ran from Imran's sense that he wanted to save those who would have the most trouble saving themselves, to Dan's desire to select those who would contribute most to society. Stephen picked the younger ones, believing they should have a chance to live longer, and David picked those who had no family because they had already learned to live on their own. Most intriguing was Dana's group's argument; like Nick, they couldn't choose at all: "How could we choose who has the right to live? Everyone's equal. It wouldn't be fair for us to pick who is more intellectual. We all have the right to live in different ways. We would pick randomly so it wouldn't be on our conscience!"

Scott L.: That would be wussing out! Our country is in a position to choose. You have to be pitiless, or you'll screw someone out that would have more to contribute.

Dan: If Einstein died, the whole world would have lost something. I'm not saying that all should die, but why pick those who have nothing to offer?

Julie: You're doing what the Nazis did—picking Aryans, the perfect race.

Dana: Just because someone may not excel earlier doesn't mean they won't have something to offer.

Justin: I've gotta use the baseball metaphor here. If I'm the manager of a baseball team I'm going to take the one shooting .350, not .150. I can't justify doing it randomly.

Imran: If you go with the argument that each life has infinite value, it doesn't matter who you pick.

I am impressed by the scope of thinking and commenting, from empathy for Varian Fry's mission to select the so-called best and brightest for visas, to the appalled reaction of students who felt that "selecting" artists and writers for visas was another version of the Third Reich's attempt to create a master race. They wrestled with important issues.

Incident at Vichy

Almost twenty years after the fall of the Vichy government in France, Arthur Miller re-imagined what it must have been like to be picked off the streets and brought into a make-shift police station for questioning—and ultimately, deported to Hitler's camps. As with his other plays—*All My Sons, A View from the Bridge,* and *The Crucible*—in *Incident at Vichy* Miller finds the vein of morality around which the events and passions bleed.

Noting that in the 1950s Miller wrote *The Crucible* about the Salem witch trials to expose the McCarthy witch hunt for communists, I ask my students why Miller would write *Incident at Vichy* in the 1960s. What was going on in the sixties that may have provoked Miller to write a play about a man who chooses to turn his guilt into responsible action?

The answer I am looking for is the Civil Rights Movement, the choice so many white people made to not just feel "liberal" guilt, but to actively get involved in marches and registering the vote. In his 1965 essay, "Guilt and *Incident at Vichy,*" Miller writes that the story around which the play is based is true; he was told by a European friend about a Jewish man picked up on the street in Vichy, France, taken to a police station under the racial laws, and handed a pass to escape, from a stranger who was not Jewish. For ten years Miller saw that anonymous stranger who gave away his pass to freedom, who took responsibility in a world he could not control. He saw that anonymous stranger when thirty-eight witnesses in Queens did not call the police when Kitty Genovese was attacked and killed and when three boys were murdered in Mississippi for fighting to make a difference.

> Who among us has asked himself how much of his own sense of personal value, how much of his pride in himself is there by virtue of his not being black? And how much of our fear of the Negro comes from the subterranean knowledge that his lowliness has found our consent and that he is demanding from us what we have taken from him and keep taking from him through our pride?"

Miller contrasts the smugness of the liberal who does not take true responsibility to the hero of the play, Prince Von Berg, who is mistakenly arrested by a Nazi "race expert": "He comes into the detention room with his pride of being on the humane side, the right side, for he has fled his Austria and his rank and privilege rather than be a part of a class which oppresses people" (72).

The play, according to Miller, is not about Nazism, but about "our individual relationships with injustice and violence." In *Incident at Vichy* Von Berg must choose whether to escape by relying on his elite status while maintaining his enlightened and liberal attitude toward the Nazi atrocities, or to take a stand against Nazi racial laws by offering his pass to a Jew condemned to die under those laws.

As Philip Brandes in a 1995 *Los Angeles Times* review of *Incident at Vichy* says, "With surgical precision, Miller's taut drama about the rounding up of Jews in occupied France during World War II pares away the comforts of detachment until we're left with an inexorable conclusion about universal complicity and responsibility for human tragedies like the Holocaust."

I assign the parts, providing a tool of the trade to each character (the play has nine male parts—which I *do* assign to females): A paintbrush to Lebeau, a painter; a screwdriver to Bayard, an electrician; a calculator to Marchand, a businessman; a beret to Monceau, an actor . . . and so on. We read and we discuss as confusing or amusing lines come up.

To discuss the play I start with the concrete: What happens in the end? Students are confused, at first. Only Von Berg remains on stage as four new prisoners are ushered in. "One plus one plus one," says Blake, referring to the quote by Judith Miller: " . . . Only in understanding that civilized people must defend the one, by one, by one . . . can the Holocaust, the incomprehensible, be given meaning." What he means is that Arthur Miller reveals the unique personalities of the original eight; by the play's conclusion, we understand the loss of each person. And now, in the last scene of the play, four more prisoners enter the waiting room; the cycle will begin again.

I move to more abstract questions: What is Miller's point? What does he want to show through this play? Some students say it is about people who live for their ideals, who will choose *not* to remain indifferent bystanders. Others say Miller shows the difference between talking about doing something and *doing* it. Still others say it is about how we choose to live in this world in which man has *not* accepted his own nature: "that he is *not* reasonable, that he is full of murder, that his ideals are only the little tax he pays for the right to hate and kill with a clear conscience" (65).

Why does Von Berg give up his pass? Students are anxious to understand Von Berg's motives—from his earlier desire for suicide when his musicians were arrested and he had to witness the indifference of his fellow countrymen, to his later insistence and need to prove that "there are people who would find it easier to die than stain one finger with this murder" (65).

Should Leduc accept the pass from Von Berg? Most students agree it depends on what he makes of his life, if he can do more good than Von Berg may have done by surviving. He is after all, students say, a doctor. He may be able to save more lives if he lives.

". . . all this suffering is so pointless—it can never be a lesson, it can never have a meaning. And that is why it will be repeated again and again forever" (61). Does Miller believe that suffering can have meaning, can be a lesson? Is that why he writes plays? Or does he believe in the innate, sad state of humans, a more existential philosophy, a Job-like philosophy—that to live is to suffer and there are no lessons to be learned?

What about some of the stage directions and images? The grimy windows (1), the Gypsy's copper pot (8), the "white cloud of feathers" that blows out of the old Jew's pillow (64–65), the major's "deadened eyes" (65), the "siren moving off in pursuit" (70)? How do they enhance the production?

I ask students to note the opening narration:

> When light begins to rise, six men and a boy of fifteen are discovered on the bench in attitudes expressive of their personalities and functions, frozen there like members of a small orchestra at the moment before they begin to play.

I divide the class into groups and ask each group to form a "tableau vivant," a living sculpture of the opening scene. We discuss how each group represents the seven characters' personalities and functions. This leads to a discussion of the importance and role of the characters.

I suggest several journal responses to help students get to the heart of the play:

- Select a quotation from the play and discuss how the quotation relates to the overall meaning. How does the quotation reveal what Arthur Miller is trying to say?

- Choose one character from the play and show his purpose. What does Arthur Miller say through this character? This response may be the beginning for a longer essay.

- Read the following paragraph from Hannah Arendt's *Eichmann in Jerusalem:*

  > And just as the law in civilized countries assumes that the voice of conscience tells everybody "Thou shalt not kill," even though man's natural desires and inclinations may at times be murderous, so the law of Hitler's

land demanded that the voice of conscience tell everybody: "Thou shalt kill," although the organizers of the massacres knew full well that murder is against the normal desires and inclinations of most people. Evil in the Third Reich had lost the quality by which most people recognize it—the quality of temptation. Many Germans and many Nazis, probably an overwhelming majority of them, must have been tempted *not* to murder, *not* to rob, *not* to let their neighbors go off to their doom (for that the Jews were transported to their doom they knew, of course, even though many of them may not have known the gruesome details), and not to become accomplices in all these crimes by benefiting from them. But, God knows, they had learned how to resist temptation. (150)

How, I ask, do the events in *Incident at Vichy* support (or not support) her insightful and ironic contention that Germans could not resist the temptation to murder and rob and that by remaining bystanders, they allowed their neighbors to go off to their doom?

These questions and journal responses will, I hope, force students to delve into the meanings of Miller's play and to consider the role of the bystander in politics.

The American Response

Unfortunately, one truth we must look at is the American response to the persecution of Jews in Europe. At a time when the government of the United States could have done something, it did very little. As Elie Wiesel said in an interview with Bill Moyers (*Facing Hate*), he is most angry at Churchill and Roosevelt because they could have warned the Hungarian Jews in 1944 *not* to board the trains, they could have at least told them what was happening in Auschwitz.

I show students *The American Experience: America and the Holocaust: Deceit and Indifference,* a PBS/The American Experience production about how and when the United States government was aware of what was happening in Europe and why and how they chose not to respond. The video looks closely at the U.S. immigration policy and at anti-Semitism in America. PBS provides an incredible website for *America and the Holocaust: Deceit and Indifference* (*www.pbs.org/wgbh/amex/holocaust/index.html*). The site opens with a photograph of the Statue of Liberty, a yellow star superimposed on her forehead. The site provides a teacher's guide, time lines, maps showing the destruction of the Jewish population of Europe from 1939 to 1945, biographies, and an enhanced transcript of the video.

"What surprises you?" I ask after we've viewed the film. Students are surprised to see signs at beaches in America that say, "No Dogs or Jews Allowed," the same signs visible in Germany and Italy. They are surprised by the lack of help offered by America despite opportunities to act: the turning away of the *St. Louis,* a ship carrying 900 German Jews, the shunning of a kindertransport (a transport of children)—because charming Jewish children turn into ugly adults. Nick comments, "There was so much anti-Semitism in Germany, but there was here, too. Why would we go help there with so much anti-Semitism here?" Students are surprised that despite warnings of the imminent destruction of the European Jewish community, the United States chose to remain indifferent, chose to remain bystanders. The U.S. reaction is contrary to everything they have come to expect from their government, and this reaction is very unsettling.

In journals, I ask students to describe their reactions to *America and the Holocaust: Deceit and Indifference.* What surprises? What do you now know that you didn't know before?

In her journal, Robyn reflects with profound sensitivity. She is perplexed by the role the United States did *not* play, the fact that we remained silent when we could have done more. As an American and as a Jew, she feels deeply the conflict between wanting to believe that we Americans are good; and at the same time, seeing the United States as complicit, no better than French collaborators in that Americans literally turned away Jews from its shores (the *St. Louis*), refused to open its immigration quotas, and did nothing to stop the incarceration and killing of Jews in Nazi concentration camps:

> The movie about America's role made me cry. I wanted to believe Anne Frank, that humans really are good underneath. The Holocaust showed man's utter evil. . . . Since kindergarten, I had been given the impression that America was the hero, the benevolent protector of little people all over the globe. I wanted the impression to be true.
>
> But it was wrong. America was only a cat with a mask on. Underneath, our country was just as vile, racist, and complicit in slaughter as Germany, perhaps in a sense even more guilty because America tried to pass itself off as a "democracy," a place with "liberty and justice for all." Germany at least openly flaunted its evil. America, meanwhile, hid its prejudice in the dark depths of the state department. . . . Elie Wiesel said, "The opposite of love is not hate, it's indifference. The opposite of art is not ugliness, it's indifference. The opposite of faith is not heresy, it's indifference. And the opposite of life is not death, it's indifference."
>
> I can't deal with America's role. I can't forgive my country.

Jackie also describes her lost idealism, yet she recognizes how by losing her innocence, she must take action to change that which she doesn't like, including the things—like prejudice and racism—that she had hoped a good and noble world could cure without her help:

> I've begun to look at how my life is now and how things have changed since the 1940s. Of course, in my average everyday life I do not witness such things as the anti-Semitism during the Holocaust, but I've become more sensitive to what goes on around me at school and around the country. With the memory of the Columbine High School tragedy still in my head, I can see that although things have changed, we still have prejudice and racism in our world. By the choices that students make to exclude one another, to separate groups by color and religion, and to judge each other on appearances, I've realized that our world can never be one.
>
> I know that I can't change the whole world, but I believe that my job now, after taking this class, is to change the choices that I make. I want to be one who stands up for those who are pushed down. I do not want to be a bystander.

My purpose in teaching about the Holocaust was never to turn my students into activists, and yet—as they study injustice they formulate their own, personal responses. They draw connections to racist and hateful behavior today—and they see the danger of allowing prejudice to spread unchecked. They see the value of adding their voices to discussions, to acting and making informed choices in a world that often prefers to shut its eyes.

5

The Ghettos

The Kolbuszowa rebbe, Yechiel
Teitelbaum, is forced to pose for a
photograph in his tallit and tefillin
(prayer shawl and phylacteries) in
front of his home in the ghetto.
Norman Salsitz, courtesy of USHMM
Photo Archives.

They did such terrible things to us that no one was surprised at
anything.

—IDA FINK

The reign of the Third Reich with their ghettos and camps was a time of sanctioned sadism, a time when the bullies went wild and were unrestrained. Why were Jews rounded up like farm animals and restricted to ghettos? Why were families systematically forced to move from their homes to apartments they had to share with several other families in the poorest section of the city? Why were food supplies cut? Why were Jews shot if they tripped or paused or didn't move fast enough? Why was it German policy to kill every Jewish man, woman, and child? Why did ordinary citizens go along with Nazi policy? Nothing makes sense.

Upon his arrival in Auschwitz, Primo Levi (*Survival in Auschwitz*) asks a German guard, "Why?" The guard answers, "There is no why here" (29). There is no reasonable explanation. Just a series of events to describe. A series of facts. Numbing, unbelievable facts. These facts are revealed in survivors' testimonies, in history books, and in the books and stories and poetry of the Holocaust.

During World War II, the Germans created more than 400 ghettos in occupied territories. The word *ghetto* originally referred to a separate quarter of the city in Venice, the Geto Nuovo (New Foundry), where in 1516, Jews were forced to live. Originally, ghettos were created to restrict contacts between Jews and Christians. By the end of the eighteenth century, the forcible restriction of Jews to ghettos was gradually abandoned; the Roman ghetto, which was closed in 1870, was the last ghetto to exist in Europe prior to World War II (Gutman 579).

Ghettos in occupied countries during World War II were designed as a transitional phase in a process leading to the "final solution" of the Jewish question. Within the ghettos people starved; they were slave laborers in forced labor camps. A number of scholars maintain that the ghettos were designed to serve as an indirect instrument of destruction, a means of physically destroying the Jews by denying them the basic necessities of life, rather than by the use of lethal weapons. The ghettos were also a way station, an organizational tool, before transport to concentration and death camps. The liquidation of the ghettos coincided with the beginning of the Nazis' "Final Solution," in the spring of 1942 (Gutman 582).

Directed by Steven Spielberg, *Schindler's List* recreates the Kracow and Plowzov ghettos. Two documentaries that show ghetto life are BBC's *The Warsaw Ghetto* (clips of often gruesome images filmed by the SS, narrated by a survivor) and The History Channel's *Kovno Ghetto* (interviews with survivors of the ghetto). One book that graphically describes the formation of the ghettos and life in the ghettos is *Maus I: My Father Bleeds History* by Art Spiegelman.

Maus I, a brilliantly rendered novel/comic/testimony, portrays the protagonists (Jews) as mice and the antagonists (Nazis) as cats. Art Spiegelman, artist and writer of *Maus I* and *Maus II,* reveals not only his father's story, but his as well: the impact of the Holocaust on the second generation. *Maus I* tells the story that leads to the camps: the coming of the war, the suffering under the Nuremberg Laws, the gathering of the Jews into ghettos, the Jews' hiding to escape *Aktionen,* and the victims' suffering from repercussions and psychic damage long after the war. *Maus II* continues where *Maus I* leaves off, and takes Vladek, Art's father, into and through Auschwitz.

Maus I offers a good entry into the literature of the Holocaust. It presents a vivid picture—literally—of life *after* the war as Vladek tells his story to his son Art, *before* the war when things were normal, and *during* the war when the Germans (cats) hunted, captured, and killed Jews (mice). *Maus I* opens with Art visiting his father to hear his story. Spiegelman explains on *The Complete Maus* CD-ROM that he drew Vladek in the present riding a stationary bike to suggest a state of pedaling without getting anywhere.

As Vladek pedals in place Art tells his father, "I want to tell *your* story, the way it really happened." Vladek responds, "But this isn't so *proper,* so respectful. . . . I can tell you *other* stories, but such *private* things, I don't want you should mention." And Art, with his hand up in the air says, "Okay, okay—I promise" (23). Then Spiegelman does what a writer does, he tells the private things. I ask my students "why" Art includes this scene. I want them to get at the truth of the book; how difficult it was for Art to get his father to talk about his experiences, and how utterly honest he is in rendering Vladek's experiences to the comic page.

In the spring of 2000, The Museum of Modern Art in New York exhibited drawings from *Maus* as examples of how American art reflects war. Art Spiegelman's drawings were shown side by side with Pablo Picasso's cartoon etchings of "The Dream and Lie of Franco, 1937," which are preliminary drawings for his "Guernica." To introduce the concept of cartooning, I bring in Xeroxed copies of Picasso's cartoons and "Guernica," his 1937 painting that depicts the bombing of Guernica, a small Spanish village during the Spanish Civil War.

My students find parallels in Spiegelman's drawings of the Holocaust and Picasso's drawings of the Spanish Civil War. I ask them to see what they can see in Picasso's "Guernica," which may be viewed and studied online at *www.pbs.org/treasuresoftheworld/a_nav/guernica_nav/main_guerfrm.html* or at *museoreinasofia.mcu.es/colecc/sala06/de0050.htm.* The PBS site offers explanations of the painting's history. I go around the room, encouraging individual students to explain the various elements of the painting: the light, the mother/Madonna figure carrying her dead child, the screaming horse, the tongues like spikes or knives, the silent screams, the bull's head, and so on. They are amazed at what they notice, and they are duly impressed by how artists have depicted war through cartoons.

To begin our study of the book, I ask students to examine the cover and to write in their journals about their discoveries. I want them to see that each line used, each color chosen, each character drawing is intentional and conveys meaning. I want my students to read the text as if reading the Bible verse by verse—to find answers and ideas in the text, to become responsible for finding questions and answers by reading without an *imposed* logic or agenda. I want students to learn to interpret literature and to trust their own interpretations.

After writing in journals, the students are ready to talk to each other in class. Writing down ideas rather than beginning a discussion cold prompts students to delve into the material and think more profoundly. Because I do not lecture, I rely on students' inquiries and responses for substance in class discussions.

What students first notice as we begin our discussion of *Maus I*'s cover is a cat's face centered in a swastika, isolated in what looks like a moon or a spotlight, a symbol of hatred and violence. Jackie says the cat's head, with its triangle of black, suggests Hitler's parted hair and his mustache. Jason, who saw the early drawings for *Maus* in a New York gallery, says the swastika was not originally there. The message he sees is of a family sticking together. Chris points out the family of two mice in shadows with the searchlight shining on them. Stephanie G. says that the mice drawings show their innocence as they huddle in fear. Robyn notes that the mice are drawn softly, in muted blues, browns, and greens, while the cat-Nazi face is drawn in uncompromising black and white. "There's a big circle, like a spotlight," Helen says. "The Jews are huddling, trying to get out of the spotlight." Leigh notes that the swastika is rising up and over the mice, and it's powerful. Leigh makes us see an arm of the swastika reaching into the heads of the mice—whom we soon know as Vladek and Anja, the parents of Artie. Jessica points out that the mice are backed up and pushed against a wall, they can't escape. "Where is the spotlight coming from?" I ask. It takes them a moment to realize it comes from the eyes of the reader!

Natalie points out to us that the subtitle, "A Survivor's Tale," has a double meaning—a survivor's tail is suggested by the homonymic association of the word. We later learn as we read that the tails, like the proverbial hooked Jewish nose, betray the mice to the Nazis. Trisha notes the German spelling of "Maus" on the cover in blood-red dripping letters. Julia P. notes the colors of the cover, except for the mice, are the overwhelming red, white, and black of the flag of the Third Reich with its red background and black swastika centered in a white circle. "Great symbolism!" says J.P., who notes the swastika, and above it the word "Maus" splattering red blood. "And the swastika, with the cat, is like the skull and bones—it means poison!"

On the back cover Jackie sees information about where the Spiegelmans were and where they are now. There's a map of Rego Park, New York, embedded in a red frame and superimposed on a dark purple, green, and brown map of Eastern Europe during the war. Mice heads over crossed bones mark various death camps: Chelmno, Treblinka, Sobibor, Maidanek, Belzek, and

Auschwitz / Birkenau. Also marked on the European map are the various cities and ghettos where Vladek Spiegelman had lived. Superimposed on the map is a black-and-white drawing of Artie the mouse lying on the floor, a cigarette in his mouth and his tail waving in the air listening to his father who sits in an easy chair. Art is listening as the tale comes out, Jackie says. Stephanie G. suggests that with Artie lying on the floor, listening to his father, there's a sense of continuity and a sense that this, though it is a Holocaust memory, takes place in the present.

Kristen asks about the significance of the two maps: "This is where Vladek lived, this is where he lives now." "Perhaps," Jessica suggests, "the geography of these maps lives in them as much as they live in the mapped land." Natalie sees the move from Poland to an Americanized city, "There's Alexander's Department Store, Kennedy Airport—he can drive there and depart whenever and for wherever he wants." Nick suggests that Spiegelman is bringing the two countries together with the two maps. Abbi says Artie and his father merge through the conversation: "The father and son are from two such different cultures."

Just from closely observing the details of the cover, my students discover what *Maus* is about. They begin to understand how Spiegelman uses his art to tell his father's story as well as his own. I want them to use their understanding to grapple with how the story unfolds within the "novel's" cartoon boxes.

I schlep a television connected to a computer to our classroom (I have to roll it from the library out over a cracked sidewalk, up a wooden ramp to our portable classroom) so we can view the CD-ROM, *Maus*, based on Spiegelman's books and notebooks. I've previewed the CD-ROM and click through the disk so we can listen to Spiegelman's explanations and Vladek's voice.

On the CD-ROM are video tapes of Spiegelman's and his wife's trip to Poland to view the places Vladek lived. There are also samples of Spiegelman's original drawings, the photographs on which he based his artwork, Vladek's explanations as taped by Spiegelman, and most important, Spiegelman's voice explaining what different boxes in the book mean.

Of particular interest is a series of drawings on pages 32–33. Spiegelman enlarges a backdrop of the Nazi flag so that the black swastika on its white background looks as if a moon engraved with a swastika embedded in the blackness of the flag rises over the town. The black background brings metaphorical night, the same image illuminated by Elie Wiesel's *Night*. The darkness of night descends and encompasses the Jews; even the moon is etched with the foreboding swastika. Drawings that show the enacted Nuremburg Laws are based on real photographs: white Stars of David and the word *Jude* (Jew) splashed on the windows of Jewish shops, a bearded old man on a horse cart, wearing a prayer shawl and carrying a sign, "I am a filthy Jew." With the click of a "mouse," the original photographs appear on the CD-ROM and Spiegelman's voice may be heard describing how he came to draw these images.

Another compelling use of cartooning explained by Spiegelman is the black-edged cartoon within the book, *Prisoner on the Hell Planet: A Case History* (100–103). "Prisoner on the Hell Planet" originally appeared in "an obscure underground comic book" (99); it is a woodblock print that shows Art in concentration camp garb going to his mother's funeral. Art accuses his mother for murdering *him:*

> Well, Mom, if you're listening . . . Congratulations! . . . You've committed the perfect crime . . . you put me here . . . shorted all my circuits . . . cut my nerve endings . . . and crossed my wires! . . . you murdered me, Mommy, and you left me here to take the rap!!! (103)

Students ask why Art would accuse his mother of murder. Through Art's trauma, the effect of the Holocaust on the second generation becomes viscerally apparent. Students also tie his calling his mother a murderer to the last image of the book where we see Art walking away from his father and muttering under his breath, " . . . murderer." Art is angry in the end that his father destroyed his mother's notebooks and in doing so, murdered Art's memory of her.

For journals, I ask students to select one or two pages from *Maus* and to examine how cartooning affects Spiegelman's message within the context of the whole book. This assignment forces students into the text. It forces them to see how image and text relate and how Spiegelman uses his art to convey meaning. In class, we go "around the room," a technique I use to allow every student to speak, as quite often, in class discussions, the shy or reluctant students do not get a chance to voice their opinions and discoveries. Students take us to separate panels and boxes within the book, essentially giving us a guided tour of *Maus I.*

Julia P. describes a series of boxes in which an SS officer kills a child by swinging his head into a brick wall. She interprets not only the significance of the drawings, but also concludes how these scenes of Nazi sadism disturb and perplex:

> Vladek tells of how the SS troops would take children that were screaming too much and smash their heads into a wall, killing them in a truly horrifying manner. The first picture Spiegelman uses to show this story has the Nazis herding children away with their hands over their heads, like prison-

ers. They are all shaded in and dark so that they blend in with the background. Then there are two images that are white and stand out. They are of a Nazi and a young, crying child standing next to a brick wall.

The next frame shows the Nazi and the child (both of whom are now darkly shaded in). The Nazi is shown swinging the child by his foot into a brick wall. In the picture you can see the force being used by the Nazi to swing the child; and then on the wall blood is splattered. It's so disturbing to see and then to actually think about it. To actually smash someone's head into a wall with *that* much force? I can't even comprehend what that would look like, much less feel like.

The last square shows the German maintaining his hold of the child's leg, only now the child is lying on the ground, dead. You can see the blood splattered all over the wall, but it's covered up by a speech bubble so that you can't see any of the more graphic detail that could have been shown.

Just looking at it disturbs me enough that I seriously have to close the book because now I'm thinking about it. Oh man . . . I just can't understand how someone could ever bring themselves to pick up a *child,* someone who's scared and hasn't even had the chance to experience life, and throw them into a wall with the only intention being to kill. I guess I'll never understand.

Abbi, herself a grandchild of a survivor, writes with sensitivity about what it means to be a survivor's child:

The cartoon, "Prisoner of the Hell Planet," is very serious and is made to look much more dramatic because the pages are much darker and have more shading. This is the only part of the book where the characters are actually portrayed as humans, not animals. It was very emotional for me to see the actual picture of Art's mother, Anja. As real as the book was to me, it had a whole new meaning when I saw her as a person, in an actual photograph. Another thing I noticed was where it says in the corner, "protect what you have," because during the Holocaust people couldn't protect what they had, and at this point [Art's mother has just committed suicide] the war is over and they still can't protect what they have.

The cartoon is also kind of scary when Vladek throws himself onto the casket and cries at Anja's funeral. The cartoon shows a scene [with Art] inside an insane asylum [wearing a camp inmate's striped uniform], which makes me wonder how the scars from the Holocaust have carried on to the next generation of people.

In writing about scenes, focusing on individual cartoon boxes, students extrapolate larger meanings. Writing about the specifics in literature—even about cartooned characters and events—helps them make sense of the whole, helps them tease out conclusions and connections, which leads to a more comprehensive understanding of the whole. Then, because students have begun to "research" within the assigned text, I feel able to assign a more rigorous essay, which forces them to deal with the book as a work of art.

The purpose of the long-term writing assignment is to force students to take another look at the text of Spiegelman's *Maus I,* to treat it as a piece of literature and to examine a single theme or motif as it runs through the book. While much of the assigned writing is in the form of journal writing to encourage more informal connections and thinking, I want students to write more formal, comprehensive essays as well.

Writing Assignment

We have discussed several themes in *Maus I.* For this assignment, pick a motif or theme and follow it through the book. Write a two- to three-page essay examining the following:

1. How is the motif or theme important?
2. How does Spiegelman use the motif or theme?
3. What are some questions or emotions the motif or theme evokes?
4. How is the use of this motif or theme effective? Is it resolved in the book? (That is, how does the motif fit with the thrust or main point of the book?) Ultimately what is the significance of the motif?

    Some suggested topics:
    - Swastika
    - Art's smoking
    - Money
    - Vladek's stationary bike
    - Art's relationship with his father
    - Art's relationship with his mother/stepmother
    - Spiegelman's use of animals for humans
    - The interior comic, "Prisoner on Hell Planet"

Exploring the relationship of cats and mice to Germans and Jews, Mike writes:

> The story of *Maus* shows the conflict of the sly and tenacious cats, out to hunt and rid the land of the mice, and of the mice, who attempt to keep out of harm's way without disturbing anyone.
>
> The Germans, or cats in this case, did what they wanted, a behavior commonly attributed to cats, and stayed on the prowl until they were satisfied that their plans were carried out. The Germans planned to rid Europe of all Jews, and wouldn't stop until they were done. The Germans, just like cats, liked to play with their "prey" before they killed them. On page 33, the center two frames show a picture of two German soldier-cats laughing at a Jew that they had made hold a sign that says, "I am a filthy Jew." Then in the next frame they beat the Jew to death. In the following frame, a sign stands at the entrance to the town stating that the town is "Jew free." Many of the Germans considered Jews "vermin" anyway, and had no trouble trying to exterminate the "infestation" of mice in their country.

Focusing on another expanded metaphor in *Maus,* Trisha describes Spiegelman's use of the stationary bike:

> In my basement, we have a stationary bicycle. All you have to do is pedal and the wheels turn round and round. You never reach a destination, because there is no way to move. Riding on a stationary bike seems to last forever, there is no end, there is no way out. In *Maus,* often when Vladek tells his story of the Holocaust, he is riding a stationary bicycle. At first glance you may see no connection from the bike to the story at all. But then it pops up again and again, until Spiegelman forces you to ask yourself why it is that Vladek is riding this type of bike. The bicycle was much more than just an exercise tool, the bicycle was the constant movement that Art's parents had to do to hide from Nazis. It was the idea that for four years there was no escape. The bike was the constant struggle that the Jews faced in the Holocaust, and it was the constant circles they made through Europe. Like the swastika-sidewalk from which there was no escape, the bike represented the fact that no matter what Jews did or where they went, they were still Jews and they were really going nowhere.

Kate examines Spiegelman's use of the swastika in its many guises:

> Threatening and disciplined are the four arms, bent perfectly at the elbows, that mark the cover of *Maus* and scatter themselves among the pages within. Though *Maus* in undeniably packed with different effectual themes and

motifs, that of the swastika stuck most prominently in my mind after finishing the book.

The swastika is flashed again at the beginning of the second chapter where it waves on the face of the Nazi flag, jagged and evil, over the Jews standing curiously below ... On the opposite page the swastika leers behind each separate box in place of the moon, peeping around corners, glowering down upon the people with an overwhelming evil.

... At one point the swastika appears as the cross section of four roads; Vladek claims, "Anja and I didn't have where to go." This scene symbolizes the huge, unavoidable power of the Nazi's by using their emblem to show the extent of their control which was stretching in all directions and from which there was no escape.

These student writers have become researchers, finding examples and passages within the text to help support their theses. Step by step, I want them to develop their own resources, to learn to research within the text to find proof. I want them also to begin to trust their own judgments before consulting with the "experts." I want them to take pride in their own discoveries rather than relying on someone else to tell them what it all means; I'm not yet ready for them to consult criticism. Later, when they have developed their own interpretation skills, then I won't mind if they consult and learn from the critics.

Additional Exercises

1. Visit the United States Holocaust Museum website for historical information on ghettos: (*www.ushmm.orgoutreach/ghettos.htm*). Assess the website. Compare that information to information you may find in an encyclopedia.

2. Visit the online exhibition of the "Warsaw Ghetto: Dignity and Defiance" at the Simon Wiesenthal Center website: (*www.motlc .wiesenthal.org/exhibits/dignitydefiance/index.html*). Read through the documents. Answer one of the questions provided at the end of the exhibit.

3. Look up the derivation of the word *ghetto* in the Oxford English Dictionary.

4. Do a search on the word *ghetto* on the Internet. What types of links do you discover? Which is the best site? Why?

5. Consider how the term *ghetto*, initially used to describe the areas of cities in Italy where Jews were confined, has been applied to "urban

ghettos" in the United States—especially during the 1960s, where minorities either chose to live or found themselves restricted due to redlining by real estate agents. Did people move to U.S. ghettos by choice or by force? What effect has "segregated" living through most of the twentieth century had on African Americans?

6. Consider how the Japanese American population was restricted to internment camps in the United States during World War II. Read *Snow Falling on Cedars* by David Guterson.

Viewing Videos

To enhance the study of *Maus I* and ghettos, I show one of two videos: *Kovno Ghetto: A Buried History* and the BBC's *The Warsaw Ghetto*. Both documentaries reveal life in the ghetto. Another video worth showing is the 1976 docudrama, *Holocaust*, based on Gerald Green's novel of that name. Though it is "Holocaust Light" in the form of a Holocaust soap opera, the film, which was originally made for television, shows life in the ghetto (Parts II and III).

I show *The Warsaw Ghetto*, a black-and-white documentary made by the BBC and narrated by Alexander Bernfes, a survivor, to provide historical background about the concentration of Jews in ghettos. The horror of starvation, indiscriminate sadism, and nude bodies heaped on carts for burial is apparent in footage shot by German soldiers for Heinrich Himmler's archive. There is something about the crassness of Himmler's wanting to document the destruction of a people—from the propaganda films to show that life in the ghetto wasn't so bad, to the filming of nude bodies laid out in front of doorsteps to be picked up and heaped in carts and there to slide down chutes into pits. Students see the resistance of Jews and the ultimate annihilation of the ghetto, street by street, by the Germans.

Hannah Arendt astutely and controversially observes:

> Wherever Jews lived, there were recognized Jewish leaders, and this leadership, almost without exception, cooperated in one way or another, for one reason or another, with the Nazis. The whole truth was that if the Jewish people had really been unorganized and leaderless, there would have been chaos and plenty of misery but the total number of victims would hardly have been between four-and-a-half and six million people. [According to Freudiger's calculations about half of them could have saved themselves if they had not followed the instructions of the Jewish Councils (125).]

I ask students to describe in journals their reactions to the videos about ghettos: What are ghettos? How are they organized? How were they used by the Germans? Why would the SS want to document the people inside the ghetto?

Megan describes the emotional effect of *The Warsaw Ghetto:*

In class today we watched a movie on the Warsaw ghetto. These ghettos were the Jewish residential quarters. They were marked off sections of towns and cities where the Nazis forced the Jews to live. There were over four hundred ghettos in Poland.

... One scene of the documentary film that stuck with me the rest of the day was the scene of the Nazis throwing the dead Jewish bodies in a large dirt pile of bodies. I couldn't believe someone would just toss the bodies in a dirt pile, just like throwing away a piece of garbage. Many questions stirred up as I watched this horrific scene: How can people be so inhuman to do something like this? Don't these people have any morals or values? How were they able to wake every morning and know that they had to kill innocent people? I don't understand what drove the Germans to this killing spree. I can't understand how people can have so much hatred towards other people just because they have different religious beliefs.

This documentary really affected me. Watching real footage of the Holocaust scared me. It is a scary thought to know that there was so much hate, and it had to end with millions of Jews dead.

Scott F. is also struck by the horrific aspect of the film, yet what bothered him was seeing the organized masses blindly supporting Hitler and the Third Reich. In responding personally to graphic scenes, he describes and analyzes detail:

The movie about the Warsaw ghetto was probably one of the most terrifying things I've ever seen in my life. It wasn't a "scary" movie, but it was horrific. The worst part about it was that the gory images of withered people starving in the ghetto weren't what terrified me ...

The most horrific parts were all the scenes of the German army marching through the streets and the masses of people hailing Hitler. Whenever I see footage of those soldiers marching straight-legged in perfect unison through the streets carrying enormous flags with the swastika on it, a chill runs up and down my spine. And to hear the people chanting, "Heil! Heil! Heil!" I get goosebumps. I don't know why all of this is so scary to me, maybe because I am just in shock that the presence of one man could fill an amphitheater that looks twice the size of the Michigan Stadium (which seats over 101,000) with people chanting his name over and over. All that power and all that evil gained Hitler an entire continent of followers, and it is simply unbelievable. I am amazed and terrified by it all.

Kate responds to the faces, to the individuals who make up the whole:

I didn't want to look into the sad faces of the 600,000 people that inhabited the ghetto, yet I couldn't take my eyes off them. They were so pale, so sickly, so skinny, and simply so desperate looking. What really amazed me were the brief moments of happiness, a smile here or there, caught on film, which showed the relentless human spirit even in the absolute worst of situations. . . . I can't imagine being forced to live under the unsanitary conditions the people in the ghetto endured. People were afraid to even touch for fear of passing lice or typhus. The stench of death and disease on the streets would certainly have made me vomit. I was aghast when I saw how the Germans were portraying life in the ghetto to the outside world, as if it were completely bearable if not happy. My stomach turned to think of the deception because in actual fact the ghetto was the ultimate picture of misery and death. It also disgusted me that the Germans filmed the suffering within the ghetto simply because they were able to. How could anyone see such human suffering and film it as though it were an athletic event? It is simply terrifying to me that people have been cruel enough to document such happenings without helping, that they would go as far as to toss down a bit of bread just to watch desperate and starving people weakly fight each other for it. . . . What brings tears to my eyes is the fact that things were so awful for the Jews after being evacuated from the ghetto that they could refer to life within its cruel walls as heavenly.

Most responding students use the words *terrifying* and *horrifying*. We somehow can't describe the events that lead to and became the Holocaust without invoking the nightmarish effects of its rendering into documentary, literature, and art. Yet, in their journal responses, students are learning to move from the abstract to the particular, from the big, encompassing idea, to the concrete, specific detail that helps us begin to see and understand.

I ask my students to research the Kovno Ghetto at the United States Holocaust Memorial Museum's website: *www.ushmm.org/kovno/index.htm*. Then we watch *Kovno Ghetto: A Buried History*, a film based on survivors' oral history juxtaposed with photographs and film clips from the ghetto. The United States Holocaust Memorial Center also has an Internet exhibition of the "Hidden History of the Kovno Ghetto." Together the two pieces of literature provide a vivid picture of the hunger, epidemics, forced labor, and "actions" in the ghetto.

Natalie personalizes what she sees in the film. She is aware not only of how she reacts to what is happening on camera, but also what is happening to her as she watches. She is unconsciously practicing "metacognition," that is, thinking about her thinking:

> The survivors speak, and suddenly the experience, the Holocaust, becomes so much more personal. We no longer hear "millions of Jews," we hear, "this happened to me and my family."
>
> I cannot get the image of the selection process out of my mind. I have this picture of standing in line and watching everyone in front of me get sent to life or death. And my little sister stands in front of me, and I know she is too weak to be spared. They tell me left and her right. There could be nothing more horrible.
>
> And suddenly in the midst of my morbid thoughts, I want the bell to ring. I want to escape from this classroom where I have such thoughts. The subject of the Holocaust is constantly paining. More death, more families separated, more ovens, more gas chambers, and more and more questions. Why weren't they warned? Why weren't they told? Why didn't they run or hide or fight? But there are no answers and I have a strange feeling that there will never be.
>
> I reach a certain point where I don't want to read or learn about it anymore. Not because it's boring or because I'm not interested, but because it's so difficult to take it in, it's so difficult to understand.
>
> So I sit here in the middle of second hour. I see a few heads collapsed on desks, and others are perplexed by the film; but I sit in my chair about to burst into tears at the thought of this ghetto being in my neighborhood or having to say goodbye to my father and knowing I will never see him again because of a war that I do not understand. Am I done now? Can I stop watching?

Another video we watch is an excerpt from the 1978 television series, *Holocaust*. I show Parts II and III, starring Fritz Weaver, Michael Moriarty, Meryl Streep, James Woods, Rosemary Harris, among others. This video shows life in the Warsaw Ghetto, including meetings of the Judenrat (Jewish Council) and the decision to resist or submit to German demands. While the film has been criticized because it is a docudrama, I use it for several purposes. First, I want my students to see how a popular television drama used documentary footage and historical material to create a soap-opera-ish film. Second, I want them to see what American viewers saw on national television, which may have triggered the beginning of a broader national awareness of the Holocaust—as *Roots* encouraged a more open discussion of racism. And third, with apologies to the purists, this is a damn good show—enjoyable and at the same time, educational.

After viewing the docudrama *Holocaust* and the documentaries *Kovno Ghetto* and *The Warsaw Ghetto,* I ask students to discuss in their journals the differences between docudrama and documentary. Which is more effective in conveying a sense of the times? Which is more compelling to watch? Why?

To force students to assimilate the material we've studied, I ask them to do what one who writes historical fiction must do—to imagine themselves or a fictitious character who lives through events they've researched and studied.

Creative Writing Assignments

Mary Berg, an American caught in the Warsaw ghetto, kept a diary of those years. In it she asks,

> Where are you foreign correspondents? Why don't you come here and describe the sensational scenes of the ghetto? No doubt you don't want to spoil your appetite? Or are you satisfied with what the Nazis tell you—that they locked up the Jews in the ghetto in order to protect the Aryan population from epidemics and dirt?

After viewing *The Warsaw Ghetto, Kovno Ghetto,* and *Holocaust* excerpts, and reading selected pieces about ghettos, write an article (500–700 words) for an American newspaper, describing what you have witnessed. Assuming you have observed what the films and literature describe, what would you want an American audience to know? Use quotations and examples in your articles.

OR

As you watch *Kovno Ghetto,* take notes on the survivors' stories. Visit the Holocaust Memorial Museum's website to better understand the Kovno ghetto (*www.ushmm.org/kovno/index.htm*). Again, take notes. Then transform your notes to an imagined diary entry, first-person account, short story, or poem to show what it was like to live in the Kovno ghetto. Turn in your original research and notes with your final paper.

Scott L. imagines an interior monologue of a Nazi, Franz, who is about to load a group of Jews from the ghetto onto a train. Franz fluctuates between his humane instincts and baser instincts:

> My God, they can't be shipped off in. . . . THAT! In all of this snow, the trip to the camp will take *at least* three days. No human can survive through that, there must be a mistake!
>
> HOLD ON THERE, What are you saying? Human? You just called those Jews human! What kind of a person are you, feeling pity for those who conspire against us, who brought about our troubles, OUR DEPRESSION! Listen to the Fuhrer, he knows what he's talking about . . .
>
> BUT THEY'RE MY NEIGHBORS!
>
> Stop saying that, they are parcels. Dammit, learn! The Jews are not human, they are rodents. Creatures unworthy of life . . . LOOK AT THEM! So smug with their rich coats and warm shoes! I'll make them pay for my suffering. I'll make them pay for my hardships!

Scott concludes after Franz clubs a boy that he is satisfied with his job. "After all, it's what the Fuhrer wants . . . he's just following orders." While Scott has given the Nazi a conscience, he tries, through the interior monologue he writes, to understand what moves a moral person to commit immoral acts. He is, momentarily, trying to "walk in another's shoes."

We also read short stories by Ida Fink who wrote two beautiful collections, *A Scrap of Time* and *Traces,* that resurrect fragments of memory. The stories, set in Poland during the war years, describe moments, nuances of scenes the history books describe with much heavier strokes. It is as if Fink paints her pictures of ghetto life with a single-haired brush, forcing us to notice details, scraps of time, and history we'd otherwise miss.

"A Spring Morning" opens with the foaming Gniezna River described as "the dirty-yellow color of beer" (39) by one of Jews in a forced march to the fields by the train station "which had recently become the mass graves of the murdered" (45). The "former secretary of the former town council"(39) overhears these words and repeats them to friends in a restaurant. The friends, members of the SS, cannot understand why a man would comment on the water looking like beer, "Maybe the guy was just thirsty," one suggests (40).

Then the point of view switches to the family of the Jew. We learn that his family is being forced from their home for the last time. During the march over the bridge the man says, "The water is the color of beer" as if he is noticing the strange concatenations of nature and appreciating its beauty. He tells his five-year-old daughter to run to a Christian milkmaid. The child is shot, and the man forced to carry her to the fields where he, too, will be shot, along with his young wife.

Issues we discuss include the comment by the man about water being the color of beer. Why do the Germans and townspeople misunderstand the man's comment? I ask. Why does the man describe the water as the color of beer? Our class discussion focuses on aesthetics, what we notice, how we want so much to capture beauty while we can. The story also betrays the tension and anxiety of a family who knows it is together for a last few hours, minutes. It is about the strong desire to live, to see the next generation live—at all costs.

I ask students to respond to "A Spring Morning" in their journals. As the family waits and prepares for their deaths, what do they think about? What do they feel? What is important? How does Fink describe the town's people's points of view? Students may want to write a version of this scene from a bystander's or a perpetrator's point of view.

Kristin says, "A Spring Morning" by Ida Fink is the first thing she's read for class that's "really, really" gotten to her:

Picture the person you love most in this world. Can't pick just one? Fine, even better. Line them up in your mind. See each one. Look at the lines on their faces. Smell them. What are they wearing? How are they standing? What are they saying that makes them the people you love?

Look into the eyes of the first one. Now hear a gunshot, watch blood spill out of their heads, hear their bones crack as their bodies fall, and know that you can never again hear their voice, see their smile. Gory, huh? Wait! We're not done. Look at the next one in your line of loved ones. I know you don't want to, you don't trust me anymore now that you know what I am capable of doing to the most important people in your life. But you have to look at the next one. Why? Because you *do* know what I can and am willing to do. And of course you want to stop me, but ignoring me won't work. I'm bigger than you. You have no control over me. So don't you want to at least say goodbye to this one? Look them in the eye. What was the last thing you did together? How did it make you feel? Take yourself there. When did you meet this person, why do you love them, how do they make you feel, what would you do without them? Got your answers? Now say goodbye. No, faster, you've got about 30 seconds before they're coming with me. Yeah, you know what I'm going to do with them. I want you to know. They are coming with me to suffer immeasurable torture for as long as humanly possible, and then I'm going to burn them to death. You know. You can't escape it. Now quickly, say goodbye. No, I'm not sorry.

... There is something heartbreaking about the fact that the people in the stories we've read thus far have no idea of their fate. We want to warn them. Then we read Ida Fink's story and it's even worse. They do know their fate. A husband and wife must say goodbye. A five-year-old girl knows people are coming to kill her. Her parents know they cannot save her.

Still, these people look for the last remnants of beauty in their lives. They search for memories instead of wallowing in fear and regret. They grasp hold of last chunks of life and spirit instead of cursing those taking them from it.

Like in the poem, "Things That Are Worse Than Death" by Sharon Olds (Chapter 2), there are certain situations that none of us can even imagine no matter what you read, hear, learn about, or even see. And if and when you do believe, you still could never fathom. And try with all your might to walk a mile in someone else's shoes, you know nothing of their real, raw emotions.

Kristin has not only imagined herself in the historical Holocaust, she has also taken on the voice of the tormentor. She imagines what it's like to watch her family destroyed. She also is able to draw parallels to other literature and to evaluate the effect of witnessing and trying to believe the unbelievable.

Two poems we read to gain a better understanding of the killing fields and reaction to Nazi hegemony are Yevgeny Yevtushenko's "Babi Yar" and Czeslaw Milosz's "A Song at the End of the World." Babi Yar, a suburb of Kiev, was the killing ground where 33,771 Jews were killed (see The History Place, *www.historyplace.com/worldwar2/holocaust/h-b-yar.htm*). There is no memorial there. Yevtushenko, a Russian poet, imagines himself to be the historical Jew—an Egyptian slave, Christ bearing scars of nails, Dreyfus behind bars, a young boy in Bialystock, Anne Frank "transparent as a branch in April." He imagines what it is like to be "every child here shot dead./ Nothing in me shall ever forget!" And he suggests the irony that as he is hated as a Jew he feels he is a true Russian. [Good websites with history, maps, associated links, and translations of the poem includes: *www.geocities.com/Paris/Rue/4017/BABIYAR.HTM;* the Simon Wiesenthal Museum website on Babi Yar: *motlc.wiesenthal.com/pages/t004/t00412.html;* and a site on Yevtushenko, including translations of several of his poems: *www.boppin.com/poets/yevtushenko.htm.*]

In "A Song at the End of the World," Czeslaw Milosz (rhymes with Chess-laugh Me-losh) writes of the beauty of the world—the things one might notice as the world ends: a bee circling clover, a fisherman mending a glimmering net, sparrows playing, a snake golden-skinned, a white-haired old man binding his tomatoes. Like T. S. Eliot's world that ends "Not with a bang,

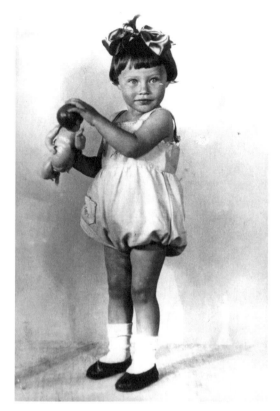

Figure 5–1. *Portrait of two-year-old Mania Halef, a Jewish child, who was later killed during the mass excution at Babi Yar. Photo by Yelena Brusilovsky, courtesy of USHMM Photo Archives.*

but a whimper," Milosz's world ends not with a bang, but a sense of lost beauty. It was written in Warsaw in 1944, the summer the Polish Resistance movement failed and Warsaw was destroyed. (Several of his translated poems may be found at *papyr.com/lizkies/milosz.htm.*)

Additional Suggested Readings, Websites, and CD-ROMs

Solly Ganor. 1995. *Light One Candle: A Survivor's Tale from Lithuania to Jerusalem.* New York: Kodansha International. (This compelling memoir is not only about Ganor's family's time in the Kovno ghetto, but also about his contact with Japanese Ambassador Sugihara who gave out more than six thousand visas to trapped Jews.

John Hersey. 1950. *The Wall.* New York: Vintage Books.

Ulrich Keller, ed. 1984. *The Warsaw Ghetto in Photographs: 206 Views Made in 1941.* New York: Dover Publications.

Jacob Sloan, trans. and ed. 1958. *Notes from the Warsaw Ghetto: The Journal Emmanuel Ringelblum.* New York: McGrawHill.

Steven Speilberg and Survivors of the Shoah Visual History Foundation. *Survivors: Testimonies of the Holocaust.* CD-ROM (to order: 800-542-4240)

Leon Uris. 1961. *Mila 18.* New York: Bantam Books. (A riveting, fictional account.)

Simon Wiesenthal Center Multimedia Learning Center Online: *motlc.wiesenthal.com /resources /education /bibliograph /ghetto.html* (for a fairly complete bibliography on *The Warsaw Ghetto*)

Yevtushenko, Yevgeny. 1944. "Babiy Yar." Yevgeny Yevtushenko *remember .org /witness /babiyar.html.*

6

Resisting

A group of Jewish partisans in Sumsk, Poland.   State Archives of the Russian Federation, courtesy of USHMM Photo Archives.

RESIST: 1. To withstand; to be proof against; to be able to repel, as disease. 2. To strive against; to exert oneself to counteract, defeat, or frustrate. 3. To withstand the action of, as the metal resists acid—v.i. To exert force in opposition; to offer resistance.—Syn. See OPPOSE.
WEBSTER'S NEW COLLEGIATE DICTIONARY

In the winter of 1942, when killing by firing squad became too messy, after the Wannsee Conference and the decision to move toward a "final solution of the Jewish question" (i.e., what to do with Jews in conquered towns) Germany designed death camps, including Treblinka, Sobibor, and Belzec. Jews were moved via cattle cars to camps devised specifically for killing—complete with gas chambers, crematorium, and a limited concentration of workers who facilitated the killing by shaving hair, processing clothes and jewels, and shoveling bodies into the ovens. Other camps, such as Auschwitz and Buchenwald and Mauthausen, were created as both labor and death camps. Besides the Jews, these camps swallowed Gypsies, homosexuals, the mentally and physically challenged, and political prisoners.

How, then, did one resist the German killing machine?

After viewing the BBC film on the Warsaw ghetto and reading *Maus* by Art Spiegelman, students want to discuss resistance. What is it? How do you resist? I divide the class into groups and ask them to define the word *resist*. I ask them to list at least five ways one could "resist" the organized effort to round up Jews and deport them to killing centers and concentration camps.

Three boys, one wearing a Naval Academy T-shirt, insist that you may only resist by picking up arms and directly fighting an enemy. Others say that resistance comes in other forms. Jordan suggests that prayer can be a form of resistance, since through prayer you may strengthen your spirituality—and thereby distance yourself from the enemy. Blake suggests that by not participating, by not fighting, by backing away, you resist by staying human and protecting your human values. Gary suggests that not snitching, not joining the Judenrat (the Jewish committee that cooperated with the Germans—in an effort to appease them and save lives) was resisting. Katie suggests that by hiding you resist—as that is disobeying. Amy points out the frames on page 109 in *Maus,* that show Tosha, who was hiding Vladek and Anja's son, Richieu, giving him poison to save him from being taken to Auschwitz. Taking your own life and the lives of your children to prevent arrest was resisting. The three boys disagree. And I ask a student who is whispering to a friend in class, "Are you resisting this lesson?" She smiles and apologizes for "resisting." This, I point out, is an example of psychological resistance. Indeed, merely staying alive in the face of Nazi threats was a form of resistance.

Resisting the Nazi decrees—to wear a star, to quit work, to not go to the park, to move to the ghetto, to starve, to board trains, to labor in camps, to die—took on many guises and forms. Some students may have a hard time understanding that one may resist by not obeying, by hiding, even by taking poison. Many believe, especially the boys, that true resistance comes from taking action to oppose—throwing rocks, taking up arms, joining the partisans. Others understand, especially the girls, that just staying alive—finding a scrap to eat, finding the spiritual strength to stop the German machine from their attempts to dehumanize—means resisting.

We look at films and literature that reveal both passive as well as active resistance. A family resists arrest for two-and-a-half years by hiding in an annex in Amsterdam (*Anne Frank: The Diary of a Young Girl* and *Anne Frank Remembered*). A Jewish family pays a Polish family to hide them in an attic (*Voices from the Attic*). A mother gives up her daughter to the care of strangers hoping her daughter will survive (*Trains*). A young man hides himself among German soldiers and Nazi SS (*Europa, Europa*). Women recount their resistance activities (*Justyna's Narrative, Daring to Resist*). Inmates of Sobibor plan a heroic escape (*Escape from Sobibor*). Courageous acts. All of them.

Many of my twelfth-grade students who saw or read *Anne Frank* in middle school greet with pleasure the opportunity to meet her again. Recently, however, Anne Frank has gotten a bad rap. She's too happy. She doesn't communicate the scope of the Holocaust. The Broadway play and Hollywood movie based on her book are de-Judaicized and prettified. Cynthia Ozick, essayist and novelist, writes in a *New Yorker* article titled, "Who Owns Anne Frank?":

> ... the diary in itself, richly crammed though it is with incident and passion, cannot count as Anne Frank's story. A story may not be said to be a story if the end is missing. And because the end is missing, the story of Anne Frank in the fifty years since "The Diary of a Young Girl" was first published has been bowderlized, distorted, transmuted, traduced, reduced; it has been infantilized, Americanized, homogenized, sentimentalized; falsified, kitschified, and in fact, blatantly and arrogantly denied. . . . Almost every hand that has approached the diary with the well-meaning intention of publicizing it has contributed to the subversion of history. (78)

Who is the real Anne Frank?
Daniel Schwarz writes:

> Anne Frank's diary has in some curricula become an annex to the horrors of the Shoah. The omission of the more uncomfortable scenes and images of the Holocaust may have helped it find a place in curricula for public schools, where it has become an appropriate tale for school children whose young sensibilities supposedly must be protected from the terrors of the Holocaust. Anne at times speaks with a sanitized diction that keeps the Holocaust at bay and, that, for naïve readers (and school boards in the 1950s and 1960s) provided a comfortable way of dealing with horrific events. Thus, if one disregards or minimizes the historical passages and the contextual knowledge we bring to the text, one can *think* one is experiencing the Holocaust without engaging in its unpleasantness. (107–108)

For a journal response, I ask students, "Do you agree that one needs the end to Anne's story for it to be complete? Do you think the diary is used to promote a more sanitized version of the Holocaust? Or do you see Anne Frank's diary and story as serving another purpose within a study of the literature of the Holocaust?"

How do we reconcile the Anne Frank who still believes, in spite of everything, "that people are basically good at heart," who also sees "the world being slowly transformed into a wilderness," hears "the approaching thunder that, one day, will destroy us, too," and feels "the suffering of millions"? How do we teach Anne Frank's diary?

For many, Anne Frank's diary is the first literature of the Holocaust they read or view. Her diary was released in the United States in 1952 and the Broadway play based on her diary opened in 1956, soon followed by the film based on the Broadway play. For me, Anne was my first and only exposure to the Holocaust—which wasn't then called the Holocaust. Yet it whetted my desire to know more. It made me care about a single person ("one plus one . . .") and it frightened me. How could a girl my age be forced to hide in an attic for two-and-a-half years? Where would I hide? How could I live with my parents and sisters without fresh air or school? For sure, I read the "Afterward," and I knew that "on the morning of August 4, 1944, sometime between ten and ten-thirty, a car pulled up at 263 Prinsengracht . . ." I knew the eight people hiding in the annex were arrested. I knew that all the residents of the annex were "transferred to Westerbork and were deported on September 3, 1944, in the last transport to leave Westerbork, and arrived three days later in Auschwitz." I knew that seven of the eight residents of the annex died in concentration camps or death marches. I knew that while Anne had hope and optimism, she still perished with her mother and sister.

For me Anne was a real person. She opened the door to my exploration of the war against the Jews. And she opens that door for my students. While many read Anne's diary in middle school, for others, this is their first exposure. I urge my juniors and seniors to read the new, complete version. We also watch the film. I want my students to know what Americans knew about the Holocaust before the wealth of literature and research was published in the seventies and eighties and nineties.

Anne Frank's diary is a beautiful book—full of the joy and angst of an adolescent's discoveries. Anne was thirteen years old when she began her diary. She was fifteen years old when she abruptly stopped. What would she have been artistically, as a writer, if her life hadn't been cut short? For she was a natural writer. Words came to her so easily, descriptions of character, of place— and of raison d'être. She knew—in the short time she lived and in the short time she wrote—what life was about. We know because we have her writing. How poignantly clear it is that in Anne's senseless death we lost someone who through her art made our lives richer. Thus, through Anne's diary and through her death, we begin to understand the devastation the Nazi racial policies wreaked.

> The diary is taken to be a Holocaust document; that is overridingly what it is not. . . . The diary is incomplete, truncated, broken off—or rather it is completed by Westerbork (the hellish transit camp in Holland from which Dutch Jews were deported), and by Auschwitz, and by the fatal winds of Bergen-Belson. It is here, and not in the "secret annex," that the crimes we have come to call the Holocaust were enacted. (Ozick, 78)

Does the diary show us the suffering of the camps and, therefore, the place where "the crimes we have come to call the Holocaust were enacted"? No, for that, we must read other books, other testimonies. But to live in fear, to not be able to make a sound during the day, to fear a thief is the green police come to take Anne and her family to the camps—this, too, is the Holocaust—the waiting to get taken, to be found, knowing what lies in store for them. And Anne did know.

Was there hope? Yes. Always. Always hope in the face of despair. It is human nature to hope for, to wish for a different outcome than the one we fear. I know every time I read or watch Anne Frank—just as I know when I watch *Romeo and Juliet* that they will die in the end—Anne will die in the end. But I hope that something will be different this time—the D-Day invasion of Normandy will succeed faster, the Russians will liberate them sooner, Anne and her family simply won't be found—and will live out the last months of the war in hiding.

We see from the diary and the film the maniacal pursuit of the Jews. We see Amsterdam emptied of its Jewish population—and even as so many Jews have fed the German megalomania and anti-Semitism and racism, we see the search for "house lice," a euphemism for Jews. The few still in hiding cannot be left in peace. They must be found. Why were the Germans so obsessed with finding every last Jew? And in the capture of the Jews, good gentiles, the righteous Christians who rescued and protected Jews, were also arrested. Something is askew in the world when even the impulse to help, to come to the aid of people in need, is squelched and quashed.

I want students to consider what their impressions of the film would be if it was all they knew of the Holocaust. For a journal, I suggest:

> It is the 1950s. You have just seen *The Diary of Anne Frank* at a local theatre. If this was all you knew about the Holocaust, what would you know? I want students to not only consider how they themselves would respond to the film of Anne's diary, but to also consider how her diary informed America of the Holocaust.

Students observe how a family in hiding lives. They see Jews rounded up down below, they know Anne's "dear vegetable man" was picked up for hiding two Jews in his house. They see Jews being marched off under guard. They see the longing for a normal life. They see Anne's family incriminate themselves for feeling too comfortable in Europe to leave when there was a chance. In a way, the film is the opposite of what we expect in a classic film—we know everything is bad and will end badly; this teases us with the good.

In the end, we see Anne and Peter gazing out of the attic window at the passing clouds. Anne says, still full of hope, "Someday, when we get outside again, I'm going to . . ." And she is cut off by Gestapo sirens—and then their arrest. Anne is arrested in the midst of her hope. The message of the film is clear. Despite her hopes and her plans, despite her vitality and love, the Germans planned to annihilate all Jews.

According to Kate, who had never seen the film before, "It was scary as Hell."

According to Jessica, "The movie was not about dying but about living."

Nick says, "It's kind of like a *Schindler's List.* Even though all died, it made you feel good."

More suggestions for journal responses for writing about the Hollywood film / Broadway play version of Anne Frank:

- Margot is jealous of Anne's relationship with Peter; she wants someone to share her feelings with, too. We, the audience, know she never will have the time or opportunity. Anne says, "I want to go on living even after my death . . ." and the phone interrupts her words. Anne says, "In spite of everything, I still believe that people are good at heart . . ." and the sounds of the sirens of the green police and imminent arrest are heard. Discuss the effect of dramatic irony and the techniques of cinematic cuts and juxtapositions that temper expressions of hope with reality.

- Anne says, ending the play and movie, "In spite of everything, I still believe that people are really good at heart." Many critics feel this is an inappropriate ending. Comment on this line as a suitable ending for the play, given what the authors knew was the true end for Anne and the Jews. Keep in mind that psychotherapist Bruno Bettelheim suggests that Anne's moving statement about the goodness of men releases us effectively of the need to cope with the problems Auschwitz presents, ". . . If all men are good at heart, there never really was an Auschwitz; nor is there any possibility that it may recur."

- Meyer Levin (the translator of *The Diary of a Young Girl*) believes that the Broadway *Anne Frank,* written by Frances Goodrich and Albert

Hackett, minimizes the Jewish elements in the diary in order to "achieve an all-embracing, consoling universality" (Graver).

Cynthia Ozick in her essay for *The New Yorker,* "Who Owns Anne Frank?" decries the erasing of Anne's Jewishness:

> ... the Hacketts' work, read today, is very much a conventionally well-made Broadway product of the fifties, alternating comical beats with scenes of alarm, a love story with a theft, wisdom with buffoonery. ... Yet this is the play that electrified audiences everywhere, that became a reverential if robotlike film, and that—far more than the diary—invented the world's Anne Frank. Was it the play, or was it the times?

Was universalizing Anne—that is, stripping her and her family of their "Jewishness" for a screenplay meant for audiences of the 1950s—a good idea? Why? Why not? Based on the film, who is Anne Frank? How did she experience the Holocaust?

- In each of the following diary entries (Critical Edition), Anne describes her reactions to the war and the persecution of European Jews:

  31 March '44 (352)

  16 June '42 (189)

  9 October '42 (273–4)

  17 November '42 (313–4)

  11 April '44 (600)

  11 May '44 (643)

  11 April '44 (601)

  22 May '44 (657)

  15 July '44 (694)

What does Anne reveal about her awareness of the war against the Jews?

Despite the criticism of the play and film, students identify with Anne—and if they look, they find much to learn about the events of the Holocaust. Lindsay writes:

I saw the frightened look in everyone's eyes when a siren wailed. I witnessed everyone's horrified looks when they heard bad news, or rather truth, from Mr. Dussel. I viewed the pain after the eight hide-aways realized their friends were taken away. I could witness Anne's heartbreak when she found out that her best friend was taken by the Nazis. By watching *The Diary of Anne Frank,* I could empathize with the victims. I always felt terrible for all who endured the pain and suffering from the Holocaust, but it hasn't felt real until now.

Julia O., herself a recent immigrant from the Ukraine whose grand-mother was in Auschwitz, writes:

> The whole point of the movie is to show people how it was dangerous to live in a place where any minute someone can find you and send you to the concentration camps. When I watch this movie I am very scared for all of them. . . . I could never understand why Jewish people should be so punished. . . . I am half Jewish and I am very hurt because in my blood I have something Jewish and my mother, she is Jewish, and I don't want anything to happen to her because I could not stand this, and nobody knows how life can change in a minute. I would never forgive Germans for doing this to my people.

Marissa writes:

> It horrified me to imagine that hundreds of thousands of families, many of them just like the Franks and van Daans, made up the six million slaughtered in the camps. Because Anne was such a charismatic and intelligent young woman, it makes me wonder what extraordinary deeds she would have been capable of had she lived.

Trisha writes:

> I am starting to get the "Holocaust Dreams." You know, the ones that put you right in the middle of it all. The ones that leave you awake in the end, in the middle of the night, in a cold sweat. They all started when we began studying Anne Frank. A young girl about my age going through the Holocaust really hit home.
>
> To me Anne was the innocence that the Nazis took away from Jews during the Holocaust. The fear that Anne felt each time the door opened, the fear that Anne felt each time the cat whined, and the fear of waiting, the awful waiting for that moment when the Nazis came. . . . In the end she had no more spirit left to fight, and she was no longer a little girl. During her time in hiding she was robbed of her innocence, her childhood, her life, and her faith in others. Anne represented to me all the Jews that were killed.

I show *Anne Frank Remembered,* a documentary video, to show the time Anne and her family spent in the annex, as well as what happened to them after their arrest. We see archival films of women exercising at the Dutch transit camp, Westerbork; we see the transports; and we see footage of life in the camps. More important and interesting, we see and hear interviews with friends of Anne who survived, who saw her in the camps, and who describe how she lived and how she died. We also see interviews with Otto Frank (Anne's father) and Dr. Pfeffer's son (Dr. Dussel). We see what Cynthia Ozick warned we don't see in the diary or the film version of the diary: we see Anne's demise, we see the devastating toll Auschwitz—and the obsessive racial laws—took.

The documentary has a website with summaries and synopses: *www.spe .sony.com /classics /annefrank /.*

Into the Arms of Strangers, a documentary released in 2000, tells of the 20,000 children whisked to England from Germany, Austria, and Czechoslovakia on the "kindertransport." Dame Judy Dench narrates; writer Lore Segal is one of the grown children who is interviewed. John Nonaghan writing for the *Detroit Free Press* says, "To say that the movie uses interviews and vintage clips to tell the story of the kindertransport makes it sound like any old night in front of The History Channel. Instead, this entertaining documentary has the wit, priceless insight and irreverent spunk of a dozen Anne Franks" (10/13/00). I'm not so sure I agree. Through we meet real people, Anne, somehow, feels more real.

Another video I show to reveal what it was like for a child to hide is *Voices from the Attic.* The voices from the attic were the hushed voices of "Aunt Sally" and her family of fifteen when they hid in a farmer's attic to escape deportation. In this documentary, Debbie Goodstein, a niece of Aunt Sally and a child of another survivor of the attic, tells a two-edged story of what happened in Europe and in her aunt's little village when all the Jews were asked to report to the railroad station for deportation; as well as the effects of the hiding on the second generation who inherited the perceptions of inferiority and defiance from their parents who hid. In 1942, Debbie Goodstein's mother went into hiding with fifteen people in a ten-by-fifteen-foot attic. Her experience, says Goodstein, "shaped her life and mine." There were always secrets, and the children—who are now in their early twenties and thirties—want to know.

The film takes us to Poland with the extended family—both those who survived and their children. We visit Auschwitz with them. We see Aunt Sally and her current family avoid walking on Jewish gravestones used to pave a road, and we see haystacks similar to those that Aunt Sally and her family hid in. We meet the family of the Polish farmer who hid Aunt Sally's family; we meet others who helped. And we learn that at liberation, Aunt Sally had to be carried out of their attic; her legs had so atrophied that she could not walk to freedom.

One part of the documentary that troubled my students was the demand of the farmer's wife for the mother's fur coat and jewelry. They were perplexed that those who broke the law to hide Jews also demanded a high payment for their services. Julie asks, "Why did the so-called good guys have to wipe the

Jews clean of every last piece of property? Didn't they see anything wrong in that? Jewish families were forced to give up diamond rings, gold, silver, and fur coats for dingy hiding places." She concludes, however, that in comparison to the Nazis, "these people who hid the Jews were like angels."

Unlike Aunt Sally, who hid with her family, Miriam Winter was a "hidden child" in that she was hidden by a family not her own and had to assume a completely new identity in order to survive. Students are moved by her memoir, *Trains*, in which she writes:

> I remember my father teaching me how to make the sign of the cross. He sat me across from himself at the kitchen table. He gave me a piece of paper on which the Lord's Prayer was written in pencil in large block letters. He told me that from now on my name was Marysia Kowalska. He ordered me to call every woman I would be with *mama* and every man *tata* and never to admit that I was Jewish or that my name was Miriam Winter. He pointed to the lining of my dark-blue winter coat, where a gold coin was sewn for a last resort. That was all.
>
> Riding away from my family in a horse-drawn buggy with a tall, blond woman I didn't know and with a boy of fourteen named Stefan, I wasn't crying. I sat deep in my seat reading by the moonlight. On a small piece of paper were words penciled in large block letters. I was memorizing the *Our Father*. My father, Tobiasz Winter, a religious Jew, gave me this Christian prayer to memorize as quickly as I could and to repeat in front of anyone who might look at me.

Fifty years later, while visiting Yad Vashem in Israel as part of a gathering of hidden children, Marian Winter traces the carved names of the towns she lived in while in Poland. A man approaches her and tells her he doesn't even know his name. She tells him that had her brother survived, he wouldn't know his name either. And, in fact, she doesn't even remember what her brother looked like.

> This meeting with a man who doesn't know his name still lingers in my heart. Like me, he had many false names; like me, he survived alone. I am still searching, but there are no traces. I have often wondered why I survived. I am all that's left of the families of Winter and Kohn; if I hadn't lived, there wouldn't be a soul to say that they even existed. I am their witness. (46)

For years Marian Winter could not cry, could not reveal her true identity. By the end of the war, she has forgotten what her mother looked like. She has forgotten what it was like to be Jewish. She can't even remember her name, only "Marycia," the new, Christian name she has had for the last three years.

Hidden children were hidden not only from the Nazis, they were also hidden from themselves. They often cannot remember their past, their parents, their original homes. Though they survived the deportations and death camps, they lost their names and their memories. *"I can't cry; I have to hide somewhere where no one will find me. . . . I shall never admit that I am Jewish. I shall not reveal who I am. This way I shall be safe."*

I show *Europa, Europa* so students can see the scope of the war from the point of view of a handsome adolescent—like them, as they say. I also show this film to illustrate how memoir is turned into art. We examine how truth is often stronger than fiction, how a director must pick and choose and order events to create a work that compels, informs, and entertains. I also hope students grasp one more story, one more way of coping.

Europa, Europa is the true story of Solly Perelman who escaped from the Germans by crossing to Russia, became a respected young pioneer communist, got separated from the Russians, and ended up hiding among the Germans, first as a soldier in the field and then at an elite German military school where he has to run at effigies of Jews with his bayonet while screaming anti-Semitic slurs.

Europa, Europa is for mature audiences. Solly has to hide his Jewishness—and goes so far as to try to undo his circumcision. These scenes are graphic; this is a European film. There is nudity and an attempted seduction by a German soldier of Solly when he is bathing. One interesting scene is when Solly, the Jew, is portrayed as a "perfect" Aryan when he gets his nose and head measured. Students may contrast this racist scene with the Holocaust Memorial Museum's Web page, which shows out of textbooks how race was "measured" (*www.ushmm.org/olympics/zca009.htm*).

While high school seniors appreciate the highly complex themes and dilemmas, this film is not for younger students.

Lindsay says, "I am having a hard time believing that the story actually happened to an actual person. Everything worked out for Solek. I wonder why he was able to have such great luck while so many others had none."

Mike says, "I really thought that the story had to be fictional, especially when a Jewish boy joins the Hitler youth and becomes a German soldier. . . . I guess that disguising yourself as a German is a pretty good way to hide from being taken to a camp or ghetto."

After we discuss what it was like to resist, to hide, I lead students through a writing assignment:

1. List ten concerns you might have if your family were going into hiding.
2. Star the most important three concerns.

3. How would you deal with these concerns? What steps would you have to take to make your escape possible?

4. Discuss these concerns with a group or with the class.

5. Now, take on the voice of Anne Frank, Aunt Sally, Solly Perelman, or Miriam Winter and write either a poem or a letter to someone who does not have to hide, yet—explaining your concerns and what *you* have to do.

Another woman who resisted arrest was Gusta Davidson Draenger. While held in a Nazi prison, Draenger fictionalized and recorded her resistance activities on scraps of paper. She memorializes the Krakow Jewish resistance in her vivid descriptions of their attempts to defy German authority. On the first page, translated by Roslyn and David Hirsch, Draenger writes,

> From this prison cell that we will never leave alive, we young fighters who are about to die salute you. We offer our lives willingly for our holy cause, asking only that our deeds be inscribed in the book of eternal memory. May the memories preserved on these scattered bits of paper be gathered together to compose a picture of our unwavering resolve in the face of death.

By reading Draenger's account, students have an opportunity to read a young woman's testament to the courage of her group of friends—their planning, their defiance, their practicality in the face of death.

Justyna describes the "akzias" by which "murder had to be committed under the cloak of 'resettlement.' Hence, violence took place without screams, coercion without a shot being fired" (109). She and her friends seem quite aware of where people are going.

Her husband Marek says, "We ought to go from city to city to alert people that there is no such thing as deportation, only a death sentence. They shouldn't delude themselves into believing it's safer to stay where they are than to run. They should try to escape while they still have the chance. And they should leave all at once and overwhelm the trains, the roads, the whole country. Think how much more difficult we could make things for the enemy."

I show *Daring to Resist*, a documentary about three young Jewish women who resisted the Nazis during World War II. The narrator tells us "Resistance against Nazi genocide took many forms besides armed combat and sabotage. Resisters found ingenious ways to hide people, change their identities, or smuggle them to safety. Teenagers were often among the first to recognize the Nazi menace, and act."

We meet Shulamit Gara Lack who lived a privileged life in Hungary before the war. When war came, she worked for the underground making false papers so Jews could pose as Christians and flee Hungary. She also helped prepare escapees for the dangerous trip to Romania, and from there to Palestine (*www.pbs.org/daringtoresist/*). She herself was betrayed, arrested, and sent to Auschwitz.

We meet Barbara Ledermann Rodbell, a ballerina living in Amsterdam, who resisted by hiding as a Christian. She distributed underground papers and helped transfer other Jews from one hiding place to another in Amsterdam. "I had always been willful and very much my own person. If I believed in something, I tried to follow up on it."

We meet Faye Lazebnik Schulman who joined the partisans as a photographer, a nurse, and a fighter. "When it was time to be hugging a boyfriend, I was hugging a rifle." Faye's partisan brigade raided her own village several times to restock food, medicine, and weapons. During one of these raids the partisans discover Faye's own house, abandoned. "What shall we do with it?" she was asked. "I won't be living here. The family's killed. To leave it for the enemy? I said right away: Burn it!"

Daring to Resist's effect is enlightening and chilling. Students want to see young women, their own ages, doing something to resist. They need to know that resistance did not always involve taking up arms, but could be enacted through both small and large gestures. They appreciate the heroism found in small acts of defiance.

A website with biographies of each of the three women interviewed, a teacher's guide, and a full transcript may be found at *www.pbs.org/ daringtoresist/*. Websites about resistance may be found at *www.ushmm .org/out reach/jpart.htm, http://.wiesenthal.com/pages/rr.html,* and *www .holocaust-trc/edures18.htm.*

Escape from Sobibor is a film that shows Jews opposing their German captors with weapons in order to liberate the six hundred prisoners of Sobibor. Sobibor was a death camp, better seen and understood in scenes from Claude Lanzmann's film, *Shoah.* However, in *Escape from Sobibor* (starring Alan Arkin) we learn how six hundred prisoners make the death camp work—and how they will only stay alive as long as there are trains bringing in human fodder for the gas chambers and crematorium. Students cheer at the end when Jews wield guns and subdue Germans. Half of the prisoners are killed as they escape. The other half survive.

Another writing assignment I suggest is to write in the voice of one of the people who resisted Nazi control: "Explain how you (as the persona of one who resisted) escaped. Consider the need to hide, to create false documents, to engage in political activities, underground work, and outright confrontation."

7

The Master Race

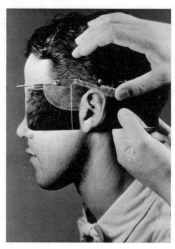

The facial features of a young
German are measured during a racial
examination at the Kaiser Wilhelm
Institute for Anthropology.   National
Archives, courtesy of USHMM Photo
Archives.

It is the very same man who is both just like us, and a mass murderer.
— OMER BARTOV

In twenty-year intervals, out of the American entertainment industry came
The Diary of Anne Frank (1956), the docudrama *Holocaust* (1976), and
Schindler's List (1996). These three films enhanced the public's awareness of
the Holocaust. In particular *Schindler's List* was released at a time when Holocaust studies were spreading across college campuses, when the body of material was growing. For the first time, a major film was released to high schools
across the nation, schools were invited to theaters to see the film, and teachers' guides were sent out. Out of the profits, Steven Spielberg has created the
Survivors of the Shoah Visual Foundation (*www.vhf.org*). He has encouraged

the recording of interviews with every living survivor, and he has turned those interviews into several full length, Academy Award-winning documentaries.

While I include *Schindler's List* as part of the Master Race chapter, I usually show *Schindler's List* at the end of the semester-long course because then my students appreciate the artistry of the film and see clearly how Spielberg incorporates so much information. There is not an unnecessary frame in the film; every shot counts and tells.

Schindler's List, directed by Spielberg, is about a man named Oskar Schindler, a member of the Nazi Party who planned to take advantage of cheap Jewish real estate and cheap Jewish slave labor to make his fortune. And he succeeded. Based on Thomas Keneally's novel, *Schindler's List,* Oskar Schindler has no conscience: he cheats on his wife, drinks heavily, bribes Nazi officials, moves into a Jewish apartment vacated when the Jewish owners leave for the ghetto, buys a Jewish-owned factory at bargain basement rates (in fact, he pays in pots produced by the plant), and uses Jewish slave labor. Yet, he turns into the good Nazi. He uses his position to protect Jews.

Oskar Schindler, in the beginning, fits our stereotype of the bad German who takes advantage of a situation—for his own good. He is one of the few, however, to cross over, to turn his evil empire into good. In a way, we see the work of Spielberg's earlier movies—the magic *E.T.* brings in his humane touch, the victory of good over evil in *Close Encounters of The Third Kind.* Schindler's victory is a victory of morality over immorality, and yes, good over evil. Until Schindler makes his final choice to give up the good life he has earned, he is like a cartoon character with the forces of Good (Itzak Stern) perched on one shoulder and the forces of Evil (Amon Goeth) perched on the other. Schindler chooses Stern. He uses Goeth.

Schindler's voice is the one clear, moral voice we hear among Germans. Through this film, Speilberg makes it clear that even in a totalitarian society, even among the elite master race, there is choice.

So much happens. Images that last for only a few seconds reveal so much—and are easy to miss. Music, events, characters, moralities, horrors, and dignities are juxtaposed against each other. "Jews always weather the storm," garbles a Nazi as he vigorously chews his meat at a dinner party. Schindler, as he moves into an elegant Jewish apartment, says, "It couldn't be better"; the Jews, as they move into a single, shabby room in the ghetto say, "It couldn't be worse." Nazis hunting Jews in the soon-to-be-liquidated ghetto stop to listen to a Jew pound last notes on the upright piano, which had been his hiding place: "Bach," says one soldier; "No, Mozart," says the other as they pause with their guns beneath the stairs. High German culture imposed during the hunt for human prey. Spielberg uses the cuts of cinematic art to contrast and expose, to force the viewer to see more, to feel more, to know more.

Pause buttons on the VCR are a great thing. I like to pause scenes to stop and talk about them with my students. What is going on? In a few seconds what do we know? The terror of the victim. The relief at not being found. The horror of accidentally stepping on the keyboard as the young man emerges from his hiding place. The panicked playing of the piano one last time, revealing through the music the ache and tension of the chase. The irony of the cultured, civilized Germans pausing to listen and identify music before carrying on with their human hunt. All this in a moment of film.

Schindler is in bed with his mistress when he is asked to rescue Stern from a train bound for Auschwitz. He leaves her behind and miraculously stops the train to pull his head accountant—who is just a number and who can be replaced by another number—from the train. And when he hears the cries of Jews imprisoned on a hot train bound for Auschwitz, in his white suit he carries fire hoses to spray the train and relieve suffering—if only for a moment. And then there's his list. When Stern tells him there are six hundred on the list, he says, "More. I want more." He even goes to other factory owners and pleads with them to save their Jews—and they refuse, preferring to take their money and run. And most heroic of all—and most incredible of all—when a trainload of Schindler Jews mistakenly arrives at Auschwitz, Schindler gets them out. He will not take "fresh, interchangeable Jews"; he wants *his* Jews. *Schindler's List* is art reinterpreting history, reflecting not only Oskar Schindler's vision and morality, but also Steven Spielberg's.

We witness the growing moral conscience of Schindler, the decay of the evil Goeth (up to his hanging after the war and his dying with "Heil Hitler" on his lips), and the determination of Jews to live. We see the horrors created by the German government to subjugate and eliminate Jews, we see a glimmer of hope in those who would fight the moral battle.

Schindler's List is often criticized because it is a story of hope, it is a story about those who survived. And Schindler *is* hope incarnate. He offers hope to "his" Jews when for the others, hope was dashed as they were loaded into cattle cars bound for Auschwitz. This movie is about the Jews who are saved, not the Jews who suffered and died. It is a story of redemption, not of suffocation. In the end, there *are* survivors. Over six thousand people are alive because Schindler saved nine hundred lives. (We even have a student in our school whose grandmother is a "Schindler Jew.") We see the survivors and their children, in color at the end of the film, walking side by side with the actors who played their roles—we see them placing stones on Schindler's grave in Israel, confirming the fictionalized events and making them real.

Some questions and topics (any of these make for good journal responses) we discuss while watching the film:

- *Schindler's List* is based on a true story, but it is not a documentary, it is cinematic art. As art, how does it construe the Holocaust? Consider that the camera's eye is the narrator. In what voice does the narrator speak? What does he want us to see? To know?

- What is the image we see of Schindler? How does it change? Consider the opening scene of Schindler dressing for a dinner party. What do we learn about him from this scene? How does his concern for appearances, for "panache," affect what he ultimately does?

- How is the film a product of America in the 1990s? Consider the importance of understanding and coming to terms with our diverse society. Consider the importance of teaching tolerance.

- How does *Schindler's List* portray the Holocaust? What does it tell us? How does it portray the ghetto? The work camps? The selections? The Nazi disregard for life? The deportations? The taking and cataloguing of jewelry and gold teeth?

- The film ends with a quote from the Talmud: "Who ever saves one life saves the world." What does this mean in the context of the film?

- Consider the eye of the camera as the narrator. What does it tell us as it moves from scene to scene?

- How are victims and perpetrators portrayed? There is an incredible sense of the "cat and mouse" nature of the hunt—the unsatisfied need to capture every last Jew. (I am always struck by the obsessive-compulsive nature of this hunt.)

- Consider the use of nudity in the film. How does Spielberg show Schindler's growth from philanderer to man with a conscience?

- What do we actually learn about the final solution? What do we learn from the scene when ashes, like snow, fall onto Schindler's car?

- When Schindler refuses to take a "fresh" load of Jews in order to save "his" women, is he acting morally? Are Jews interchangeable? Consider the morality of saving only those he knows or loves.

- What is the effect of filming in black and white? Consider how Spielberg uses color, particularly the child with the red coat, to show the universal through the particular. Why do we see the charming child in the red coat? Is Spielberg giving meaning to one child's life within the scope of one-and-a-half-million children murdered?

- At the end, in color, the actors walk beside the real survivors to lay a stone (a Jewish custom) on Oskar Schindler's grave. What is the effect?
- How does Steven Spielberg use his art to reveal the Holocaust? In this journal response I want students to consider how art renders truth. What happens in a screenplay based on facts that is different from a memoir? What devices does a director use to move and inform his audience?

Ben and Robyn notice the Jews' hiding places and their juxtaposition with the urgency of the Germans' search. Ultimately, even though the Jews are caught, Ben notices how Spielberg vindicates German inhumanity by exulting the Jews' humanity—through art.

Ben writes:

I was amazed at the hiding places that families had. One family hid beneath their floor and had a rug that was pulled over to disguise their hiding spot. Children hid in cabinets and under beds. German officers ran from room to room shooting their bullets at any spot that looked like a hiding spot. They tore up furniture and beds searching for Jews. One thing that amazed me was how the Germans treated searching for the Jews as a game. It was as if it were hide and go seek, except if they won, the Jews died. Another scene that amazed me was when the boy got caught coming out of the piano. After realizing he'd be found, he began to play. It was his way of leaving this planet with pride—and music.

Robyn writes:

Today we watched *Schindler's List.* It made me cry. The man stepping from his hiding place to play Bach in the final moments of his life. The beauty of it. That beauty in that moment made me cry.

Afterwards, I desperately wanted to talk. Wanted to sit down at a coffeehouse with a caramel mocha, sit with this boy, touch his wrist and ask, "Why are there people like you? Why are there people so beautiful they'd dedicate the last minutes of their lives to Bach? Why can't I hate the human race absolute? The race as a whole, so hideous, but its individuals are so beautiful. Yet, these same individuals orchestrated the death camps, the marches, the human experiments. What kind of people are we?

What kind of people are we?

Lindsay writes, focusing more on the movie's total effect:

The movie was very scary. What affected me the most was when I saw one of the Nazis wake up and take his shooting practice out on the Jews in the concentration camp. Watching him kill anyone walking in his path so easily was appalling. The worst part was knowing that this was a normal daily routine as well, and his girlfriend didn't even care about it! The pictures throughout the movie were so graphic. The screams were real, the suffering was real, and the hatred was real. I felt as if the Holocaust had really come to life. I was witnessing everything and could do nothing. I felt helpless, horrified, and scared.

Such is the effect of art. It pulls us in and makes us think it is real, even if it is not. As we enter a good film, a good book, we are there, and as Lindsay says, the screams are real, the suffering is real, and the hatred is real. Through art the Holocaust comes to life.

While I would *not* want to see *Schindler's List* as the *sole* Holocaust "lesson," it is possible to weave the film into almost any part of the curriculum: It portrays the ghettos, the work camps, the Nazi disregard for life, the deportations, the taking and cataloguing of jewelry and gold teeth, the morality and justice of that oppressive world where the German was lord and the Jew was slave.

I appreciate *Schindler's List* more every time I watch it.

The Final Solution to the Jewish Question

Most agree the decision to implement the final solution to the Jewish question came at the Wannsee Conference (pronounced Von-Say) on January 20, 1942. The film *The Wannsee Conference* re-enacts, from the minutes of the Wannsee Conference, what took place. The U.S. Holocaust Memorial Museum web site (*www.ushmm.org/outreach/wannsee.htm*) describes the Wannsee Conference and also provides time lines, pronunciation guides, and a historical context. The minutes of the meeting may be found at several web sites including: *www.historyplace.com/worldwar2/holocaust/h-wannsee.htm*, and *www2.h-net.msu.edu/~german/gtext/nazi/wanneng2.html*.

As a journal response I suggest students assume the role of a high-ranking German officer:

You have the minutes of the Wannsee Conference in hand. You must implement it. Write a memo to your subordinates telling them what you know and what must be done. OR, if you prefer, you may try to find the "voice" of a German officer with a "conscience" and write a poem or a letter describing your reaction. Consider who you are writing to, your relationship with that person—and that this is a top-secret document. You could be in grave trouble if your superiors find out you are leaking information. Can you take that risk?

Another way to understand the German soldier's attitude about participating in the killing is to read excerpts from *The Good Old Days: The Holocaust as Seen by Its Perpetrators and Bystanders.* Of particular interest to my students was the war diary of Blutordensträger Felix Landau, titled "Once Again I've Got to Play General to the Jews."

In this German soldier's diary entry students read the account of an ordinary soldier's love for a woman with whom he is having an affair, while at the same time he is carrying out orders to shoot several thousand Jews a day. How do we understand the mind of a perpetrator? How could he do what he did?

My students are perplexed. Blake asks, "How could he split his personality?" Dan, ever more practical, answers, "Work. He's just at work. When he's not killing he operates like a normal person." Scott L. adds, "He was probably normal growing up. It's the same as hunting. The people he's killing aren't people. He's been taught through propaganda that they're not human so he doesn't think of what he's doing as taking life." Dan throws back, "He thinks he's doing the world a service. He's getting rid of vermin." Dana, the first female to enter the discussion, says, "He needed that normal life when he wasn't killing. He doesn't think of himself as being inhuman or a bad person, he's thinking of what he's doing as getting rid of a problem." Tal adds, "He's desensitized like everyone else. Just like the Jews in the ghetto who could load the dead onto wagons without thinking, he's numb. He has no conscience."

I bring up Daniel Goldhagen's theory exposed in his book, *Hitler's Willing Executioners,* that ordinary Germans perpetrated the heinous crimes of the Holocaust. I ask my students if they agree with Goldhagen's contention that not just Nazis, but ordinary Germans and Poles and Ukrainians and Lithuanians carried out the final solution. None were coerced. All could have chosen not to participate. Therefore, Goldhagen says, we should not say the crimes were perpetrated by Nazis, but by Germans. Hands shot up. "NO!" Students echo. "It was a totalitarian society. It's not fair to blame all Germans. Some Germans were good." But, I ask, didn't German society allow and participate in the decimation of Jews? Weren't they part of a racist state? Isn't there a parallel between those who lived in the United States during the years of slavery? Weren't they also part of a racist state if they weren't fighting for abolition?

My students surprisingly don't buy that argument. A biracial student says, "If you sit by and watch, then you're not guilty. No one's obligated to say that something's wrong. If anything's going to hurt you, you shouldn't have to participate." Amy shakes her head, "If there's slavery and you're not speaking out against it, you're justifying others who do have slaves."

Students accuse me of not listening to their arguments as I jump around the room hearing different students' arguments. I try to explain that I am only trying to provoke. I want them to think and respond. I wonder if, perhaps, I have done too good a job of asking students to refrain from judgment by understanding some of the decisions people made—to not take in Jewish children, to not let Jews hide in the barn, to remain bystanders or witnesses. I have carefully tried to teach students to understand and empathize with the predicament of making moral decisions based on circumstances we cannot always understand—the fear that your own children will be killed if you hide Jewish children, the fear you yourself will be sent to a concentration camp if you protect someone who is trying to escape.

Ultimately, though, we must judge, because I do believe there is a greater morality. What if everyone had refused to cooperate? Then could Nazi policy have been as effective? Look at what happened in Denmark when the king decreed that all Danes would save their Jews by ferrying them to neutral Sweden.

I introduce Lawrence Kohlberg's six stages of moral development. (Among many websites, *luna.pepperdine.edu /gsep/class/ethics/kohlberg/* may be helpful. For a more extensive discussion, see *The Meaning and Measurement of Moral Development* by Lawrence Kohlberg.)

Kohlberg's famous dilemma concerns a man named Heinz whose wife is dying from a rare form of cancer. There is a drug available that may save her life. Kohlberg asks, "Should Heinz steal the drug?" There is no "right" or "wrong" answer. Answers pro or con help the researcher determine the interviewee's moral stage of development.

The dilemma I pose to my students is one they have witnessed in several documentaries: Two Jewish children are looking for a hiding place. They knock on the door of a farmhouse in Poland and plead to be taken in. The farmer's wife knows that there is a law that will condemn her and her family if she takes in the children. She has children of her own to protect. Should she hide the children?

> Stage One: A person makes moral choices based on rewards and punishments. (We will kill you if you take in Jews, we will give you two kilos of sugar if you turn one in.)
>
> Stage Two: One makes moral choices based on a tit for tat—I'll do for you if you do for me. (I'll hide you if you pay me; I won't hide you if you won't pay me.)
>
> Stage Three: A person makes moral choices based on one's relationships—for friendship or love or family. (I can't hide you, I'll endanger my own family, or I'll hide you because you are my friend.)

Stage Four: A person chooses to act based on the laws and good of the society. (I can't hide you because there is a law; if I break the law, everyone might break laws.)

Stage Five: As the Constitution of the United States provides, laws may be broken if they are unjust—and if one is willing to bear the consequences. (I'll hide you; if I get caught, I will willingly go with you to Auschwitz—this whole organized mess is wrong. We should do what we can, including civil disobedience, to change the law.)

Stage Six: This is the stage to which only Gandhi, Martin Luther King, and a few select others have arrived—one makes a decision for the good of all. (I will hide you, I will set an example, I hope everyone follows my example; that way, the German ideology will prove ineffective.)

According to Kohlberg, morality may be relative as one moves through the stages of moral development, but when—and if—one reaches the final and sixth stage, there is only the decision that is for the good of all—the universal, morally just decision.

Thus, I explain to my students, the farm wife who is afraid to take in Jewish children justifies her decision because her own children's lives could be endangered. In a way, her own human instinct to protect children is claimed by the dark Nazi forces—she is taught, as Hannah Arendt suggested,

> The law of Hitler's land demanded that the voice of conscience tell everybody: "Thou shalt kill," although the organizers of the massacres knew full well that murder is against the normal desires and inclinations of most people. . . . Many Germans and many Nazis, probably an overwhelming majority of them, must have been tempted *not* to murder, *not* to rob, *not* to let their neighbors go off to their doom . . . . " (150)

In one class, students overwhelmingly condemn those who would not take in the young children. A student suggests that if no one had cooperated with the German racial laws, then the Nazi program to kill all European Jews would have been ineffective. In another class, students feel tremendous sympathy for the farmer's wife who could not put her own family at risk to save strangers, who in fact was forced to *not* follow her natural, human instincts for fear she, too, would be a victim. The Nazis, we decide, deprived even those who followed them of their basic instinct to behave humanely.

We return to our discussion about the culpability of all Germans for the crimes against humanity. Students are still unwilling to assign guilt to the nation as a whole. They say: "Everyone did not participate." "Some were good." "Some protected Jews."

I ask, "If all Germans were not Nazis, is Germany responsible as a nation for the atrocities committed during the war? Should they have been responsible for reparations?"

To this, the answer is "yes." And to further provoke my students, I ask, "Is America, then, responsible for reparations to the descendants of former slaves?" To this, the answer is unclear—and quite controversial.

Einsatzgruppen Killing Squads

To further understand the mass shootings of the Einsatzgruppen, I refer students to The History Place for an eyewitness account of an Einsatzgruppen massacre: *www.historyplace.com/worldwar2/holocaust/h-engineer.htm.* The account is vivid and effectively renders the horror of what the witness saw:

> . . . An old woman with snow white hair was holding a one year old child in her arms and singing to it and tickling it. The child was cooing with delight. The parents were looking on with tears in their eyes. The father was holding the hand of a boy about ten years old and speaking to him softly; the boy was fighting his tears. The father pointed to the sky, stroked his head and seemed to explain something to him. At that moment the SS man at the pit started shouting something to his comrade. The latter counted off about twenty persons and instructed them to go behind the earth mound. Among them was the family I have just mentioned. I well remember a girl, slim with black hair, who, as she passed me, pointed to herself and said, "twenty-three years old." I walked around the mound and found myself confronted by a tremendous grave. People were closely wedged together and lying on top of each other so that only their heads were visible. Nearly all had blood running over their shoulders from their heads. Some of the people shot were still moving. Some were lifting their arms and turning their heads to show that they were still alive. The pit was nearly two-thirds full. I estimated that it already contained about a thousand people. I looked for the man who did the shooting. He was an SS man, who sat at the edge of the narrow end of the pit, his feet dangling into the pit. He had a tommy-gun on his knees and was smoking a cigarette . . .

For many students, this description of the nonchalance of the SS soldier crystallizes the shutdown of normal human response in those assigned to kill Jews. They are moved by the witness's observations. I want to tap into their reactions. I ask, "What do we know about the witness? How does the witness describe what he sees?"

Katie H. observes:

> To me, the saddest part of the passage was when a young girl passed by the engineer, and as she passed by him she said, "Twenty-three years old." She was so young and innocent, yet old enough to know that she was on her way to her death. This tears at my heart. . . . And I will never forget the description of the SS soldier sitting on the edge of the pit, his feet dangling over the edge. He sat there with a gun on his knee and a cigarette in his hand. He is so detached and unconcerned with the thousands of dead bodies lying in front of him.

Another way I ask students to deal with the graphic words of the engineer is to write a poème trouvé—a found poem from the lines of this account. That means they may use verbatim the lines found in the passage we read; their job is to "lineate" the lines in a more poetic way, forcing us to notice what we might not have noticed by reading the passage in paragraph form.

We also read the letter from Gerda Weissmann Klein's friend, Erika, about the killing that took place in her ghetto. In contrast to the above account, this account is told from the point of view of a victim. It is an incredible letter, written in the last moments of life, describing sadistic killing in the streets:

> Finally we met a young man who told us the tragic tale. Old people, young people, and children all had been taken to the marketplace. There they had undressed and lain naked on the stones, face down, and the murderers on horses and brandishing guns trampled on that screaming human pavement. Many were killed by the horseshoes, the whips left bloody traces. After the initial thirst of the sadists was satisfied, those who remained alive had to march naked outside the town. They had to dig their own grave and stand on the rim until a hail of bullets killed them. Strangers embraced as they went to sleep forever. . . . The moon was shining. We saw a great square grave, half open yet, a mountain of naked bodies in it. Many we recognized. We found my mother. She was all bloody. We did not find my little brother. I found Henek, the one I loved more than life, who was to be my husband. I kissed his dead face. Not one tear did I shed in that grave. Only my heart died. Do you know what? If they would come tomorrow and kill my father I would not care. I would not cry. I would be glad for him. I wish they would kill me. (69–70)

For a journal response, I ask, "What does Erika reveal about the 'action' in her town? How do the actions of the SS affect the survivor? Why does Erika wish they would kill her?"

And finally, I share with my students one of the most graphic and moving accounts of the Einsatzgruppen killing outside the Kovno ghetto. In the words of Solly Ganor's thirteen-year-old friend, Cookie, "a ghost" who returned from the pits of the dead and dying,

> Lithuanians and Germans with rolled up sleeves and red faces were loading and firing into the mob. You could see the yellow flashes from the barrels, and a veil of blue smoke drifting over the field.
>
> It was a scene out of hell itself. There were hoarse shouts, and women's screams—shrill, and children and babies crying and barking dogs. It stank of sweat and urine and excrement as terrified bodies just . . . let go. . . .
>
> Then we were at the pit. It looked like thousands of bodies, one on top of another, screaming and writhing, begging the Germans to finish them off. A vision of hell. A vision of hell. . . .
>
> We were right in front of the guns. Bullets were buzzing around me like angry bees, but all I felt was the crush of the mob behind me. Then I felt myself falling with Lena [a good friend] still clinging to my arm. She was gripping me with terrible force. There was a look of horror in her eyes, and she was trying to say something. But only a croaking sound came from her lips. A gaping hole appeared in her throat, and a stream of blood gushed out over her breast. Then I felt a weight fall on my head, knocking me into merciful oblivion. . . .
>
> I tried to suck in some air, but there wasn't any. Something enormously heavy was pressing down on my head, pushing my face into something soft and cold. The return to reality was the most terrifying experience imaginable, for the reality was that I was buried alive. (176–177)

Solly's friend then tells how he escaped the pit: Mr. Jablonsky's body covered his, Mr. Jablonsky tells Cookie he must escape, he must tell the others and warn them, "You must go, dear child, and bear witness," and then he asks Cookie to do one more thing—"Please don't let them bury me alive . . . take the body above me and cover my face with it. You must press down hard. I won't last long" (180).

How do we even begin to discuss this chilling account? There is silence, and then rage. All we can do is acknowledge that this happened. All we can do is hope—if we have anything to do about it—that it won't happen again.

To complement our discussion of the complicity of ordinary Germans, I again bring up Stanley Milgram's theory. Milgram, a professor at Yale

University in the 1950s, wondered if the evil deeds of Nazis were the result of their own personal defects or if normal people have the capacity for evil if the situation for evil is powerful enough. Milgram designed an experiment to see how far ordinary people would go in following orders—even if following orders meant inflicting high levels of pain on others. Subjects, as "teachers," were asked to administer increasing levels of shock to "learners," who were really paid actors in on the experiment. "Teachers" were told they were testing memory, and that if the "learner" didn't learn, they were to inflict an electric shock. Forty experts predicted that most "teachers" would not go past 150 volts, that only one in a thousand, the sadists, would go all the way to 450 volts. In fact, two-thirds of the subjects went all the way; the majority would not disobey. None got up to help without permission of the experimenters. Milgram concluded that blind obedience is *not* limited to the fascist mentality, but rather, is controlled by situational forces. *The Power of the Situation* explores several experiments that show how people will obey and follow directions, even if the directions are to perform sadistic acts toward others.

We try to make sense of Milgrim's theories in light of the conclusion of the judges at the Nuremberg Trials and the Eichmann Trial: that each individual is responsible for his or her own choices.

And then there are the Holocaust deniers, believers in a master race who blasphemously say the Holocaust did not exist. In the spring of 1996 in Britain, Deborah Lipstadt, a professor at the University of Georgia who wrote a book called *Denying the Holocaust: The Growing Assault on Truth & Memory,* was sued for libel by David Irving for saying in her book he was a Holocaust denier. They went to trial in the spring of 2000, and Deborah Lipstadt was vindicated. *Nova: Holocaust on Trial* is a PBS video that provides not only a reenactment of the libel trial, but also a good overview of the development and implementation of the final solution.

The backbone of the film is its portrayal of what the final solution was about—how it was organized, set up, and constructed. The history of Germany's systematic killing begins with archival footage and a discussion of the Einsatzgruppen who moved with the German army in June 1941, as they swept into the Soviet Union and the Eastern Front. Einsatzgruppen killing squads murdered 1.5 million Jews by gunfire. We witness the development of mobile gas vans that in 1942 systematically killed by carbon monoxide 97,000 people in five weeks. Irving admits in court that the killing was in reality, not experimental, but systematic. And finally, as the genocide reached its climax in 1942 with the "liquidation" of the ghettos, we see the development of Zyklon B gas and more efficient gas chambers. Irving denies that Jews were gassed at Auschwitz. He claims the crematory would have required more coke than was delivered. And chillingly, the defense shows evidence that once the fires of the ovens reached full intensity, they could burn for days without adding more coke—they only required fat and flesh and bone. At least one million Jews were murdered at Auschwitz.

The website *www.pbs.org/wgbh/nova/holocaust/timeline.html* provides a time line of Nazi abuses. It also includes the director's story (*www.pbs.org/wgbh/nova/holocaust/making.html*)—how he came to make the film, his fears, his obligations, the research, and his facing the horror of visiting Auschwitz; a bibliography and list of Holocaust links on the Web, as well as the complete transcript (*www.pbs.org/wgbh/nova/transcripts/2711holocaust.html*). The website also provides information on the "scientific" experiments done on humans, including many children. This film is worth showing to visit the arguments of Holocaust deniers—as well as the profound implications of their arguments. The facts presented through archival and recently shot footage clearly refute David Irving's contentions.

At this point, if they haven't already, students may want to examine the hate sites on the Web and watch *Hate.com,* a BBC/HBO documentary. (See Chapter 3.)

To keep students tuned into the film(s) as they watch, I ask them to take notes. As follow-up, I suggest they visit the time line provided by PBS: *www.pbs.org/wgbh/nova/holocaust/timeline.html.* To understand the sequence of events, I ask them to select the five most important dates and events in the construction and implementation of the Final Solution. Then I require that they explain *why* these events are important.

Another journal response I suggest is to write a letter to an editor refuting David Irving's contentions—that the Holocaust is an invention of Jews seeking sympathy, that Hitler never knew about the Holocaust and Jews were not systematically killed by gas. Students should refer to evidence from the film (they may quote from the transcript found at *www.pbs.org/wgbh/nova/transcripts/2711holocaust.html*). Perhaps they will understand, by writing a letter, what it means to protest, what it means to speak out. Writing a letter is also a way to simply process information in a productive and meaningful way.

8

The Camps,
Part I: Night

Young survivors behind a barbed wire
fence in Buchenwald concentration
camp, April 11, 1945.   National
Archives, courtesy of USHMM
Photo Archives.

"I saw it—saw it with my own eyes"

—ELIE WIESEL

I always have trouble approaching and teaching *Night* by Elie Wiesel. I treat it
with, perhaps, too much reverence. For me, it is the story of my former
mother-in-law. (She would object to my saying this.) It is the story of every
child separated severely and unjustly from family. It is the story of cruelty
inflicted and pain and sorrow sustained. It is, ultimately, the story of one
young man's survival. How do I teach something so personal?

In my Honors Humanities class I am concurrently teaching *The Iliad*
and we are discussing Achilles' pain when he learns of the death of his friend

Patroclos. He prostrates himself to the ground and covers his face with dust and ashes—much as Job does when he learns of the deaths of his children. We discuss suffering and the pain of loss. And I cavalierly assign a three- to five-page paper asking students to discuss why and how man suffers: "In both Job and in *The Iliad,* characters rue the day they were born. Why? What does it mean to suffer? What is the existential state of suffering? Are there lessons to be learned or is suffering simply part of the state of being human?" I think this is a good question for that class. And though I make a somewhat similar assignment in my Holocaust Lit class, it's different. I can't distance myself from the material enough to ask generic questions—even though these philosophical questions are raised in discussion every day. I can't abstract, I can't generalize—because the literature is still too close, too personal.

Several years ago, walking down the hall of a school, I overheard a teacher assigning a paper on *Night.* She told her students she expected a five-paragraph paper with an introduction ending in a thesis, three paragraphs that prove three ways Elie suffered, or three ways the Nazis were cruel, or three ways Elie helped his father, or three ways Elie found to survive—and a conclusion. I stood outside that teacher's classroom fuming. How can you reduce Wiesel's experiences to a five-paragraph paper? How can you organize and simplify such a complex rendering of suffering and loss? I vowed I would find a way to get students to genuinely and authentically understand and assess Wiesel's 109-page story.

My assignments are simple: Read the book, keep a journal. Sometimes I am more specific: Write a journal entry after every chapter or write three journal entries during the course of the book; respond honestly; describe what you observe; describe how what you read affects you, what you think about, what you question, what you associate. Sometimes I ask them to write about a quotation they find effective. Sometimes, I ask them to pick out a paragraph of prose and lineate it as a poem. I want them to read the text carefully—to see what Wiesel is saying, to see how Wiesel conveys his experience.

For many students, *Night* is their first exposure to Auschwitz. We have, in fact, added *Night* to our tenth-grade English curriculum at Groves—and at Seaholm—so that every student in our schools reads the book before graduating. As we hope a good, literary book will do, *Night* grabs the attention of students and never lets go until the end. Like *Catcher in the Rye,* it is a coming-of-age story. Like *Antigone* or *Oedipus,* it forces students to grapple with universal questions of good and evil. Like *1984* and *Brave New World,* it asks, What kind of society do we live in? What kind of social system have we devised? And above all else, *Night* asks us to consider what it means to be human.

Night opens with a warning to the Jews of Sighet to flee—that the Jews of Sighet ignore. How can one believe that what Moshe the Beadle says is happening to Jews is true? Then, the Germans arrive, and the Jews are forced into ghettos, and then onto trains—and to Auschwitz. No one even knows what Auschwitz is. It is, at first, merely a train station. At Auschwitz, the narrator sees his mother and sister for the last time. And as he and his father are marched by the flames of a burning pit, Wiesel's life turns to one long night:

> Never shall I forget that night, the first night in camp, which has turned my life into one long night, seven times cursed and seven times sealed. Never shall I forget that smoke. Never shall I forget the little faces of the children, whose bodies I saw turned into wreaths of smoke beneath a silent blue sky.
>
> Never shall I forget those flames which consumed my faith forever.
>
> Never shall I forget that nocturnal silence which deprived me, for all eternity, of the desire to live. Never shall I forget those moments which murdered my God and my soul and turned my dreams to dust. Never shall I forget these things, even if I am condemned to live as long as God Himself. Never. (32)

When we gather for our class discussion, students don't speak right away. This is the kind of book that moves them. They read it in a couple of hours. They are silenced by its story. To spur discussion, I ask each student to comment on one thing observed in the text. Each student must either ask a question or comment on a passage they found particularly effective. Usually, a single comment provokes a string of responses:

- No one believes Moshe the Beadle—how could they not listen? Why didn't they leave?
- They were told to pack. They just do it. They move from ghetto to ghetto. They had two chances to leave, Elie has a chance to stay in the hospital at the end—it seems so unreal to have so many chances, and yet the naivety—Elie never blames his father for pushing them on.
- In the beginning, their rights were slowly taken away. They had such hope, such strong hope. But they had to wear the yellow star, have their own police—there's a theme of hope (78).
- The children thrown into the pit of the fire is so disturbing (p. 30). It was sick.
- Madame Schacter sees fire, and no one wants to believe her.
- No one could believe the Germans actually wanted to get rid of the Jewish "race." We discuss whether Jews are a race. They're just like everyone else, my students say. You mean Caucasian with eyes and nose

and ears and mouth? I ask. I tell them how in middle school—here in this district, I thought I was like everyone else, though I was one of about five Jews in the school. I could "pass," yet I was afraid of being different, afraid of telling my friends I went to a temple instead of a church—and so when asked what church I went to, I said, "Beth El," without telling them that Beth El was a temple. Students comment you can be Jewish, Christian, and still be white. We talk about a recent *Newsweek* in which there are two pages of photographs of the 1920s and 1930s racial profiling in America of "white" people—Jews, Rumanians, Italians, Hungarians, Gypsies, Armenians. We talk about black Jews—Ethiopian Jews who have immigrated to Israel in the last ten years; the Lemba in South Africa who carry the Jewish gene for the priestly tribe, the Cohanim. We wonder what is race? What is religion?

- How the Nazis effectively dehumanized the Jews and transformed them into dogs. Humans are animals in desperate situations, the savage scene on page 96—so contrary to human nature.

- Night as a metaphor. "Never shall I forget that night, the first night in camp, which has turned my life into one long night . . ." (32).

- I don't understand, throws in Tyson: Did the Nazis have the Jews hypnotized? Tyson is descended from Chaldean (Iraqi Christian) parents; he is a big, handsome boy, a football player. "I would fight," he says. "Why didn't they fight? Were the camps set up to put them in a trance?" Tyson asks an important question. A question many students want answered: Why didn't the Jews fight back? (See Chapter 6 on resistance.) Many of the students had answers for Tyson. Tim suggests, "Nazis made examples of people who didn't DO what they were told. Fear made it easy for Germans to do what they wanted to do." Trisha says, "We'll never understand the power the Germans had." Natalie adds, "Jews were being put in camps and starved to death. We can see how people would be numb."

- The humanity of Juliek's playing his violin to the dying—amidst this horror there's this music, there's beauty—the Jews were forbidden to play German music, and when just before he dies, Juliek plays the one thing they couldn't take away from him, it's his last stand—they say music is the inner soul.

Based on our discussion of how humanity was found in the midst of death as Juliek plays his violin, the next day I bring in a CD of Beethoven's violin concerto in D, op. 61. I don't want to take up a lot of class time, but I want my students to hear what Juliek played for the dying prisoners. I want them to imagine a young, frail boy playing forbidden music, beautiful music, for the last time. I play the second movement in which the violin solo is plaintive and mournful. It makes me weep. My students' response to the music is more profound than I expected. Stephanie G. calls it "serene, calming." Janet, a violinist herself, says, "His soul is in his bow." Leigh says, "Juliek's music took him to another world, lifted him. When you listen to music, you feel like you're in some beautiful place. It shows how much Juliek wanted to live."

How do we ask authentic questions about this book? I ask students to write down a question for the next day's discussion. They return with big questions:

- How did Elie's father change?
- How does Elie change?
- Why don't people believe the Germans mean what they say?
- How could the Germans throw babies into a burning pit? What does that show about them? About the breakdown of civilization?
- How do they maintain their humanity in the face of inhumane treatment?
- Did luck or strength of character affect survival?
- What reasons do they have to live? Why do they bother? What is the meaning of life?
- What do we learn about man's cruelty to man (92)?
- How can a father become a burden? When does a son abandon a father to survive?
- Why does Juliek play his violin? What do we learn about man's struggle to live? To find beauty in life? What does it mean to be human?
- How does Elie's belief in God change? What about the trial of God? What does it mean to be angry with God? What is God's role in the Holocaust according to the prisoners?
- What does Wiesel mean when he writes, "From the depths of the mirror, a corpse gazed back at me. The look in his eyes, as they stared into mine, has never left me" (109).
- Wiesel writes about being led from the train past a ditch where "they were burning something . . . little children. Babies! Yes, I saw it with my own eyes. . . . I pinched my face. Was I still alive? Was I awake? I could not believe it. How could it be possible for them to burn people, children, and for the world to keep silent (30)? Does Wiesel ask us to make moral judgments?

Students are moved both by our discussions and by the book itself. Their writing helps, as always, to clarify their thinking. Especially with a book that evokes such an emotional response, I want and hope students will be able to break down their visceral reactions into ideas they can define and elaborate. For journals, I suggest students respond to one of the questions we discussed in class. Or they may select and write down a quotation they find particularly moving or effective and describe what the quotation means within the context of the book.

J.P. writes:

On page 62 there is a powerful passage that reads: "Where is God now? . . . Where is he? Here he is—he is hanging here on the gallows. . . ." To me this is a midway climax for the story. We can see that here Elie loses his faith in God through the tragic death of an innocent boy. I would consider myself a fairly religious person and can understand how horrible this event must have been that he lost all hope in God. With this section of the book I get the complete feeling of how lost Wiesel really was during this time. There is nothing to look towards anymore.

Natalie writes:

How could one possibly find any hope in a concentration camp? How is there a God in a concentration camp? How can one be optimistic about human nature when one has seen so much evil? . . . I cannot get the selection process out of my mind. I have an image of standing in line and watching everyone get sent to death or life. And my little sister stands in front of me, and I know she is too weak to be spared. They tell me left and her right. There could be nothing more horrible. And suddenly, in the midst of my morbid thoughts, I want the bell to ring, I want to escape from this classroom where I have such thoughts. The subject of the Holocaust is constantly paining.

In reading *Night*, I kept saying to myself, "How much more do I have to take?" Wiesel doesn't spare his audience. I remember thinking as I read this book, "How would my family act?" "How would we survive?" And I think that's where it gets so incredibly unbearable. This happened to real families. Neighborhoods that look like ours. I cannot imagine hearing a siren and looking out my window and seeing a German police car race down my street to pick up my Jewish neighbors. I cannot imagine it.

Trisha writes:

I liked this book because there was no turning back once you started reading. There was no escaping once you reached the camps. . . . One of the first things Elie saw and described in the camp was a picture that I felt through my bones and smelled through my nose. This was the scene of the children, the babies being thrown into the burning pit. All I could see was innocent children crying and crying, and I saw their bodies burning. I will never forget that this is what the Holocaust was.

Another writing option I offer is to write a "found poem." Since Wiesel's prose is so dense and poetic, students may find a passage within the text, and lineate it as if it *were* a poem. I want them to give fresh meaning to the words by forcing us to focus on the first and last words of the line. I want them to consider the rhythm of the lines, to use line breaks as a mini-comma to make us pause—to make us see. I also remind them that in writing a "found poem," they must attribute the lines to the original writer.

Julia P. takes a few simple lines: "For more than half an hour he stayed there, struggling between life and death, dying in slow agony under our eyes. And we had to look him full in the face. He was still alive when I passed in front of him. His tongue was still red, his eyes were not yet glazed. Behind me, I heard the same man asking: 'Where is God now'?"

By breaking the lines, making us pause at particular words, she creates new meaning:

"THE HANGING"
after Elie Wiesel

For more than half an hour
He stayed there,
Struggling
Between life and death,
Dying
In slow agony
Under our eyes.
And we had to look him
Full
In the face.
He was still alive
When I passed in front of him.
His tongue was still red,
His eyes
Were not yet glazed.
Behind me, I heard the same man
Asking:
"Where is God now?"

Julia Porter, from Night, *p. 62*

To provide further background to our study of Wiesel, I show *To Speak the Unspeakable: The Message of Elie Wiesel*, directed by Judit Elek. The documentary follows Elie Wiesel to Sighet, the town he was born in and the town from which he and his family were wrenched. Wiesel walks with us through Auschwitz as passages from *Night* are read. The film ends with Wiesel accepting the Nobel Peace prize. Another video, which shows Elie Wiesel "in person," is *Facing Hate with Bill Moyers and Elie Wiesel* (see Chapter 3). Students always comment of Wiesel's overwhelming presence and wisdom.

To better understand what arrival at Auschwitz looked like, students may look at several moving photographs taken by the SS of women and children waiting for selection (see the front cover), men dressed in striped prison garb after delousing, and piles of abandoned suitcases and coats for "Canada"—the warehouse of acquisitioned goods. These photographs may be seen at the Yad Vashem archives: *www.yadvashem.org.il/Auschwitz_Album/*. (See the poetry exercise in Chapter 9.)

Another video that gives a sense of what life was like for Hungarian Jews is *The Last Days,* produced by Steven Spielberg's foundation. Hungarian Jews were deported in the spring of 1944. They were among the last Jews of Europe to be arrested and deported. Most were gassed immediately. This documentary traces the stories of five Hungarian survivors, including Tom Lantos, a U.S. congressman from California. The stories are moving and effective. The three women survivors tell of losing their material things, being packed into cattle cars and sent to Auschwitz where they saw their families for the last time. Irene Zisblatt tells of how her mother gave her diamonds for an emergency. When she saw that she would have to give them up at the entrance to Auschwitz, she swallowed them. She had to swallow them more than once. And now, she wears them in a tear-drop shape on a necklace.

Students agree this documentary effectively shows the story of the war against the Jews. It is one of many comprehensive films that tell the story—from before the war, to the camps, to liberation. Many, after seeing the film, say it is the "best" film they have seen. They say that, thank goodness, many times about many films!

Responding to the film, Abbi, the granddaughter of a survivor, writes:

> After watching *The Last Days* I think I really saw the damage that Hitler and the Nazi Party did to people. It was really troubling for me to see all those people taking their families back to what can only be described as Hell on Earth. For most of those people, what happened to them has made them who they are today and has damaged them just the same. . . . I'm seventeen and I know that I'm too young and too weak to be faced with a situation half

as bad as what these heroes went through. I think they are heroes because we look at soldiers who kill and call them heroes, but these people prevailed by staying alive, that is the only way they fought back. Today if I was asked whom I admire the most in the world, I would have to say the survivors of the Holocaust.

Art Spiegelman's *Maus II: And Here My Troubles Began*, the sequel to *Maus I: My Father Bleeds History*, tells what happens to Vladek when he is captured and sent to Auschwitz. I suggest the book for outside reading and extra credit. Art Spiegelman shows through his cartooning how Vladek survived. He makes us understand what it means to be infested by fleas—his magnified drawing of a flea makes us itch as we examine the squirmy legs and pincers. He shows graphically how the barter system worked in the camps. We see how Vladek "organized" and bartered to save his wife. And we see how the experiences of Vladek affected his son, Artie. This book, though harrowing, is easy to read.

Why Focus on the Jews?

Students often ask, Why do we focus on the Jews in our studies? Weren't there others killed? The answer is yes. Gypsies. Homosexuals. Political prisoners. Soviet prisoners of war. As Elie Wiesel says, "All victims were not Jews, but all Jews were victims" (Kingdom 174). This statement forces us to examine the ethnic quality of the Holocaust, the unique demonization of the Jews as a people, the arrest, imprisonment, and death assigned to innocent, nonaggressive people. We turn to Martin Gilbert:

> Between 1939 and 1945 the Germans killed many millions of non-Jewish civilians in Germany itself, and in every occupied country, often in massive reprisal actions or after prolonged torture. The shooting down in cold blood of unarmed, defenseless Greeks, Poles, Yugoslavs, Czechs, Russians, and men, women and children of a dozen other nationalities, all of them civilians who had taken no part in military action, was a feature of Nazi rule throughout Europe. Among those murdered were as many as a quarter of a million Gypsies, tens of thousands of homosexuals, and tens of thousands of "mental defectives." Also murdered, often after cruelties of tortures, were several million Soviet prisoners-of-war, shot or starved to death long after they had been captured and disarmed.
>
> As well as the six million Jews who were murdered, more than ten million other non-combatants were killed by the Nazis. Under the Nazi scheme, Poles, Czechs, Serbs and Russians were to become subject peoples; slaves, the workers of the New Order. The Jews were to disappear altogether. It was

the Jews alone who were marked out to be destroyed in their entirety: every Jewish man, woman and child, so that there would be no future Jewish life in Europe. Against the eight million Jews who lived in Europe in 1939, the Nazi bureaucracy assembled all the concerted skills and mechanics of a modern state: the police, the railways, the civil service, the industrial power of the Reich; poison gas, soldiers, mercenaries, criminals, machine guns, artillery; and over all, a massive apparatus of deception. (Holocaust 824)

Tadeusz Borowski's story, "This Way for the Gas, Ladies and Gentlemen," is not an easy story. It is one of the few stories we read written by a non-Jewish, political prisoner. According to the introduction of the book by the same title, Borowski was arrested at the end of April 1942. He was "lucky." "Three weeks earlier 'Aryans' had stopped being sent to the gas chambers—except for special cases. From then only Jews were gassed en masse." I think it is important for students to understand that though all prisoners suffered severely in Germany's concentration camp system, only Jews were designated for extermination. It is also apparent from reading the stories of Borowski—and of Heinz Heger (*The Men with the Pink Triangle*)—that prisoners who were not Jewish were able to receive sustaining packages from family and friends. On the second page of "This Way for the Gas . . ." the narrator describes slicing neat loaves of crisp, crunchy bread. "Sent all the way from Warsaw—only a week ago my mother held this white loaf in her hand . . . dear Lord, dear Lord . . ."(30).

Borowski's story begins, "All of us walk around naked." He takes us immediately into Auschwitz following delousing and ironically says, ". . . our striped suits are back from the tanks of Zyklon-B solution, an efficient killer of lice in clothing and of men in gas chambers" (29). I ask students to tell me about the "tone" of the speaker's voice. What is he trying to tell us? How is his voice different from Wiesel's? He is not speaking as only a victim, but also one who takes advantage of a situation—if possible. There is a double edge to the speaker's voice as he describes the ugliness and horror of the camp—as well as his ability to take advantage of the situation. The narrator works in "Canada" (see photographs at *www.yadvashem.org.il/Auschwitz_Album/*). Working in Canada means taking suitcases out of the hands of arriving Jews. It means going though the suitcases to plunder the last things owned by the soon-to-be-gassed transports, giving gold and jewels and clothing to the SS and salvaging food for themselves.

"What if there aren't any more 'cremo' transports?" I say spitefully. "Can't you see how much easier life is becoming around here: no limit on packages, no more beatings? You even write letters home. . . . One hears all kind of talk, and dammit, they'll run out of people!"

Henri, the narrator's friend who talks with a mouth full of sardines, says, "They can't run out of people, or we'll starve to death in this blasted camp. All of us live on what they bring" (31).

How utterly appalling to my students. This is not the Auschwitz they know. Here is a prisoner who hopes for more transports that will be sent directly to the crematory, who will stand to gain from their loss of goods and life, and who fears "they" will run out of people! We discuss a new dimension of the Holocaust and the camps—the horror of needing and wanting others to die to sustain one's own life. Suddenly, we must redefine reality as it existed in the camps. We learn how prisoners themselves collaborated.

The narrator finally says to his friend, Henri,

"I am furious, simply furious with these people [the transported Jews]— furious because I must be here because of them. I feel no pity. I am not sorry they're going to the gas chamber. Damn them all! I could throw myself at them, beat them with my fists. It must be pathological, I can't understand . . ."

We must ponder a new idea. The fury the narrator feels because he must work in Canada because of the Jews who are to die. And he feels no pity. He wishes to beat them himself. Why? Why does he feel such anger? And what does his anger show about his own personality—and the complex nature of the camp?

Borowski describes a young woman who denies her own child. "It's not mine," she cries. Already, the woman who will soon be gassed has removed herself from the life of her child—she refers to him as an "it." "She is young, healthy, good-looking, she wants to live." And the child keeps crying, "Mama, mama, don't leave me." A Russian prisoner picks up the woman who wants to live, knocks her down, then throws her on the truck of those to be gassed. Then he throws the child at her feet. There is no escaping the horror of the camp—even if one is a prisoner who has some power and some food.

During our discussion of the story Dan says, "Everyone would like to believe that in the camps there was a brotherhood of prisoners, but there was not." In fact, we wonder if it is even more horrible to become part of the enemy you hate in order to survive. Borowski takes us through the looking glass to see the twisted, distorted reality imposed by the camps. He committed suicide six years after his liberation.

For further reading and extra credit, especially for students interested in the plight and fate of homosexuals in the Third Reich, I suggest they read *The Men with the Pink Triangle: The True, Life-and-Death Story of Homosexuals in the Nazi Death Camps* by Heinz Heger. This sensitive memoir describes the antihomosexual legislation beginning with Paragraph 175 of the criminal code, which outlawed sodomy in Germany in 1871. (Paragraph 175 was not repealed until 1969.) Heger describes how the law against "degenerates" was enforced by the Nazi regime, how homosexuals were arrested and sent to concentration camps, and what they had to do to survive.

And in a little-known chapter of history, the arm of the SS reached even into the American army and plucked out its Jews to serve the German genocidal rage. When American GIs from the 106th Division were taken as prisoners of war, Jewish and Jewish sympathizers were selected by Germans to go to Berga, a concentration camp. Dr. William Shapiro, a medic attached to the 28th Infantry Division, taken for his Jewish name, reports in an interview with the *New York Times* (4/17/01), "I traveled the same road as an American prisoner of war as the Jews of Europe. I was put in a box car, starved, put on a death march." Out of 2000 American POWs, 350 were selected for Berga; out of the 350 selected, seventy died.

In the spring of 2001, Academy Award winner Charles Guggenheim began making a documentary about the American GIs caught in the Nazi maelstrom; were it not for a foot infection, he, too, would have likely have served with them in Europe and Berga.

9

The Camps, Part II:
Survival in Auschwitz

What Does It Mean to Be Human?

Roll call for newly arrived prisoners, mostly Jews, arrested during the "Night of Broken Glass" pogrom, at the Buchenwald concentration camp. Buchenwald, Germany, 1938.   American-Jewish Joint Distribution Committee, courtesy of USHMM Photo Archives.

While *Night* is a minimalist rendering of Elie Wiesel's experiences, a beautiful book, cut from the original 900 pages written in Yiddish, *Survival in Auschwitz* by Primo Levi offers an almost scientifically observed picture of Auschwitz, and most of all a portrait of what it means to be human—to attempt to retain one's humanity in the midst of the most dehumanizing force in history. The original title in Italian of *Survival in Auschwitz* is *Se Questo e un Uomo*— *If This Be a Man*. As we read Levi's book, we ask ourselves, What does it mean to be human?

Levi is our Dante, taking us into the burning world of the German Lager (concentration camp). How, despite the German effort to strip man of all his humanity, does a human being prevent his own destruction? How does one "resist" the enormous effort of the Nazi machine to dehumanize him, to make him unworthy of life?

To prepare for the reading of this powerful book we watch *The Garden of the Finzi-Continis* to see what life was like for Italian Jews as racial laws began to affect them, and we read several poems from Primo Levi's *Collected Poems*.

Vittorio de Sica's film, *The Garden of the Finzi-Continis,* which won an Oscar as Best Foreign Film in 1971, opens in Italy in 1938 when Mussolini's anti-Semitic edicts began to isolate Jews from their communities. We see the wealth of the aristocratic Finzi-Continis—and the utter sense of loss as Jews are gradually separated from their tennis club, their school, their local library, their friends, their homes.

Students are struck as they watch this film by how similar the protagonists in the film are to them. These are the beautiful people—who, as Jews, receive no special treatment. The wealthy are transported to Auschwitz, too. Students get caught up in the love story between Georgio and Micol. As Marissa says, "The Finzi-Contini family were often portrayed playing tennis or lounging in their lavish home. They lived in their own carefree world of decadence and wealth. As assimilated as they were, they always imagined their money would save them."

Next, we read several poems by Primo Levi, starting with "Shema," which is printed just after the author's preface in *Survival in Auschwitz:*

"SHEMA"

You who live secure
In your warm houses,
Who return at evening to find
Hot food and friendly faces:

    Consider whether this is a man,
    Who labors in the mud
    Who knows no peace
    Who fights for a crust of bread
    Who dies at a yes or a no.
    Consider whether this is a woman,
    Without hair or name
    With no more strength to remember
    Eyes empty and womb cold
    As a frog in winter.

Consider that this has been:
I commend these words to you.
Engrave them on your hearts
When you are in your house,
when you walk on your way
When you go to bed, when you rise.
Repeat them to your children.
Or may your house crumble,
Disease render you powerless,
Your offspring avert their faces from you.

Levi asks us who live in our safe, warm houses, who return in the evening for hot food and friendly faces to consider if this is a man "who works in the mud/who knows no peace/Who fights for a crust of bread/Who dies at a yes or a no." He asks if this is a woman "Without hair or name/With no more strength to remember. Eyes empty and womb cold/As a frog in winter." Levi's "Shema" echoes the prayer every religious Jew says every day, a prayer asking God to "listen," followed by the V'ahavta, a prayer that professes love of God:

Hear (Shema), O Israel: The Lord is our God; the Lord is One.
And thou shalt love the Lord thy God with all thine heart, with all thy soul, and with all thy might. And these words, which I command thee this day, shall be in thine heart: And thou shalt teach them diligently unto thy children, and shalt talk of them when thou sittest in thine house, and when thou walkest by the way, and when thou liest down, and when thou risest up. And thou shalt bind them for a sign upon thine hand, and they shall be as frontlets between thine eyes. And thou shalt write them upon the doorposts of thy house and upon thy gates. (Deuteronomy VI, 4–9)

The words of the command to teach of God's covenant are followed in Deuteronomy by a series of curses:

But it shall come to pass, if thou wilt not hearken unto the voice of the Lord thy God, to observe to do all his commandments . . . that all these curses shall come upon thee and overtake thee:
Cursed shalt thou be in the city, and cursed shalt thou be in the field. Cursed shall be thy basket and thy store. Cursed shall be the fruit of thy body, and the fruit of thy land, the increase of thy kin, and the flocks of thy sheep. Cursed shalt thou be when thou comest in, and cursed shalt thou be when thou goest out. (Deuteronomy XXVIII, 15–19)

In "Shema," Levi curses those who would not "consider that this has been."

Some questions I ask: What is Levi saying? Who is the speaker? To whom does the speaker speak? Who is the implied "you"? How does Levi define a man? Why does he ask us to consider "whether this is a man"? How low can a man go before he hits bottom, before he is no longer human? What is it that Levi wants us to teach our children? Why does Levi curse us if we do not meditate about how this came about? Students begin to see what Levi is getting at when he states in his original title, "If this be a man." They begin to define what it means to be human—to be able to return to a warm house, hot food, and friendly faces in the evening; to NOT have to work in mud, to NOT have to fight for a crust of bread, to NOT have to die because of a yes or a no; to have hair, a name, even the strength to remember. We also discuss the moral imperative Levi stresses in the poem: to meditate on these words and to teach them to our children; to NOT forget. And then, we begin our reading of Levi's opus, *Survival in Auschwitz*.

I assign pairs of students to teach each chapter to the class. Though they are responsible for reading the whole book, I ask them to carefully read over their chapter, to look closely at the text. What is it saying? I ask them to take us through the chapter so that we can understand what is important:

- Consider and describe what is at stake in the chapter.
- Find a quotation (or two) you feel is emblematic of the whole. Tell us why.
- How are the concerns of the chapter resolved or dealt with?

This assignment provokes profound and important discussion. These chapters are difficult for twelfth-grade students to process. They miss important points that come out in discussion. And yet, they find ideas with which the class grapples and comes to terms. The thread that we pull throughout our discussions is, What does it mean to be human? What must man do to maintain his humanity and dignity in the face of ironclad oppression?

Levi opens his book with an author's preface. He says he has written the book to furnish documentation for a quiet study of certain aspects of the human mind:

> Many people, many nations—can find themselves holding, more or less wittingly, that "every stranger is an enemy." For the most part this conviction lies deep down like some latent infection; it betrays itself only in random, disconnected acts, and does not lie at the base of a system of reason. But when this does come about, when the unspoken dogma becomes the major premise in a syllogism, then at the end of the chain, there is the Lager. . . . The story of the death camps should be understood by everyone as a sinister alarm-signal. (9)

We begin our discussions with a single question: How do you live a sane life in an insane world? Very quickly Levi learns that language lacks words to describe the "demolition of a man":

> Nothing belongs to us anymore; they have taken away our clothes, our shoes, even our hair; if we speak, they will not listen to us, and if they listen, they will not understand. They will even take away our name: and if we want to keep it, we will have to find ourselves the strength to do so, to manage somehow so that behind the name something of us, of us as we were, still remains. (27)

Levi says in prose what he has suggested in "Shema":

> Imagine now a man who is deprived of everyone he loves, and at the same time of his house, his habits, his clothes, in short, of everything he possesses; he will be a hollow man, reduced to suffering and needs, forgetful of dignity and restraint, for he who loses all often easily loses himself. (27)

Thirsty, Levi reaches for an icicle outside the window. A guard brutally snatches it away. Levi asks, "*Warum?*" (German for why). The guard answers, "*Hier ist kein warum*" (there is no why here) (29). Levi learns it is better not to think (37). Yet, he determines that he must survive to tell the story, to bear witness, "and that to survive we must force ourselves to save at least the skeleton, the scaffolding, the form of civilization" (41).

Primo Levi, a chemist by training, uses his powers of scientific observation to describe the absurdity of what went on in the camps. It is as if, explains Rabbi Aaron Bergman (who visited my classes), "The sun started coming up in the east or gravity only worked three days a week. We get through our days based on certain assumptions: if we are nice, people are going to be nice back; people will stop their cars at traffic lights; we trust that at a construction sight, no one will throw a brick at us." German law is suddenly kaput as logic and order are taken to absurd extremes.

Ultimately, Levi invites the reader to contemplate the possible meaning in the Lager of the words "good" and "evil," "just" and "unjust": "Let everybody judge, on the basis of the picture we have outlined and of the examples given above, how much of our ordinary moral world could survive on this side of the barbed wire." He asks us not to judge those who made decisions inside the Lager that they would not have been forced to make outside the camp. He reminds us of Hannah Arendt's words, that laws were turned inside out by the Germans, that the prohibition against murder became the commandment: Thou must murder—or be an accomplice to murder—to survive.

In one of the most beautiful chapters of all—and one of the most difficult for students to understand—Levi tells the story of walking to pick up a vat of soup. On the way, he is trying to reconstruct and recite Dante's "Canto of Ulysses." Like Juliek who plays his violin to the dying in *Night,* Levi recites poetry to his friend, Pikolo: "As if I also was hearing it for the first time: like the blast of a trumpet, like the voice of God. For a moment I forget who I am and where I am" (113). In the midst of the mud, of the dying, of the starving, Levi finds the beauty of literature, of what it means to be human:

> Think of your breed; for brutish ignorance
> Your mettle was not made; you were made men,
> To follow after knowledge and excellence. (Dante)

In these lines from Dante, Levi confirms what it means to be a man. A man is not made for "brutish ignorance," but rather to follow after "knowledge and excellence."

How to make students understand this? And indeed, I want to *make* students understand. I feel this appreciation of literature, of beauty, of art is an underlying premise for what I most want to accomplish as a teacher. I search for ways to pull them in. So far, they don't get it, even after reading the lines aloud in class and discussing what they mean. "Haven't you ever read a great book that just stops you? A passage that makes you say WOW!? Writing that is so beautiful you want to cry?" I meet blank stares. They shake their heads. No one. No one has read anything that has moved them to tears. No one has read anything that has made him catch his breath. I reach for a way to make them understand.

"What about movies? Or music? Have you ever watched a movie that has moved you or listened to music that just stops you with its incredible beauty?" I tell them how I weep when I hear Vivaldi's "Four Seasons" or watch a male ballet dancer leap through air. And then, finally, they get it. A lot of hands go up. Now, they can relate—and they tell me about music by Jay-Z and Mozart, films like *Titanic* and *Braveheart.* "When I see Mel Gibson yell 'FREEDOM'! it makes me tingle," Blake says. Alyssa says, "Good dance makes me cry." And for the next fifteen minutes or so, we discuss what moves them, what constitutes an aesthetic experience, how art is so important to their lives and to their sense of what it means to be human.

Survival in Auschwitz evokes life and the enduring quality of men (in this case, Levi, isolated from women, writes only about men) in the camps. We learn how bread is money, how it is hoarded to be traded for an extra soup or cigarette, which can be traded for extra bread. We learn the importance of leather shoes, of avoiding selection, of sleep. We learn the importance of a good friend, a warm place to work.

In the last chapter, "The Story of Ten Days," we learn how Levi survived during his last days in the Lager. He speaks of becoming a man again when someone shares his bread with him. That first human gesture of kindness is the moment that marks the change by which those who had not died "slowly changed from Häftling (half persons or prisoners) to men again" (160). The book ends with a note of hope—hope that Levi will see a friend from the camp, again.

[For an excellent critical essay in the *New Republic*, see Michael Andre Bernstein's review of *Primo Levi: Tragedy of an Optimist* by Myriam Anissimov: *www.thenewrepublic.com/archive/0999/092799/bernstein092799.html*]

We move from our discussion of *Survival in Auschwitz* to a brief discussion of *Speak You Also: A Survivor's Reckoning* by Paul Steinberg. I suggest students read this book for extra reading, "extra credit." In Primo Levi's memoir, *Survival in Auschwitz*, Steinberg is the barely fictional Henri who brazenly does what he needs to do to survive. *Speak You Also* is Steinberg's response. Unlike most Holocaust memoirs, Steinberg's writing is edgy; there is a brashness to his writing that makes you feel this could be written by the kid who blocks for the football team or is great at slipping out of holds on the wrestling team. His voice compels us to read on—his story is the story of a seventeen-year-old boy who gets caught in Paris—and ends up in Auschwitz where one's lifespan, if not cut short immediately, is exhausted in three to four months. "We'd left feelings and friendships by the wayside. Withdrawn inside himself, each man was fighting for his own survival. The dehumanizing machine had worked like a charm. Our existence had been reduced to vileness and humiliation" (27).

As a journal response, I suggest students contrast Steinberg's perceptions of the Lager with Levi's. Consider how Henri, condemned by Levi as self-serving, explains his actions. Consider Levi's contention that there is a different morality on "this side of the barbed wire."

Another exercise I suggest to my students to help them visualize the camps and crematorium is to look up the drawings by David Olère on the Internet. David Olère is one of the few Sonderkommandos to survive. A Sonderkommando was one who worked in the crematoria loading bodies into the ovens. No photographs were taken of what happened in the crematorium. David Olère through his sketches and paintings, which are reproduced in *David Olère—The Eyes of a Witness*, was published by the Beate Klarsfeld Foundation in Paris in 1989. Olère has painted the horror of starved humans digging graves, marching out to work, supporting each other as they falter toward the gas chamber. The drawings may be found at *fcit.coedu.usf.edu/holocaust/resource/gallery/olere.htm*.

To use the research, to interpret and reflect, I ask students to bring in a photograph (or a copy of a painting by David Olère) that they have either found in a book or they have downloaded from the Internet. Good sources for photographs are The Auschwitz Album at *www.yadvashem.org.il /Auschwitz _Album /*, the History Place found at *www.historyplace.com /worldwar2/ holocaust /timeline.html#eng,* the United States Holocaust Memorial Museum (*www.ushmm.org/*), and Yad Vashem (*www.yadvashem.org.il /collections/ index.html*). Then, I lead students orally through the following steps. I give them five or so minutes to write before moving to the next direction:

1. Describe what you see happening in the painting or photograph.

2. Speak as if you are a person in the photograph or you are at the scene, but you cannot be seen—and describe what you *know* is happening, what is *really* going on. What do you see? Smell? Hear? Touch? Taste?

3. Is someone speaking? What are they saying? Write a dialogue that you hear, or write the monologue that is going on in your head.

4. What happened just before this instant was frozen on film or paper?

5. What happened just after this moment?

6. Now step out of the voice of the person in the picture. Does this scene remind you of anything you have ever experienced yourself—either personally or vicariously (on the news or in a book or movie).

7. Look through your notes. Underline the best chunks of writing and use the material to write a poem. No rhymes allowed!

Bethany writes in her exploratory writing:

I feel dirty and hurt. The way I have to wash up in a pool that is filled with germs and not being able to wash my body properly is just disgusting. The area surrounding me is very muddy and filthy. There is no privacy when I am cleaning up. I am going crazy here. We are taken from one camp and put into another. I dread waking up in the morning and knowing I have to suffer through another day that never seems to end. Each day is like a year.

I suggest lineating the lines into poetry. I suggest considering the rhythm of her lines, thinking about breaking the lines into stanzas, cutting "dead wood"—words that do not contribute to the effect of her poem. She writes:

"A DISPLACED PERSONS' CAMP"

Hagenau, Germany, May 30, 1945

I feel dirty and hurt.
I have to wash up

in a muddy and filthy pool
that is filled with germs.

There is no privacy.
I am going crazy here.
I dread waking up
in the morning and knowing

I have to suffer
through another day
that never seems to end.
Each day is like a year.

Bethany Putnick

It is amazing what simple lineation does to meaning. There is now a rhythm to Bethany's lines. There is a dirge-like quality to the movement of words, a repeated "ur" sound in "dirty" and "hurt" and "germs" and "suffer." There is a dread of waking up in the morning and knowing—that pause on "knowing" forces the reader to see that the speaker doesn't want to know what she must know about her life, about the past years. And still, wakefulness is never ending; a day is like a year. And the title adds meaning, tells us where and when—and forces us to acknowledge the Holocaust, which is never mentioned in the poem.

Based on a photograph of unending lines of people shouldering caskets, "a funeral of inmates who could not be saved or who were killed by the SS before liberation," January 27, 1945, Julie wrote the following:

"'FREEDOM' AT AUSCHWITZ" (JANUARY 27, 1945)

I carry my brother;
my best friend,
my last reason to live,
on my shoulders.

He was only seventy pounds
when he passed away,
but his weight
seems unbearable.

I follow an endless
line of coffins,
a flowing river of souls

Figure 9–1. *Funeral of inmates who could not be saved or who were killed by the SS before the liberation of Auschwitz. National Archives, courtesy of USHMM Photo Archives.*

I am a survivor,
but for what?
No one to love,
no family,
no future.

I envy the dead.

They no longer
have to struggle
or be reminded
of their nightmares
they lived in
every day.

Julie VanHelden

I am impressed by Julie's insight into the sensibilities of the survivor, the sense that a survivor lives—and doesn't live, that what a survivor experienced will never go away. I also appreciate the speaker's sense of her brother's "un-bearable" weight at only seventy pounds. I applaud her for her ability to em-pathize with people she has only read about or seen in videos.

And finally, I assign the type of paper most students dread. I want them to synthesize and develop their thoughts. I want them to get practice writing the more formal types of essays they will have to write for college. And I want them to reach some conclusions about what these important books mean and suggest to us.

Writing Assignment: *Survival in Auschwitz and Night*

Choose one of the following questions/prompts. Please write a three- to five-page well-reasoned, well-developed essay. Include direct quotations and interpretation of those quotations in your essay.

1. Why are *Survival in Auschwitz* and *Night* among the most effective Holocaust narratives? What devises, techniques do the authors employ to transmit their experience? What are they doing in the act of transmitting their experiences? How do they communicate Levi's and Wiesel's stories?

2. Compare *Survival in Auschwitz* with *Night*. How are they similar? Different? Is one more effective than the other in communicating the experience of the Lager? Why? Why not?

3. Trace a motif through the text of either *Night* or *Survival in Auschwitz*. Some motifs you may want to consider include:
   - What it means to be human
   - Night as a metaphor
   - Faith
   - The father–son relationship(s)
   - Food
   - Relationships in the Lager
   - Role of the Kapo
   - Survival
   - "Organizing"
   - Language

4. Compare *Night* and/or *Survival in Auschwitz* with "The Book of Job." Consider the existential meaning of human life in the face of suffering.

Holocaust Films

Night and Fog (1946) was one of the earliest documentaries, produced at the same time the Nuremberg Trials of doctors, judges, and SS officers were going on to provide proof of what happened. The film is in French with subtitles. It has been criticized because it does not focus on the crimes specifically against Jews, but on the crimes the Germans committed against humans. In thirty minutes it covers deportations (without pointing a finger at French collaboration), camps, and liberation. The footage is graphic and not advisable for young students.

The United States Holocaust Memorial Museum offers some cautions about using graphic films in the classroom:

> A main concern of educators using audio-visual materials on the Holocaust is that graphic footage depicting people who were starved, tortured, or killed can be upsetting to viewers of all ages. Videotaped eyewitness testimonies often contain vivid descriptions of the horrors encountered by victims. When the horror is presented, it should be done in a judicious manner, and only to the extent necessary to achieve the objective of the lesson. Teachers should remind themselves that each student and each class is different, and that what seems appropriate for one may not be for all.
>
> Students are a "captive audience." When educators assault them with images of horror for which they are unprepared, we violate a basic trust: the obligation of a teacher to provide a "safe" learning environment. The assumption that all students will seek to understand human behavior after being exposed to horrible images is fallacious. Some students may be so appalled by images of brutality and mass murder that they are discouraged from studying the subject further. Others may become fascinated in a more voyeuristic fashion, and subordinate further critical analysis of the history to the superficial titillation of looking at images of starvation, disfigurement, and death. (*www.ushmm.org/education/ov.html*)

I hesitate before showing *Night and Fog* to my twelfth-grade students. I tell them the film is graphic, they will see skeletons still in crematory ovens, bodies stacked like cordwood for burning, and heaped, naked bodies swept by bulldozers into a common grave. I ask if they can handle watching the film. All say they can. Then I still advise them that if images are too intense, to avert their eyes or put their heads down on the desk.

The film's first twenty-eight minutes or so reveal through edited black-and-white footage the history of concentration camps, beginning with support for Hitler in 1933 to deportations to the camps and their crematories. The voice-over is somewhat sardonic, the subtitles a bit hard to read; however, my students tell me that what they missed in the subtitles they could see in the footage. Most effective are the stacks of shoes, spectacles, bowls, and the mounds of human hair—juxtaposed by bolts of felt selling for 15 pfennigs a kilo. It is as if the point of the film is to show those who may have slept through the war what was happening in their backyards. The film ends with footage of Germans saying, "I am not responsible." We think the point of the film is to say we are all responsible.

I ask my students to write when the film is over. I offer a few prompts: Who was this film made for? What was the original purpose of this film? Now, what do we get from it? Do we need to see the graphic footage to understand? Why do you think this film was made in 1946, one year after liberation, at the time of the Nuremberg Trials of the doctors and judges and SS officers?

It is so hard to discuss a film like this without stating the obvious. I hope that as they write, the ideas will come and feel fresher, original. As they write—and they don't want to stop after even fifteen minutes—I take pleasure in watching and walking around the room to see what they are writing. Finally, I interrupt and ask if we can talk. Now they have ideas and are anxious to state them.

Scott L. says he feels somewhat desensitized by recent images he's seen of death in the camps. This time, he turned his head out of respect. "They were people," he says of the naked, bald bodies.

Blake says the music was not gruesome horrible music, more like "Peter and the Wolf." He notes how Alain Resnais contrasts flowers and fields with the horror of the barbed wire and camp. He then says that because he saw so many people getting on trains at train stations, he began to understand how the people could "not know," how they could board trains as if they were at an airport, as if they were really going somewhere.

David says, "These are real people. It's hard to make the transition between what's real and not real. We've seen so much death in movies and on television."

Tal says, "We're seniors. It's okay to see it. If we don't recognize the reality of history, it will be forgotten."

And Julie adds, "It's more important to see these images than not to see them. We shouldn't censor. You can't leave out these parts."

Dan responds, "I felt like I *had* to watch, unlike Scott. I understand why people don't want to see it, but I felt I owed it to the people who were there, who didn't have an option not to look. If we can turn it off, then we're going to believe it wasn't so bad."

And Charlie writes in his journal:

To say that we have to "bear witness" to the atrocities of the Holocaust is stupid and overdramatic. The history books bear witness, so do all of the historians. Who are we? We are just students. It doesn't really matter if we see them or not. Because I haven't seen some of the worst images, I will not be any less passionate in saying that the Holocaust was horrible and should never happen again.

There is a separation between actually seeing something and just hearing about it. Seeing things directly certainly affects the emotions more, but it also leaves us more scarred. Through merely hearing about something we can know that it occurred, we just don't have to deal with all of the emotional distress that goes with seeing it. (Sometimes I suppose emotional distress is a good tool, but in this instance I just think it's unnecessary.) There are definitely instances where is it better to see, but when it comes to the dead bodies of victims of the Holocaust, I think it is enough to just hear about them.

I'm impressed by my students' reactions. They are mature. They have grappled with the difficulty this film presents. And they seem to understand its impact and importance. In fact, in later discussions, they tell me this is among the most important and impressive Holocaust films they have seen.

I segue from our discussion of the massive piles of human hair seen in *Night and Fog* into Primo Levi's poem, "On Trial," to discuss Levi's portrayal of a businessman who turned human hair into bolts of felt.

"ON TRIAL"

"My name? Alex Zink." "Where were you born?"
"In Nuremberg, that illustrious ancient city.
Rightly famous, honest judge.
First, because certain laws were passed there
That are of no interest here.
Second, for a debatable trial.
Third, because the best toys
In the whole world are produced there."
"Tell me how you lived,
And don't lie. It would be useless here."
"I was hard working, Your Honor.
Stone on top of stone, mark after mark,
I founded a model industry.
The best buckram, the finest felt
Were made by the Zink Company.
I was a humane and diligent boss:
Honest prices, generous salaries,
Never a complaint from my customers.
And above all, as I was telling you,

Figure 9–2.   *Bales of the hair of female prisoners found in the warehouses of Auschwitz at the liberation. National Archives, courtesy of USHMM Photo Archives.*

The best felt produced in Europe."
"Did you use good wool?"
"Extraordinary wool, Your Honor,
Loose or in braids,
Wool of which I had the monopoly.
Black wool and chestnut, tawny and blonde;
More often gray or white."
"From what flocks?"
"I don't know. It didn't interest me;
I paid for it in cash."
"Tell me: have your dreams been tranquil?"
"Usually yes, judge.
Though sometimes in my dreams
I've heard grieving ghosts groan."
"Weaver, stand down."

by Primo Levi

"What is happening in the poem? Who is on trial? Where?" I ask. Initially, a student suggests this is at a Nuremberg trial. "Look more closely, what does he say about Nuremberg?" I say. Ahhhhh! Zink refers to Nuremberg as that illustrious city where, first, "certain laws" were passed that are of no interest here. Certain laws? The Nuremberg Laws? Those racist laws forbidding the rights of citizenship to Jews? (See Chapter 3.) Why would those laws be of no interest "here"? Second, Nuremberg is famous for a "debatable trial." Why are the Nuremberg Trials debatable, according to Zink, the man on trial? Does he not agree with their premise—or outcome? And third, Nuremberg is famous for the toys it produced. Do not these references suggest that this is a different sort of trial? Perhaps, students suggest, the judge in this case is St. Peter—or God.

Now, what is the trial about? We look closely at the "wool" the weaver used. "Loose or in braids . . . Black wool and chestnut, tawny and blonde;/ More often gray or white." As Charlie says, "He would have to recognize that the hair is obviously not from sheep." And yet, when the weaver is asked, "From what flocks?" he answers, "I don't know. It didn't interest me." Why? What is Levi saying in this poem? Is he talking about the choice not to see? Not to know? Is he passing judgment on those who "blindly" benefited from the insane policies of the Third Reich? By the end of our discussion my students understand—and are appalled. Perhaps Levi's injunction (in "Shema") to repeat his words to our children is what teaching the Holocaust is all about.

Another harrowing film I show, *Shoah,* has no archival footage. The entire nine-and-a-half-hour documentary was filmed on location in Poland (at former death camps), New York, Tel Aviv, Switzerland, and Germany. Claude Lanzmann interviews perpetrators, bystanders, as well as victims of the Holocaust. Simone de Beauvoir writes in the preface to the film's text, "Neither fiction nor documentary, *Shoah* succeeds in recreating the past with an amazing economy of means—places, voices, faces. The greatness of Claude Lanzmann's art is in making places speak, in reviving them through voices over and above words, conveying the unspeakable through people's expressions."

The interviews are chilling and enlightening. Itzhak Zuckermann, a survivor of the Warsaw ghetto, says, "I began drinking after the war. It was very difficult. Claude, you asked for my impression. If you could lick my heart, it would poison you."

To guide students in their assessment of the film I offer the following prompt:

What does Lanzmann accomplish with his documentary? Consider:

- the film's slow pace
- the interviews
- the focus on language

- the photographic focus on landscape and people
- the individual stories
- the juxtaposition of victim and persecutor and bystander
- the geographic scope
- the film's sheer length
- the testimony
- the lack of archival footage
- the effect of the slow accumulation of detail

The film begins at Chelmno—a killing center where 400,000 Jews were gassed in vans. Of the men, women and children murdered at Chelmno, only two survived. Lanzmann's film opens with an interview of Simon Srebnik who was thirteen years old when he began work at Chelmno. I usually show the third of five cassettes. We meet Srebnik in front of a church at Chelmno where he uncomfortably stands among the townspeople who remember the "Jews." Then a van rides down the road where over 400,000 were gassed and then dumped.

We watch scenes in which a former German SS officer describes in numbing detail how Treblinka was designed so that the Jews did not know that when they got off the train they were walking straight through a tunnel to a gas chamber. We also meet Abraham Bomba, who survived by cutting hair in the gas chamber at Treblinka. Working in a barber shop in Tel Aviv, speaking in English, Bomba describes cutting the hair of women he knew—and being unable to tell them that they would live for only a few more minutes. From this film, students see and hear witnesses describe the indescribable. They are upset that Lanzmann pushes the survivors to tell their stories, no matter how painful:

Lanzmann: What was your impression the first time you saw these naked women arriving with children?

Bomba: I tell you something. To have a feeling about that . . . it was very hard to feel anything, because working there day and night between dead people, between bodies, your feeling disappeared, you were dead. You had no feeling at all . . . some of the women came in on a transport from my town of Czestochowa, I knew a lot of them. I knew them; I lived with them in my town. I lived with them in my street, and some of them were my close friends. And when they saw me, they started asking me, Abe this and Abe that—"What's going to happen to us?" What could you tell them? What could you tell?

A friend of mine worked as a barber—he was a good barber in my hometown—when his wife and his sister came into the gas chamber. . . . I can't. It's too horrible. Please. [Bomba is choking back tears.]

Lanzmann: We have to do it. You know it.

Bomba: I won't be able to do it.

Lanzmann: You have to do it. I know it's very hard. I know and I apologize.

Bomba: Don't make me go on please.

Lanzmann: Please. We must go on . . .

Bomba: They tried to talk to him and the husband of his sister. They could not tell them this was the last time they stay alive, because behind them was the German Nazis, SS men, and they knew that if they said a word, not only the wife and the woman, who were dead already, but also they would share the same thing with them. In a way, they tried to do the best for them, with a second longer, a minute longer, just to hug them and kiss them, because they knew they would never see them again. (Shoah 116–117)

Julia O. says, "It's so mean, why does Lanzmann have to push him?" Jessica snaps, "Hey, there is no why." Lindsay comes to Julia's defense: "I didn't like how he was on the brink of tears. There was so much emotion. Why couldn't Lanzmann have stopped the tape?" Julia O. responds with attitude in her strong Ukrainian accent, "He was trying to show how hard it was so many years ago. I'd say, you know, you have to take your camera and leave." She breaks the ice. The class laughs.

Peter, who audited my class as a community service assignment helping another student with Down's syndrome, says, "Most filmmakers cut or leave only the speech parts. They might cut the tears. But Lanzmann kept the camera running, and we get a sense that we're there. We really know what it's like." Nick adds, "Watching the video was like watching it happen. Jessica summarizes the class's experience: "A lot of movies today are brain candy. Shot after shot in this film makes your brain work."

In her journal Lindsay writes:

Wow! I don't know how else to describe my opinion on the documentary other than wow! Everything that happens throughout the documentary was so powerful. Actually being able to see a Nazi and hear him talk about the Holocaust was frightening. I couldn't believe that he could still live like he did after knowing that he was a hated murderer. He [Franz Suchomel, SS Unterscharführer] remembered the song that he forced the victims to sing, the procedure that killed thousands of Jews each day, and the exact number of people who died by his command. He seemed like he was proud of what he had done. He felt no remorse. Watching his expression as he argued over two or three million people who died made me so angry. He says, "It was only two million." Only two million. How many doctors, scientists, teachers, artists were in that two million?

Al writes:

I found the reactions of the non-Jews of the time strange. They acted like nothing had happened and all the hatred had been erased in one clean swipe.

I am impressed at the sensitivity and thinking among my students. They have tuned into a very difficult film. They have been moved by documentary footage. They understand and appreciate not only the story Lanzmann is telling, but also the process of his filming and "forcing" survivors to speak.

Comic Relief

For a little comic relief (and it's necessary!), I show an excerpt (about 10 minutes) from *The Producers* written and directed by Mel Brooks. I show the "Springtime for Hitler" scene, the Broadway extravaganza in which the chorus, dressed in skimpy uniforms, goose-steps around the stage in the shape of a swastika to a resounding Broadway theme song. The audience—and my students—are aghast.

"How can you make fun of the Holocaust like this?" they ask. And so we discuss the effects of comedy—how it took a Jewish producer and writer to address the angst and make fun of Hitler. Actually, the horror of the camps is never mentioned, rather, it is the humor poked at Hitler and all those who chose to joyously follow him. We talk of the times—the film came out in the late 1960s. Was the country ready for it then? Why in the sixties could we finally make fun of the very serious events of the forties? And isn't humor, after all, a way of turning horror on its head, of reducing it so we can laugh about it?

And we discuss the effects of humor: If you can laugh at something, it's not as bad at it seems.

Dom: It's not like you're making fun of the Holocaust. It shows that people can talk in a not so oppressing manner.

Nick [noting that Hitler is made out to be a weirdo]: Hitler is not a joke. You can't make fun of it. Hitler is pure evil. There's nothing funny about him.

Abbi: I could be way off, but people use humor to get through hard times. Even though I don't think it was offensive, Hitler hurt people, and this movie makes light of a the situation at a time when books and memoirs are coming out.

Peter: When you make fun of something, you deflate it. You take the power out of it.

Al: It's like the "n" word. When my cousin says it or when Gloria Naylor says it, it's a term of endearment, it's a compliment when used among ourselves. We deflate the meaning of the word. But my dad still won't let me say it. When I was a kid, I got a basketball hoop. Kids came over to play and I used the word. My father beat me. To him the word has so much meaning.

Abbi: I don't want to say it's okay to say it. Even when I hear black kids say it, it makes me uncomfortable. My dad takes my CDs away. He doesn't want my sister to hear it. To me, it's a degrading word, it's like another Jewish kid calling me a kike.

J.P.: It has lots of meaning, but you can tell if it's used affectionately or not. It's a scary word.

Kristin: It's kind of like that with other words, bitch and slut. I know it's terrible, but my friends use them all the time.

Lindsay: You have to know who you're saying it to. You deflate the word when you use it. You take the power out of it and you can laugh—and you can live more comfortably.

We tie these thoughts back to the film. Laughter deflates a powerful situation. Like letting air out of a balloon—humor pokes a hole in the power of something—and it isn't as scary afterwards.

And finally, in relation to our discussion of humor and the Holocaust, I show the last hour of *Life Is Beautiful.* All semester long, students have asked to see the 1999 Academy Award–winning film. "It's beautiful," say students who saw the movie in the theater or on their home VCRs. "It's a touching story."

Once at the pseudo-concentration camp, Guido (Roberto Begnini) creates an imaginative game for his son: the first one to get one-thousand points will win a tank. He protects his son from abrasive German orders, he even lands a job as a waiter in an officers' dining room and gets his son placed in a German nursery school where he is well fed. Somehow, Guido manages to profess his love and health over the camp P.A. to his non-Jewish wife—who has voluntarily joined their deportation. And there is never any dirt or blood on their prison uniforms. The set is surreal—a set that resembles Auschwitz's formidable brick walls and entrance. But the bunks are clean—and when Guido has to do "prison" work, we see him carrying anvils up stairs to a furnace—a less than apt metaphor for the back-breaking labor of concentration camp inmates. In the end, Joshua does get his tank—a real U.S. army tank that picks him up from the side of the road of refugees—where he is reunited with his mother.

About the film, Robyn says, "I really liked this film when I first saw it. But it's not really a Holocaust film. How was there enough bread for the boy not to starve? How could he be hidden? How could he go to his father and demand that he would not take a shower"?

Stephanie S. says, "It's not the Holocaust."

I suggest that it was more a simulation of the Holocaust, a lovely story of a father and son set in a "camp." But why?

Robyn astutely suggests, "Perhaps it could have been set against another, fictitious genocide? This story almost denigrates those who let their children perish, those who could not play a game and keep their children alive."

Their perspective is interesting. They judge the film by two criteria—as a story and as representative of the Holocaust. They unanimously feel this is not a "Holocaust" film. It dilutes the experience. The Holocaust is a mere backdrop for another story, for an opportunity for Begnini to clown. But they also feel that the film contained a good story—and perhaps would be better served against a different setting.

Rap Music

The next day Nick comes to class with a CD in hand. It is Wu-Tang's "Killa Bees." He thrusts the CD into my hands and insists that even though "Killa Bees" is a rap tape with a parental advisory of explicit content stamped on the cover, there's a Holocaust song—with no offensive content— on the CD and I ought to play it for the class. I do. And we are impressed by the sensitivity and morality of the content. "Never Again" (cut 12) begins with a Yiddish accented voice intoning Hebrew prayer, the blessing over wine. Then the rapper's voice dedicates the song to the countless victims and their families "forced into a slave," and says, "Never again shall we walk like sheep to the slaughter." Now, heard in the background is the Israeli national anthem, "Ha Tikva," the hope. The rap song ends with the Hebrew prayer, "Shema," the prayer religious Jews say every day and before death. And then we hear gunshots. (The lyrics are available at *www.OHHLA.com/anonymous/wu_tang/theswarm/nevagain.wtg.txt*).

The students listen to every word, and then ask, "Can we hear it again?" Scott L. raises his hand and asks if he can go download the words for us from the media center. I let him go. In ten minutes he returns with the words copied for each student. We listen again. "Feel this/ To all those races, colors, and creeds, every man bleeds/for the countless victims and all their families/of the murdered, tortured and slaved, raped, robbed and persecuted—Never Again!" It is almost a mini-history of the Holocaust.

We discuss the parallels to American slavery. And we discuss the sensitivity the song has with regard to the Holocaust. In general, my students are impressed—and think a rap song like this might reach out to educate people about the Holocaust. Alyssa says, "It's exposing people. There're so many points smushed into the song. If I had never heard of the Holocaust, I would know a lot about it." Dana, however, suggests that it's probably better to know something about the Holocaust before hearing the song, because then the words would have even more meaning. Bo says the beat is so strong, like a march through history that won't stop while the violins in the background are so slow, so sad, so melancholic. And Blake suggests the song is inspirational: "Never again."

10

The Camps,
Part III: The Women

"Women after delousing"   Yad Vashem, "The Auschwitz Album"

"We Have Nothing"

—LIVIA BITTON-JACKSON

What Is the Nature of Evil?

It is said that as we study the Holocaust, we study the nature of evil. Evil suggests the opposite of good; it suggests cruelty, the dehumanization of man. Evil is what Satan does when he strips Job of his children, his animals, his fields, and his belongings—in order to test him and prove to God that a good man only has faith as long as he has his things. Not so with the Holocaust.

There was no bet. Only a satanical urge to strip humans of all they have, of all they are—for no ulterior purpose, not even a bet.

What was the nature of evil in the world of the Lager? What was the nature of evil in the systematic creation of ghetto, train schedule, deportation, slave labor, and crematorium? How can we examine evil in the context of its practice by a whole nation?

Primo Levi tells us that among the forty-five men deported with him, only four returned. Livia Bitton-Jackson tells us that from over five hundred people—"parents, siblings, grandparents, uncles, aunts, and cousins, friends, neighbors, storekeepers, and teachers, toddlers, and teenagers"—deported from her town of Samorin, only thirty-six survived—thirty-two girls and boys and four adults (216). Gerda Weissmann Klein tells us that of the four thousand that began the three-month-long death march into Czechoslovakia with her, fewer than 120 survived.

The killing was systematic, and those who survived the first selection, those who had a chance to live a little longer, were stripped of everything— their clothes, their shoes, their hair, their names—not to mention their families, men sent one way, women the other, children another. After the shower, after having their hair shorn, survivors were tattooed and given striped pajamas and shoes, usually wooden, to wear.

We observe an entire nation cooperate in the racist policies of the German government (Chapters 3 and 4), and we see the implementation of a final solution by functioning administrators who followed and handed down orders from Berlin. Hannah Arendt tells us that those who worked in the administrative hierarchy, who claimed they were simply following orders in the practice of "human wickedness," taught us "the lesson of the fearsome, word- and thought-defying *banality of evil*" (252). But at its very root, evil in the camp is sadistic and cruel: men and women deprived of everything, becoming "nothing."

When Elli Bitton-Jackson (*I Have Lived a Thousand Years*) arrives from Auschwitz to Augsburg to work in a labor camp, the German soldiers (not members of the SS) say, "We expected a transport of women from Auschwitz. . . . Are you from Auschwitz? Were you sent instead of the women?" And the interpreter for the women says, "We are from Auschwitz. And we are women" (149). Their appearance must have been shocking: shaven heads, loose fitting pajamas, skin and bones. "But where is your luggage?" the officer asks.

"We have no luggage, *Herr Offizier*," the interpreter says softly, "We have nothing."

There is even laughter among the women who in Hungarian, a language the officer cannot understand, quip that their luggage will be sent special delivery, that they left their golf clubs in Auschwitz. Laughter in the face of nothing.

The officer is incredulous. "You have no luggage at all? No personal belongings? How can that be?"

"No," the interpreter repeats. "We have nothing."

The German officer who welcomes this transport has no idea what his SS counterparts are inflicting on humans in Auschwitz. He tells them that they will be treated better in Augsburg. And indeed they are: white sheets, golden yellow soup served in clean porcelain bowls. Real food in real dishes served at a table with real silverware. Five days later, when the SS guard arrives, the white sheets are removed from the beds, food has turned into tasteless mush, and the table and benches are removed so that they eat crouching on beds or sitting on the floor.

How, I ask my students, could a world reduce humans to "nothing"? How was it possible? Over and over, in the literature of the Holocaust, we witness this reduction, this desecration. Levi asks what happens to man when he is stripped of everything? At what point does he dissolve, become a Muselmann, and die? The evil of the Holocaust was perpetrated by men and women, it was sadism sanctioned by the state for no other purpose than to humiliate and dehumanize.

Primo Levi describes these "drowned" men:

> . . . If I could enclose all the evil of our time in one image, I would choose this image which is familiar to me: an emaciated man, with head dropped and shoulders curved, on whose face and in whose eyes not a trace of a thought is to be seen. (Survival 90)

I ask my students to define evil.

Dan suggests evil is about power. Tal suggests that there is pleasure in inflicting pain in the context of the Holocaust. Evil is the inclination to do bad, to do wrong. Blake asks if this inclination is instilled in us or if it is innate. He suggests that everyone has evil in them, and it is a constant fight to suppress our evil instincts, to behave morally. Charlie says that evil comes down to selfishness: perpetrating evil means doing something to hurt others for personal gain or pleasure; "Evil," he says, "is unconscionable."

Dan counters that evil is often unmotivated. Tal suggests evil is often random, a power trip.

Dana says, "We all have a balance of evil and good in ourselves."

Charlie agrees that all of us have evil tendencies. "The Holocaust," he says, "allowed people to tap into the evil in themselves. They got to do all this crazy stuff. You had the freedom to *do* things you normally can't. During the Holocaust you were allowed to be evil. It was as if an ideology of evil was enforced."

There was, I suggest, based on my students' comments, an inversion and perversion of values. For ten years the ratchet of evil was cranked up, beginning with the Nuremberg Laws, leading to sanctioned racism, ostracism, and ultimately, annihilation.

We take a break from our discussion to write in journals. I think this topic is important enough that I want students to think and write on a personal, deeper level.

Charlie writes in his journal:

Evil is doing things that hurt others in order to bring personal gain or pleasure to yourself. I believe everyone is innately selfish. Extending this selfishness to the point of hurting others in order to help yourself is evil. I don't think everyone is innately evil. We all do, however, have the potential to be evil. It's just a matter of "letting go." Society has placed on everyone restraints concerning what is acceptable behavior.

In Nazi Germany, society as a whole "let go," as they say. An environment was created where no one had to worry about getting caught, and the standard in society was evil. They were encouraged to hate and hurt and kill. The Nazi's were living out a sadistic fantasy in which I think a lot of people over the course of history deep down inside wish they could have taken part. Not everyone who has felt this is necessarily a bad person. Evil is like a drug. It's an indulgence that is immediately pleasurable, but in the long run is a horrible, horrible thing.

Blake writes:

Evil remains within us all. It festers and dwells deep within our hearts and minds, constantly battling with our Jiminy Cricket consciences. But just because the evil is present, it does not mean that it will ever show itself to the world. Children whose parents instilled strong morals and raised them with a gentle nurturing hand in a sound and healthy environment, are usually less likely to show an evil side.

We move from a fairly abstract discussion of evil to witnessing evil's effects through film and literature. After our study of "men" and how they experienced the camps, we watch a thirty-nine minute Academy Award–winning short documentary, *One Survivor Remembers,* about Gerda Weissmann Klein. As the film begins, students in this semester's class are still talking. I stop the film twice to get their attention. Still, there are students turned around, chatting. I am angry that they do not respect the material as I do, and hurriedly point to a seat on the other side of the room for one student, and pick up an algebra book from another student's desk, and French homework from another student's desk. I want the students to know how serious this is. I want them to pay attention. "Take notes," I say. "Note taking will help keep you awake." And if that prod doesn't work, I threaten, "I'm going to collect your notes and grade them."

Gerda Weissmann Klein was restricted to the basement of her home in Bielsko, Poland, in September 1939, when the German SS moved into her town. She was fifteen years old. Within days, Jewish men were forced to register for forced labor, and her brother disappeared forever. She felt completely betrayed, as if she were home and not home anymore. In June of 1942, the Jews of Bielsko were deported. She saw her parents for the last time. That morning, her mother made her cocoa, "which didn't taste particularly sweet." They were loaded on trucks—she jumped off to join her mother and was told, "You are too young to die." The final solution had begun.

With two friends she is sent to a slave labor camp where for two-and-a-half years she worked on looms to make fabric for the military. In January of 1945, the girls were sent on the "death march" to Czechoslovakia. She saw girls breaking off their toes "like twigs" due to the three months of exposure to cold. Of four thousand girls who began the march, fewer than 120 were alive when Americans liberated the vacant bicycle factory where they rested. Gerda Weissmann weighed 68 pounds when she showed an American soldier, her future husband Kurt Klein, the remains of the women whose gaunt, skeletal bodies and faces are revealed in photographs and film footage. "Noble be man, merciful and good," Gerda says ironically to her American rescuer as she sweeps her arm over the stark landscape of starved survivors.

As my students become involved in the film, and it is engrossing, they become silent—and moved. When it is over, I want to know what impression it made on them. Many say it was the best film they've seen in Holocaust Literature. (They say this about most of the films we see.) "What's important about this film? What is the purpose of a film like this?" I ask. I expect them to see the whole picture—the devastation of one young woman and her family as a microcosm of the devastation of six million. I want them to see the utter cruelty and evil perpetrated for no purpose.

Instead, they surprise me by citing details from the film, and as we discuss the details, we build a fuller picture of what happened. Bo is struck by the bet—how Gerda bet her friend Suse that the war would end in six months, and she lost the bet for a quart of strawberries and whipped cream. Alyssa comments on how the realists had a harder time surviving. Daydreamers with imagination could go on; realists, according to Dan, felt more hopeless. Blake says, "It showed how lucky you had to be, no one person had more chance than another to survive. There's such a thin line between life and death. What saved her was a pair of boots." They are beginning to understand the serendipity of survival as well as the cruelty and sadism of the German SS.

Gerda Weissmannn Klein's autobiography, *All But My Life,* tells in more detail the story of Klein's six-year ordeal as a victim of Nazi cruelty. (A study guide is available from Hill and Wang Academic Marketing.)

After viewing the film about Gerda Klein, a student reports seeing the Kleins interviewed on *Nightline* about their new relationship with Columbine High School after the shooting of twenty-two students. Stuart writes in his journal, "Because of her experiences from the Holocaust, Klein has gotten involved with the students and staff to help them cope with their own terrible tragedy. Especially widespread is the question of 'Why me?' Just like Holocaust survivors, survivors at Columbine have had a hard time figuring out why they survived and others didn't."

In class we turn to Livia Bitton-Jackson's *I Have Lived a Thousand Years,* with its description of the total destruction of a living human being. And in the face of that destruction, the will to live. Students appreciate Bitton-Jackson's writing style as well as her storytelling. This is *Night* from a woman's perspective.

The title, *I Have Lived a Thousand Years,* comes from a scene Bitton-Jackson describes. Upon liberation, a middle-aged German woman approaches her and says, "At your age, it must have been difficult."

> At my age. What does she mean? "We didn't get enough to eat. Because of starvation. Not because of my age."
>
> "I meant, it must have been harder for the older people."
>
> For older people? "How old do you think I am?"
>
> She looks at me uncertainly. "Sixty? Sixty-two?"
>
> "Sixty? I am fourteen years old."
>
> She gives a little shriek and makes the sign of the cross. In horror and disbelief she walks away, and joins the crowd of German civilians near the station house.
>
> So this is liberation. It's come.
>
> I am fourteen years old, and I have lived a thousand years. (205)

She is fourteen years old, gaunt, starved. And she looks like an old lady. How could that happen?

I Have Lived a Thousand Years is beautifully written from a teenager's point of view. Livia Bitton-Jackson was thirteen years old when she and her family were arrested. This book is equally compelling for middle school students as well as high school students. Told from the young woman's point of view, students say they feel swept up by the narrator's voice, they identify with her and feel like they are living through her ordeals.

To discuss this book, it is perhaps best to begin with the basics of a literary discussion. The simple questions first: Where does the story take place (setting)? Who is the narrator (voice)? How does she change (character)? What happens in the book (plot)? What are the major themes? As questions move from the concrete to the more abstract, students begin to grapple with the real issues the book presents.

- How can man be so evil?
- How can one survive with nothing?
- How important are relationships with friends and family?
- How could this happen?

Gisella Perl's *I Was a Doctor in Auschwitz* contains several vignettes and stories of her work and observations. Her stories are vivid and morally acute. "Childbirth in Camp C" is about women who arrive in Auschwitz pregnant. "The poor, young women who were brought to Auschwitz from the various ghettos of Hungary did not know that they would have to pay with their lives and the lives of their unborn children for that last, tender night spent in the arms of their husbands" (80). Pregnant women were asked to step forward when they arrived at Auschwitz. They were promised doubled bread rations and better living conditions. And then Perl had an errand near the crematories and saw "with her own eyes" what was done to the women:

> They were surrounded by a group of SS men and women, who amused themselves by giving these helpless creatures a taste of hell, after which death was a welcome friend. They were beaten with clubs and whips, torn by dogs, dragged around by the hair and kicked in the stomach with heavy German boots. Then, when they collapsed, they were thrown into the crematory— alive. (80)

The sadism Perl describes is unbelievable, as if in the camps it was a prerequisite for becoming a guard. Why do we read these horrifying stories? We see descriptions of unimaginable cruelty over and over. Unfortunately for students of Holocaust Literature, this is what they must read to know. This is the essence of what humans (were they human?) did to other humans. Over and over, we witness as readers the degradation of humanity—both within those who perpetrated these crimes and those who were the victims of these crimes. This evil pervades almost every exchange between the SS and the prisoner. We witness what happens to men and women if their evil instincts remain unchecked, even encouraged. We witness what happens to men and women who struggle to maintain a thread of dignity in the face of this utter abuse.

On dark nights in dark corners, "in the toilet, on the floor, without a drop of water," Perl delivers the women's babies.

> No one will ever know what it meant to me to destroy these babies. . . . I prayed to God to help me save the mother or I would never touch a pregnant woman again. And if I had not done it, both mother and child would have been cruelly murdered. God was good to me. By a miracle, which to every doctor must sound like a fairy tale, every one of these women recovered and was able to work, which, at least for a while, saved her life. (82)

Students are anxious to discuss the morality of abortion in the camps. While the class seems evenly split between those who under ordinary circumstances are divided on the abortion issue, they must come to terms with the aggravated circumstances in the camp. Even the most stalwart believers in the right to life had to concede that in the camps, as Levi suggested, morality must be judged from a different vantage: We—who live in warm houses and who find hot food and friendly faces each evening—cannot judge the morality of the Lager by standards that exist because we live in a civilized society.

Sara Nomberg-Przytyk's book of poignant vignettes, *Auschwitz: True Tales from a Grotesque Land* is not widely read; however, her vivid writing takes our breath away. In "Old Words—New Meaning," Nomberg-Przytyk describes the perversion of language and the barter system in the women's camp; in "A Living Torch" she describes children thrown live into fires; in "The Little Gypsy," she describes a four-year-old Gypsy boy favored by Dr. Mengele—and the overnight destruction of the Gypsy family camp of 20,000 men, women, and children. It is one of the few stories of Gypsies that we read. In story after story, SS cruelty and perversion come to light. It is as if Nomberg-Pzrytyk casts her searchlight into darkened corners to illuminate what she saw in that truly grotesque land of Auschwitz.

We read several of these vignettes aloud in class. I want students' full attention. I don't want to have to "trust" them to do their "homework." Reading in class forces all students through the material; it forces them to hear—and to see the words. And Nomberg-Przytyk's words are powerful. After reading through "A Living Torch" and "A Little Gypsy" students are silent. I don't know whether to break the silence with one of my prompting questions to try to get them to speak, or to allow the silence to envelop us. After a few minutes I speak. I tell them I am uncomfortable breaking the silence, that as a teacher, I have this compulsion to have conversation in the classroom, to discuss the issues. And yet, perhaps we need to honor the silence, to *not* try all the time to define what we are feeling, to let the overwhelming sense of despair and shock and sadness sink in. Nomberg-Przytyk and Perl push us to "the other side" of good and evil. They force us to confront our morality in the face of survival.

"Where do you put this new knowledge in your scheme of what you know about the world?" I finally ask. It is a big question. But then again, these women's stories force us to ask the big questions.

Dana suggests that it's easier to deal with yourself when you're taking care of other people. She is speaking about the differences in the way women seem to deal with life in the camps. In the stories we read, women seem more caring. Blake agrees. He speaks of his mother, how even in the supermarket, she tries to start caring conversations with other women in the line.

I refer my students to Gisella Perl's "The Value of a Piece of String." In this story, Perl recounts how finding a pair of size 10 men's shoes would save her life—if only she could find a piece of string to lace the shoes to her feet. She is referred to an old Polish man who has a piece of string—and she tries to barter her daily bread for that string. He wants "her" and gropes her "womanhood." She flees without the string and vows to "remain a human being to the last minute of my life—whenever that would come." To remain human she organizes the women to tell about their former lives:

> To my surprise they listened with rapt attention, which proved that their souls, their minds were just as hungry for conversation, for companionship, for self-expression as mine. One after the other, they opened up their hearts, and from then on half our nights were spent in conversation.
>
> Later, as we came to know one another better, we invented games to keep our minds off the sordid present. We recited poetry, told stories of the books we had read and liked, sang songs, in a low voice, with tears in our eyes, careful that the Blockova shouldn't hear us. (59)

Students notice a drastic difference in women's and men's perceptions of camp life. Students see an emotional side, a concern for sister prisoners that is different from the men's concerns. Interestingly, in the men's voices, we see them fighting for themselves. In the women, we see that though they fight for themselves, there is more sharing of bread, more looking out for a friend, more "mothering."

As we looked at Lawrence Kohlberg for some understanding of moral development, we also look at Carol Gilligan who examines Kohlberg's theories and shows their lack of attention to women's issues. In Gilligan's studies

(*In a Different Voice*), she shows that as women develop morally, their concerns often focus on care for family and friends. (Ergo, the farmer's wife caring more for her own children than the Jewish children and the moral issues surrounding hiding, as well as the care we witness among women for each other in the camps.)

Still, I don't feel we have even begun to address the big issues. And the bell has rung. We have to wait until our next meeting to continue our discussion. I really want to know how these stories fit into the way my students see the world. Do they disrupt? Do they tear apart assumptions of good and evil? Do they simply reveal a side of life, of human behavior, that we'd prefer not to see? And conversely, as we visit what appears to be base and sadistic cruelty, we witness at the same time an almost heroic, as well as stoic, behavior among the victims. We witness the will to live no matter what. We witness a gracious perseverance in the face of abject evil. I am reminded of Faulkner's last words in *The Sound and the Fury:* "She endured."

In journals, I ask students to define evil through *images* we have visited in literature and film. I ask, What "picture" do you see in your mind that epitomizes the evil of the Holocaust? What does evil look like? Feel like? Taste like? Smell like? Sound like? I want them to use all their senses to evoke the essence of the Holocaust, of evil incarnate.

A prior journal assignment asked students to try to define evil. They did, in fairly abstract terms. Now, I want them to try to see what evil looks like dressed up in its flesh, in all its clothes. I want them to synthesize their abstract definition with what they have read and seen. I want them to put a face, and action, to what it means to be evil or to experience evil. And interestingly, from the images the students describe, we gain a glimmer of what they understand to be the evil of the Holocaust: SS guards kicking the abdomen of a pregnant woman; Mengele telling a dancing boy to sing, rewarding him with candy, then pushing him with his own hands into the oven; trusting, innocent, unsuspecting pregnant women tossed alive into the flames of the crematory; Irma Greise, an SS guard, ripping a "beautiful" woman's breast with her whip and then gleefully watching the painful operation to repair the damage; wheelbarrowing live children into a pit of fire; an SS soldier shooting one thousand people, then sitting on the edge of the pit of death to enjoy a cigarette.

In description after description what we begin to see is someone intentionally hurting an innocent person, inflicting undeserved pain and death. It is this quality of cruelty to innocence, of depriving one of life—of trust and faith in taste, smell—the normal functioning of the world—that enhances our sense of gravity, or lack thereof. Evil pulls one into the black hole of horror—a blackness without justice or dignity or redemption.

Imran, a student with a highly developed sense of morality, writes that Gisella Perl's stories were "by far, the most disturbing pieces of literature" he's read in this class:

> Just think, how could someone kill newborn babies either by suffocation or by disposing them into crematoriums *as a job?*
>
> Many times, we are not doing the Holocaust justice by saying "Six million Jews, eleven million total died." Stories such as these serve as constant reminders that the Holocaust was unique in its cruelty and terror and should be regarded as the ultimate form of dehumanization that a society could possibly commit. Regardless of what can be said about the inherent nature of humans, it is clear that the Holocaust was an event that transcended all forms of compassion, humanity, and sanity.

These stories with their images of evil are what good writing is about.

Our discussion of image, of how a writer shows rather than tells, prepares us for our reading of Cynthia Ozick's astounding story, "The Shawl." We are better able to appreciate her art as she deftly describes a mother and what appear to be her two daughters in a camp. (In the sequel, "Rosa," we find out Stella is Rosa's niece.) We read the story aloud in class. I want my students to hear the rhythms and sounds of Ozick's writing.

Once again, when we finish reading, there is silence in the classroom. Finally, Blake says, "It's kinda weird." And more silence. As teacher, I take over and ask a basic question: "What is this story about?"

They tell me it is about a girl who makes her sister die. Gary says, "It's immoral and cruel for fourteen-year-old Stella to take away fifteen-month-old Magda's shawl, to want to eat her! You don't do something to take away the life of your sister." But then, Charlie says, "Stella wanted to survive. She was fourteen. Her sister was going to die anyway." I ask, "Is Ozick condemning or showing what existed?" And then we talk about how in the camp, conditions were *so* severe that normal morality broke down; the rules were different. Again, we note how Primo Levi asks, "how much of our ordinary moral world could survive on this side of the barbed wire" (86). Gravity has stopped working. We talk about how absurd it is to try to judge the morality of those who were forced to live behind the "barbed wire."

Dan suggests the story is about necessity, the way "The Lemon" by Arnost Lustig is about how a boy who had to deface his father's body to pry out his gold tooth to buy a lemon for his dying sister. His sister's life was more important, and forced him to make moral choices he would never have made under normal circumstances. "Stella," Dan explains, "is reduced to a situation in which she wants to live—even at the expense of her sister's life. She did it out of dire need."

"What else is Ozick's 'The Shawl' about?" I ask. We have barely scratched the surface in our discussion, and the bell will ring in five minutes. Someone volunteers that the story is also about a mother and her daughter, a mother who will do anything to protect her fifteen-month-old daughter, and how the rules of the camp stop the mother from acting on her basic instincts to feed and to protect her child. The mother's nipples not only dry up, but even after her daughter's death when the "steel voices went mad in their growling, urging Rosa to run and run to the spot where Magda had fallen from her flight against the electrified fence," the mother cannot move. "She only stood, because if she ran they would shoot, and if she tried to pick up the sticks of Magda's body they would shoot, and if she let the wolf's screech ascending now through the ladder of her skeleton break out, they would shoot" (10).

Isn't this, then, the evil of the camp, the robbing and depriving a person not only of life—but also her human instincts, her mothering instincts? To sleep Stella must rob her cousin of her blanket, depriving Rosa of her daughter—so that she will probably never sleep. How then does Ozick convey the camp experience? She never "tells" us that the place was an evil place. How then, does she "show" it? Ozick crosses a magical line in her descriptions of people who were transformed by their experience. Their hunger, their weight loss, their weightlessness:

> Rosa did not feel hunger; she felt light, not like someone walking but like someone in a faint, in a trance, arrested in a fit, someone who is already a floating angel, alert and seeing everything, but in the air, not there, not touching the road. As if teetering on the tips of her fingernails. (4)

We also notice how Rosa has disassociated herself from her experience. She "did not feel hunger, she felt light, not like someone walking." She is there and not there. She is in a faint, in a trance, already a floating angel—seeing everything, but above it all. Not even touching the road, as if, and Ozick has separated this last simile into a fragment that stands alone, "teetering on the tips of her fingernails"—an impossible feat. It is as if she has separated herself from what is happening, blocked the present in terms of how she physically experiences it, and yet, she is aware of everything—almost as if she is on drugs—morphine, for example, given to cancer or AIDS patients to stop their pain, separate their minds from the pain in their bodies. She also shows us how a victim experiences the camps: she is there and not there. She has separated from the reality in order to survive it. Gerda Weissmann Klein suggests in *One Survivor Remembers* that those who were too in touch with reality did not survive, those with imaginations could remove themselves from the horror of their experience.

When Magda is carried on the black domino shoulders of the SS guard, she is a speck, no bigger than a moth. When she is "swimming through the air" toward the electric fence, she is traveling through "loftiness" and looks "like a butterfly touching a silver vine."

This transformation of flesh into air reiterates the flesh burned into ash, the "floating smoke that greased Rosa's skin." It also reminds us of the magic in an Isaac Bashevis Singer story or a Mark Chagall painting. I show students a picture of "The Birthday" by Marc Chagall, his painting of a man floating through air as he kisses his wife, to show what art does as it pushes image, making it more real, making it surreal—like Rosa feeling as if "teetering on the tips of her fingernails." ("The Birthday" by Chagall may be seen at *www.mcs.csuhayward.edu/~malek/Chagal1.html.*)

I ask students to reread the story over the weekend, and to find at least five images or descriptions that reveal something about life in the camp. On Monday we discuss how image affects meaning: "Even the laugh that came when the ash-stippled wind made a clown out of Magda's shawl...." We discuss how rhythm of language imitates walking, marching: "... Stella wanted to be wrapped in a shawl, hidden away, asleep, rocked by the march, a baby, a round infant in arms." And we discuss how vivid metaphors enhance understanding: "In the barracks they spoke of 'flowers,' of 'rain': excrement, thick turd-braids, and the slow stinking maroon waterfall that slunk down from the upper bunks...." We begin to see how art interprets history; how art via language and rhetorical devices helps us understand and see and feel—just a little more. We talk of how Ozick never "tells" us what to think or feel, as an artist she "shows" us and takes us there and forces us to experience what her characters see and feel.

There is a sequel to "The Shawl," called "Rosa." In it, we meet Rosa again, retired in Miami Beach. She has not forgotten Magda. In fact, she writes her daughter letters as if she were alive. In "Rosa," Ozick imagines the survivor forty years after liberation living with her vibrant memories, memories so real, they supersede the "normal" life she is trying to live.

To grasp the enormity of what one person went through, I ask students, once again, to ponder the stories as a poet might. Sometimes poems are written from the point of view of the person who is "told" a story or who observes. Good examples are the set of poems described in Chapter 2 by Siamanto,

Willa Schneberg, and Sharon Olds. In each of these poems, the speaker speaks of what he or she "heard." What stories have you heard in literature or film or even on the nightly news? How could you describe one tale? One story? Who did you hear it from? Could you believe what you heard? What were you told? What details do you remember? See? Use as much sensory description— sight, hearing, touch, taste, smell—as you can.

Another type of poem, a "persona" poem, is written from the point of view of someone who is *not* the poet—we get into and identify with another's persona, another's proverbial shoes, and imagine what it must have been like to see the world as the imagined person sees it. I ask students to pretend they are someone we have read about or viewed in a video. I ask them to write that person's story from his or her point of view. What does the person observe? See? What is happening around her or him? Who else is in the scene? What are they doing? How are "you" reacting? What do you do? Think?

We next read Nobel Prize poet Nelly Sachs' "O the Chimneys." Sachs and her mother found refuge in Sweden in 1940. Explaining her writing, Sachs said: "I have constantly striven to raise the unutterable to a transcendental level, in order to make it tolerable, and in this night of nights, to give some idea of the holy darkness in which the quiver and the sorrow are hidden" (*www.interlog.com/~mighty/special/nelly.htm*).

Because my students have trouble understanding "O, the Chimneys," I begin by asking them to think about what image or metaphor, for them, epitomizes what they know about the Holocaust. We list several images: ash like snow (as in *Schindler's List*); fire—how it engulfs; a blond-haired, blue-eyed SS soldier with a pitbull; a pile of shoes; stacks of bodies, a brick wall; wooden bunks lining walls of barracks; and open, empty ovens. Then we read the poem together—more than once.

For my dead brothers and sisters

O, THE CHIMNEYS

And though after my skin worms destroy this body,
yet in my flesh shall I see God. Job, xix, 26

O, the Chimneys
On the ingeniously devised habitations of death
When Israel's body drifted as smoke
Through the air—
Was welcomed by a star, a chimney sweep,
A star that turned black
Or was it a ray of sun?

O, the Chimneys!
Freedomway for Jeremiah and Job's dust—
Who devised you and laid stone upon stone
The road for refugees of smoke?

O the habitations of death,
Invitingly appointed
For the host who used to be a guest—
O you fingers
Laying the threshold
Like a knife between life and death—

O you chimneys,
O you fingers
And Israel's body as smoke through the air!

I need to explain who Job is—how Satan made a bet with God that Job would not remain righteous if deprived of his family and all his worldly goods. With his children dead, his livestock gone, his fields demolished, Job rants at God. He does not understand why he must suffer. We talk about Sachs' focus on the small to portray the large—chimneys as a metaphor for the crematory, fingers as metonymy for the hands and bodies of people who laid the threshold of the crematory, the threshold like a knife between life and death. I have an excuse to teach simile, metaphor, metonymy, and synecdoche. The poem itself takes marvelous turns—from chimneys on "ingeniously devised habitations of death," to "Israel's body" drifting "as smoke" to the welcoming of that smoky composite of Jewish bodies by a star or a ray of sun blotted out by smoke. "Israel's body" follows the same "freedomway" as Jeremiah and Job's dust, which paved the way for Jews who suffer.

The speaker addresses the chimneys: "Who devised you and laid stone upon stone / The road for refugees of smoke?" She sarcastically compares the crematory to a living room "invitingly appointed / For the host who used to be a guest." The host—which we think is death—now lives in the well-appointed room and is no longer an infrequent visitor, but one who lives there and claims all who cross the threshold. Ultimately, this is a poem of lamentation, of loss, of transcendence as the speaker blames the chimneys and the fingers that laid the stones of the chimneys for making "Israel's body as smoke through the air!" By the time we have finished explicating the poem, students see the devastation wrought.

Another book I show my students is . . . I Never Saw Another Butterfly . . . : Children's Drawings and Poems from Terezin Concentration Camp, 1942–1944. This slim volume contains a collection of poems and drawings by children while they were inmates of a "model" concentration camp. There is a stark awareness of both the beauty and the cruelty of the world around them.

Websites regarding women and the Holocaust may be found at *www.holocaust-trc.org/edures35.htm, www.interlog.com/~mighty/, www.interlog.com/~mighty/valor/valor.htm,* and *www.holocaust-trc.org/edures.htm#contents.*

11

On Forgiving

Witness Zivia Lubetkin Zuckerman testifies during the
trial of Adolf Eichmann in Jerusalem, May 3, 1961.   Israel
Government Press Office, courtesy of USHMM Photo
Archives

"What would I have done?"

—SIMON WIESENTHAL

What does it mean to forgive? How can we forgive? Who can forgive? What
must one do to pay penance for sins? Forgiveness is a difficult concept in the
context of the Holocaust. Can one be forgiven for participating in mass murder? Can one be forgiven for murdering one thousand? One hundred? Ten?
Can one be forgiven for killing even a single person? Where do we draw the
line? Who should stand trial? What kind of justice do we, can we, seek?

Tribunals of men created the Nuremberg Trials to seek justice. But was
there any justice? Was hanging the perpetrators any way to make amends, to
compensate for all the death and loss? At least in the war crimes tribunal, humans used laws to make clear how the civilized hoped to live, and the court

attempted to punish evil perpetrators countenanced and supported by the German state during the reign of the Third Reich.

How do we, mere students and teachers of the Holocaust, come to understand justice and forgiveness? How do we search our own souls to know if we could forgive the crimes of mass murder? How do we come to understand—if we even wish to—the mind of one who participated in the murder of many? How do we understand how it felt to be a Jew asked for forgiveness?

To provoke discussion and thinking about the act of forgiving—what it means to forgive, when it is appropriate to forgive—we read Simon Wiesenthal's *The Sunflower: On the Possibilities and Limits of Forgiveness.*

The Sunflower is an autobiographical story/allegory written by Simon Wiesenthal. A young concentration camp inmate, Simon, is asked to the bedside of a dying SS soldier. Karl tells of rounding Jews up, locking over three hundred in a three-story house where they had previously unloaded petrol, and setting the house on fire:

> When we were told that everything was ready, we went back a few yards, and then received the command to remove safety pins from hand grenades and throw them through the windows of the house. Detonations followed one after another. . . . My God! (42)

Karl says they had their rifles ready to shoot anyone who dared to jump from a window. Karl and his cohorts shot at men and women and children who tried to escape being burned alive. Then Karl asks forgiveness from Simon. Simon, who has listened to the SS man's story, walks away in silence, without offering forgiveness.

Twenty-five years later, Simon Wiesenthal still ponders whether the SS man deserved forgiveness:

> The crux of the matter is, of course, the question of forgiveness. Forgetting is something that time alone takes care of, but forgiveness is an act of volition, and only the sufferer is qualified to make the decision.
>
> You, who have just read this sad and tragic episode in my life, can mentally change places with me and ask yourself the crucial question, "What would I have done?" (98)

The story and question are followed by a symposium in which almost fifty theologians, historians, writers, philosophers, and survivors respond to Wiesenthal's question. Most students can read and appreciate the parable/ story that Wiesenthal relates. The symposium may be a bit difficult for middle school students—however, they may want to write and conduct their own symposium.

After we read the first part of *The Sunflower* I ask students to respond in their journals to Wiesenthal's final question: "You, who have just read this sad and tragic episode in my life, can mentally change places with me and ask yourself the crucial question, 'What would I have done?'" I ask students to consider not only how *they* might respond, but also examine the issues Wiesenthal exposes through his brief narrative.

The next day we discuss their responses. Should Simon forgive the German soldier who participated in the burning of a house full of Jews, who shot any Jew who tried to escape? In our discussion, students wrestle with the big questions: What does it mean to forgive? Are there any times a person may not be forgiven? Can one forgive without forgetting? Should one forget? Who is responsible for the Nazi crimes? How much responsibility does a single Jew have for granting forgiveness? Who is entitled to forgive? God? The person sinned against? A judge? How can there ever be justice? Should one who seeks to be pardoned be pardoned just because he wants it? What does it mean to take responsibility for one's actions? Should one forgive to grant the penitent peace of mind?

Mark H.: It's pretty tough to put yourself in his shoes.

Mark W.: You can't really put yourself in his shoes. From my perspective, it's difficult. Personally, I would have looked at the boy and felt he was at the wrong place at the wrong time. Peer pressure kicked in, propaganda came into play and affected everyone. I don't really think he knew what he was getting into when he joined the Nazi youth. When he asked for forgiveness it was his way of showing he had a heart.

Helen: Yes, there was probably some peer pressure, but I don't accept the peer pressure as something as drastic as that. I don't know if I would forgive him. It would be different if *he* was saying "I'm sorry."

Mark W.: Saying I'm sorry and asking for forgiveness are two different things. Forgiveness is wanting closure.

Helen: It's kind of insulting. The soldier is insulting Simon. Simon's not left with anything.

Jessica: We can't choose one person to ask for forgiveness from a whole race. We can't look at one German and forgive.

Kristin: We're taught to be good. In Germany they were taught to be bad. If we were Germans, then every single one of us would have joined the Nazi Party.

Stuart: I don't think he should forgive. He has no obligation.

Kate: If he would have apologized, it would have been different. Why would he change if he wasn't dying? It's different to accept an apology as opposed to taking the more positive step of granting forgiveness.

Anup: I don't think he should be forgiven.

Helen: We're giving the SS man too much sympathy. I wouldn't totally blame them. To begin with, you have to want to kill. I don't think if a KKK guy or skinhead tried to organize a mass killing that we would go along with it.

Mark W.: The SS soldier's asking for forgiveness is like a slave-master who sold or killed your family who asks for forgiveness.

I ask, as we finish our day's discussion, which has filled the entire hour-and-a-half, "Could you forgive Karl?" Twenty-one of my class of twenty-six students could *not* forgive; four were not sure, only one could forgive.

For the next class, I ask students to read through at least five voices from the symposium. I don't want them to read others' opinions until they have formulated their own. Then, I ask them to pick from those they read, whose opinion they would like to represent in a second symposium the next day. They do not have to agree with the person whose views they choose to represent. I assign "parts" and ask them to dress up in the guise of the person they plan to represent. Just a hat or a prop will do. I ask the students to speak in the voice of the person whose commentary they will represent. "Please summarize your position. Read us at least one quote you feel epitomizes the writer's stand. Then the class—from the vantage of whom they represent—may ask questions about your stand." When they arrive in class, the seats are arranged in a circle. I give each student a piece of paper to fold into threes. They write the name of their "character" on one panel, and their name on another panel. If they revert to their own voice, I ask them to turn the sign, so we know whose opinion they are representing.

Our discussion the next day is heated and intense. Nuances become important. I never realized from how many angles we could see the problem of forgiveness. Students represent other voices well, from "Primo Levi" who says, "When a crime is committed, it is forever irreparable. The pain of the dying man feels not as painful as the pain *he* caused. If Simon forgives, he inflicts a terrible moral violence on himself," to "Abraham Joshua Heschel" who says, "Jewish law states that you can't forgive someone for something he did to someone else. Even God can't forgive. God can only forgive those who sin against *Him*," to "Jose Habe," a Franciscan nun of the Iroquois who says she *would* forgive, "No one memory should hold us down. Without forgiveness, memory will tear us apart," to the "Dalai Lama" who would forgive, but would not forget.

Students are engaged and excited as they present the ideas of the symposium, and in effect, conduct their own. For almost ninety minutes we race through ideas about culpability, responsibility, penance, and forgiveness. Finally, I ask, "Can you buy a German car? Can you forgive the German people?" Opinion is divided.

Students continue to address these questions in their journals. The range and depth and scope of their comments visit many nuances the dilemma of *The Sunflower* poses.

Some excerpts:

Ben: Does everyone deserve to rest in peace? Does everyone deserve to die with a cleared conscience? My answer to that question is NO. Not everyone deserves to rest in peace. People make choices in life and those choices follow them forever. If I were put in the situation of Wiesenthal, I, too, would not forgive the dying SS man. How could I? Those people, the Nazi Party, slaughtered Jews as if they were flies on the wall. . . . I don't think killing is a crime that deserves forgiveness. Whether you are sorry for your actions or not, you still killed another human being. In my beliefs, humans are not the ones who decide when other human beings should leave the earth. God does that. The Nazi Party tried to play the role of God, and for attempting that, they all deserve punishment.

Julia P.: I asked myself what I would have done if it had been a different situation, something that had happened to African-Americans here in the United States. What if, during the time of slavery, a slave owner called me into his room on his deathbed and asked me to forgive him on behalf of all the blacks in America. Undoubtedly, I would think about all the horrendous things that had happened to my people as a result of people who owned slaves. Lynchings, beatings, verbal/physical/sexual abuse, degradation . . . the list would just go on and on. True, I never experienced this firsthand, but I have heard stories from members of my family who witnessed segregation and racism. The emotions would have been strong, but I still came up with the same response to the SS man's question. I would have forgiven him. . . . Honestly, I believe that it would have been a horrible thing to have denied Karl some sort of peace before he died. He was honestly sorry and he was suffering from guilt.

Helen: Even though this SS Officer is on his deathbed, I would still feel no sympathy. I would ask him, "And am I supposed to forgive you for killing my mother? My father? My sister? My cousins? What about my grandparents? And my pets?" I would show him that I would have no reason to feel obligated to owe him or any Nazi anything.

I find it way too convenient that this officer only came forward to ask the forgiveness of "any old Jew" when he is on his deathbed. . . . If he sincerely felt sorrow, grief, and regret for the awful things he had done—including shooting children—then I wonder why he didn't just decide at an earlier time that he was sorry for these things instead of waiting for death to come knocking and send him into a panicked fit of regret.

To ask for forgiveness is a very selfish thing to do. When the SS officer asks the Jew—a victim—for forgiveness, I think that the Jew should find this extremely insulting. Demanding forgiveness is like asking for something for yourself. When someone grants you forgiveness you are at peace with yourself and can move on. No one should ever feel at peace for what happened in the Holocaust. Some say "forgive but never forget," I say, "move on, but never forgive."

Simon owed this officer nothing. I would want the officer to die knowing that what he did was unforgivable. It wouldn't be fair to let him die in peace when I know that as a concentration camp prisoner I am going to likely die a violent, furious, painful, unfair death at the hand of someone just like the man lying in the bed begging for forgiveness.

Natalie: This man is a Nazi soldier who has most likely saluted Hitler or joined in with the cheers and rallies of other anti-Semites. He has put on a uniform and gone out and killed someone because he was Jewish. This man has contributed to a genocide, and in one point of his life, he probably thought that the Jews deserved to be wiped out. Instead of forgiving this man, I would suggest to him that he pray until the moment he leaves this Earth and that his God is more merciful than humans can possibly fathom. If not, he'll be waiting in a long line with other SS soldiers to burn in hell.

Robyn: There are two major things I would have done differently, had I been in Wiesenthal's place. First, I probably would have accepted the present of the watch and such which Wiesenthal was offered after the Nazi's death. Such a gift might enable me to buy food or a better work shift, to put off death a little longer. If the Nazi's death can bring good things to me, I should accept those good things. Pride seems rather pointless in the camps.

Now, to the question of forgiveness itself: I think I, like Wiesenthal, would not forgive. I doubt, however, I would have enough dignity to leave in silence. More likely, I would be unable to prevent myself from screaming and berating the dying soldier.

The man who acts with guilt is perhaps worse than one who acts without. At least those Nazis who killed because they honestly believed Jews were evil were doing what they thought was right. They were ignorant. Ignorance can be excused. The man who knows what he's doing is repugnant, yet goes ahead and does it anyway, however, should never be forgiven. This man recognizes that what he's doing is wrong, evil . . . and does it anyway. Because he doesn't want his peers to think he's a wimp. Because some general tells him to. Because he doesn't have the courage to speak up. He goes ahead and murders hundreds of people, innocent men, women and children, knowing that it is wrong, because he doesn't feel like speaking up. That, I believe, is true evil.

Does the man's guilt save his victims? No. Does it help their families? No. Does it have any purpose at all? No. So, why should the fact that the man is guilty, "repentant," give one any reason at all to forgive him? If the man felt guilty, he shouldn't have committed the atrocity. But he chose to anyway. Now he will have to live—and die—with that guilt. Without forgiveness.

All these student writers have grappled with big issues. They have considered what it means to forgive in the context of horrible, unforgivable crimes. They have pondered and wrestled. They have rendered an opinion. They have assimilated and processed what I have tried to teach.

A related journal response I offer is to consider the ending to Sara Nomberg-Przytyk's story "A Living Torch," about the murder of children at Auschwitz. Nomberg-Przytyk ends with the following question:

> The next day the men told us that the SS men loaded the children into wheelbarrows and dumped them into the fiery ravines. Living children burned like torches. What did these children do to suffer such a fate? Is there any punishment adequate to repay the criminals who perpetrated these crimes?

I ask students to answer Sara Nomberg-Przytyk's question, keeping in mind all they know about the suffering in the camps. Obviously, her first question is rhetorical. Her second is also. But I ask them to ponder her question. Is there any justice for one who burns or orders the burning of children? What is that justice within the realm of a civilized, humane system of law?

12

Aftermath

The Chain Is Not Broken

Jewish youth liberated at Buchenwald lean out the windows of a train, as it pulls away from the station.   Robert Waisman, courtesy of USHMM Photo Archives

The first words my ex-husband said when our daughter was born at Sinai Hospital were "Hitler did not prevail, the chain is not broken. She is a gift for my mother." Then he handed her to me to nurse. We named her Sari after one of the sisters my mother-in-law lost. Sari had a heavy burden to bear—as did her father who was named for his mother's father, a WWI soldier in the Hungarian army, a father of six, who was gassed the day he arrived in Auschwitz.

The war ended in 1945. The last displaced person's camp closed in 1948. And yet, the memory of life still invades the thoughts and dreams of survivors—and their children. One cannot move on through life without the invasion of distilled memory. Almost fifty years after liberation, Paul Steinberg says in a chapter of *Speak You Also*, a memoir about his experiences in the camps, "It's already a month since I began writing, and I'm starting to feel the effects of my plunge into the depths. My sleep grows more and more troubled.

As I lie awake at night for hours, my disconnected brain dredges up images I thought were dead and buried. That's how the faces of Dr. Ohrenstein and others have come back to life. My memory is sweating, oozing."

In a Spiegelman panel from *Maus II*, Francoise, Artie's wife, sighs and says, "I'd rather KILL myself than live through all that . . . everything Vladek went through. It's a miracle he survived." Artie, Vladek's son, answers, "Uh-Huh. But in some ways he DIDN'T survive" (90).

Though survivors and their children may live outwardly normal lives, the inner turmoil and memory persists. Students need to understand that the effects of the Holocaust are long lasting—into the next and even the next generation.

In his excellent foreword to *Witness: Voices from the Holocaust*, which contains the transcript from the film of the same name, Lawrence Langer writes,

> The saddest legacy of all for those still alive is an inability to escape from the tainted memory that still hovers over their daily existence. When one witness exclaims that the Passover she celebrates with family and friends is "not the same," that "something is missing," that she wants to share it with "someone who knows me really," she evokes a severed intimacy whose absence still fills her with yearning. (xviii)

My students recognize that for survivors the Holocaust didn't end when they were liberated. What they witnessed lives on in memory—and behavior. Charlie recalls the end of *Night*, "All Elie sees is a skeleton when he looks in the mirror. He was alive and not alive. In a physical sense, he exists, but in another sense, he feels dead inside." Tal suggests that survivors live through so much trauma. "They have post-traumatic stress syndrome," she says, recalling things she studied in her psychology class.

In another panel from *Maus II*, Artie and his wife Francoise listen in the night to Artie's father's loud moans: "AAWOOWWAH!" "Wh-What's that noise?" Francoise asks. "Oh, nothing—just Vladek . . . He's moaning in his sleep again. When I was a kid I thought that was the noise ALL grown-ups made while they slept" (74). The nightmares persist.

Even into the second generation. One night my former husband woke me from a deep sleep and with wide-eyed fear ordered me to wake our daughters, get them dressed, and take them over to our neighbors. "You're dreaming," I told him. "Go back to sleep."

"Don't you hear the tanks and the planes? They're coming for us. Take the children next door. They're righteous gentiles, they'll hide them for us."

I begged my husband to wake up: "You hear traffic on Woodward, the 3 A.M. train." Still, he was insistent that the Nazis were coming for us. It was

1985. Forty years after his mother was liberated from Auschwitz. Memory lives on—even in the second generation.

To understand the force of memory, how it invades our thoughts and dreams without warning, I ask my students to do a three-part response journal. First, I ask them to write their most vivid memories, the ones that float before their eyes when they least expect them, the thoughts that spring up in images and words and remembered deeds. I ask, "What do you see? What do you 'dream' when you're daydreaming? What recurring dreams do you have at night? If it helps, put your head on your desk and just let thoughts float through your mind for the next ten minutes of so." (And I turn off the lights.)

Then, I ask, "What do you know about your parents' past? What three major events come to mind? How do you know these things? Did they tell you? Did others hint at what they went through? Did you simply surmise what happened from their actions?"

And then, I ask, "What do you know about your grandparents' past lives? What stories have your heard about them?"

I want students to recognize how selective memory is. I want them to visit for themselves their own recurring memories. To hold—through their writing—the moments that normally float in and out of their vision. I also want them to understand how much (or little) of their parents' and grandparents' memory is passed down to them.

With a sense of what it means to remember—how selective and ornery we may be about what we remember—and also how real and vivid memory is—we turn to the recorded memories and stories of survivors. What remains from the horror? How do they go on with their lives? What gets passed down to the next generation?

We revisit *Maus I* and *Maus II*. This time, we look less at the events of the past that Vladek describes to Artie and more at *how* Artie is affected by his father's past. We also look closely at Vladek himself to see how his actions in the present are affected by his ingrained memory of the past.

In the first page-and-a-half of *Maus II, A Survivor's Tale: And Here My Troubles Began*, Artie's wife says, "I only converted to make Vladek happy." Artie responds, "Yeah. But NOTHING can make him happy" (12). It is as if no matter what his children do, they cannot reach the inner core of Vladek and change the past for him. His memories are always there and always affect his state of happiness. Two pages later, on the way to visit Vladek, Artie confesses to Francoise, his wife, "I can't even make any sense out of my relationship with my father. . . . How am I supposed to make any sense out of Auschwitz? . . . Of the Holocaust? . . . When I was a kid I used to think about which of my parents I'd let the Nazis take to the ovens if I could only save one of them . . . usually I saved my mother. Do you think that's normal?" Francoise tries to reassure him that "Nobody's normal" (14), and yet, we have to wonder if some people are more "normal" than others—if the Holocaust didn't inflict a particular "normalcy" on its survivors, and on the children of its survivors. In the very next frame, Artie's thoughts leap to his dead half-brother when he wonders if he and Richieu would have gotten along had he lived. The past is ever present. Even in the end of the book, in the second to last frame, Vladek calls Artie Richieu. Vladek, almost fifty years later, confuses his living son with his dead son, with what Artie calls his "GHOST-brother."

The act of writing of his father's history is also a way of entering his father's past. Scenes of the past set in Auschwitz overlap scenes set in a summer bungalow colony in the Catskills. We move easily in and out of memory and present. Together the fluidity of movement recreates the addled mind of the survivor who hoards wooden matches, keeps the gas on in the oven because it's free, offers to make his guests tea with a tea bag drying from prior use, and tries to glue together a broken dish. The present is never safe or secure. The past always intrudes.

Another way to try to understand what it is like for a survivor is to read Primo Levi's description of his post-Auschwitz experiences in *The Reawakening,*

> It is a dream within a dream, varied in detail, one in substance. I am sitting at a table with my family, or with friends, or at work, or in the green countryside, . . . yet I feel a deep and subtle anguish, the definite sensation of an impending threat. And in fact, as the dream proceeds, slowly or brutally, each time in a different way, everything collapses and disintegrates around me, the scenery, the walls, the people, while the anguish becomes more intense and more precise. . . . I am in the Lager once more, and nothing is true outside the Lager. (207–208)

I want students to consider how "nothing is true outside the Lager," even when he is sitting at a table with friends or family, at work, or in a green field. I want them to question, "What is the new, real truth? Why is all else illusion? What *is* that truth of the Lager according to Levi? Wiesel? What is the experience outside the Lager like for a survivor?"

Meeting a Survivor

I have qualms about asking someone who lived through the Holocaust to tell us what happened. For some, it is dredging up memory they may not want to touch. If, however, you live in a major city, there are probably volunteers who willingly come into classrooms to talk to students about what personally happened to them. Despite hoping the literature will convey to my students the depth and extent of the Holocaust, speaking to a live person seems to have a profound affect on them. Said one student, "It was like shaking hands with Michael Jordan—the survivor was real. I could look her in the eye. And I knew what she told me was true."

Our students still don't quite believe what they see on television or read in books. Seeing, for them, is believing. Unfortunately, within the next ten to twenty years, the generation who survived the Nazi years will no longer be with us (most survivors are now in their seventies and eighties). Nitasha writes in her journal, "We are the last generation to be able to hear from a survivor firsthand, and to have that is so fortunate. Twenty years from now, there will be no more survivors for students, like us, to listen to."

In most major cities of the United States, there is a Holocaust museum. Staff at these museums go out of their way to arrange for classroom speakers. If it is not possible to contact a survivor to speak, there are places students may access videotaped footage of survivor testimony. As a literature, the survivor testimony is authentic and reveals—if we carefully watch facial expression as well as listen to stories—the survivor's experience. Though taped, we see real people telling their all too real stories.

The Fortunoff Archives at Yale University contain some of the first tapes made by survivors, many of them still in their forties and fifties. These tapes are somewhat unusual now, as we are used to thinking of survivors as "old" and these tapes show younger people remembering what it was like. The Archive has series of edited videotapes available for loan to schools and community groups, based on the Archive's collection of testimonies (*www .library.yale.edu /testimonies /homepage.html*).

Another wonderful source for hearing survivors' voices is *holocaust .umd.umich.edu /*. Dr. Sid Bolkosky, a Professor of History at the University of Michigan-Dearborn, interviewed over 150 survivors. On the website are eleven compelling interviews posted with printed transcripts. Each interview covers the time before the war, during the war, and after the war. In listening to these interviews one can hear the silences, the confusion, the trembling, the weeping, and the strength in survivors' voices. The voices convey not only the story of what happened, but also what it's like to remember and to tell.

Abraham Pasternak on what it was like to come to America after the war:

> . . . I stayed in a hotel in New York and I went out for a walk. I don't remember what the name of the street or anything. And I looked in the windows and I see those big hams, it must have been a butcher shop and bread and all kinds of stuff, oh my God! So much food! And as I looked at

the window I started to proceed a little further down the street and I see a tall policeman coming in front of me. I immediately went into my pocket and I was ready to take out my identification card and to show him that look I am here legitimately. [pause] It was, coming over here was a daze . . . coming in from, from, from hell and all of the sudden you are in paradise . . . that is the only way I can put the two things together.

. . . And they [relatives in Los Angeles] asked me to come down there, and I went down there and uh, the first time I saw them, the first thing they said to me, "I don't want to hear anything about a concentration camp, because I know everything about it." I was stunned. Really I was disappointed. You don't want to know about your parents? Or you don't want to know about . . . why the hell did you bring me here all the way? But then the other brother, pumped all the information from me.

. . . My first sentence in English was this. "If you laugh, everybody laughs with you and if you cry, you cry by yourself." . . . I didn't know what I really wanted. The only thing I do remember, I wanted was to go in a corner and cry.

Erna Gorman and Abraham Pasternak, who each spoke to different classes of mine, are interviewed on this valuable site. Videos of the interviews are available through interlibrary loan.

In 1994 after filming *Schindler's List,* Steven Spielberg established the Survivors of the Shoah Visual History Foundation with an urgent mission: to chronicle, before it was too late, the firsthand accounts of survivors, liberators, rescuers, and other eyewitnesses of the Holocaust. Recording more than 50,000 unedited testimonies, the largest undertaking of its kind, the Shoah Foundation launched its mission to create a multimedia archive to be used as an educational and research tool. The archive is comprised of 200,000-plus videotapes filled with more than 100,000 hours of testimony. To watch the entire collection straight through would now take about thirteen years and six months (*www.vhf.org/*).

Spielberg's foundation has also produced a CD-ROM titled *Survivors: Testimonies of the Holocaust.* On it are the chronological stories of several survivors, supported by historical documentation and footage. Several videos, which splice together footage from these interviews, have been produced including *The Lost Children of Berlin* and *The Last Days.*

A very good video that introduces students to survivors is *Witness: Voices from the Holocaust,* which takes us through the survivors' stories, from the beginning of the rumblings of war to the ghettos, deportation, and the camps. This film condenses four hundred hours of testimony from the Fortunoff Archives to an hour-and-a-half, to tell the story of the Holocaust. As we watch, I ask students to be aware of how survivors speak of their experiences.

After Liberation

Students ask what happened after the Holocaust. A good video to show the years between liberation (1945) and the establishment of the state of Israel (1948) is *The Long Way Home.* The film, which won the 1997 Academy Award for Best Documentary Feature, examines the postwar struggle of the tens of thousands of displaced Jewish refugees. The film, narrated by Morgan Freeman, shows the people who lived in displaced persons camps in the two to three years before leaving Europe to find new homes. The film portrays how difficult immigration was—how hard it was to come to the United States or England, how impossible it was to go to Palestine until the British withdrew and statehood was declared. Even after the war, no one wanted the Jews.

Most alarming is a statement by General George S. Patton. He claimed that if the Jews were not kept under guard in the D.P. camps, they would spread around like locusts. Earl G. Harrison, Dean of the University of Pennsylvania Law School, was appointed to find out how the U.S. Army was treating people they liberated. Patton is quoted as saying, "Harrison believes displaced persons are human. They are not. They are lower than animals." I pause the film so that my students can digest those hateful words—spoken by a United States general after the war. Patton was promptly replaced by Eisenhower.

The Israeli film, *Under the Domim Tree,* shows beautifully and engagingly the stories of several "hidden children" as adolescents in a group home in Israel in the early 1950s. By watching the film, students see how difficult it was for adolescents (their age) to integrate into a new, unthreatening world. We see two boys who survived by hiding in Polish woods revert to animalistic survival skills and run like howling wolves when there is a full moon. We witness arguments over German reparations: Are payments from the former Nazi state blood money or money to be used to construct a new life? We see a girl who escapes from abusive adopted parents and claims she can't remember her own mother and father and brother from whom she was separated when she was three or four years old. And we see the narrator, a native Israeli, whose mother is in a psychiatric hospital for imagining she, too, was in the camps, though she was not. The film portrays life after the horror, life in the nascent state of Israel.

To help students watch and understand *Under the Domim Tree,* I ask them to take notes, to notice how the pain of the years of the war resurfaces in the present. Much of this is subtle—a flinch, withdrawal, an abrupt remark. Some pain is more overt—a suicide, howling like wolves, joy in finding a lost father—and sadness at losing him again.

For journals, I ask students to think about what it is like for those who survived the Holocaust. How are their lives affected by recurring memories and events? How do they attempt to live "normal" lives in the face of their pasts? How is *Under the Domim Tree* about memory—lost memories, invasive memories, and retrieved memories?

Lindsay writes in her journal about the film:

> Seeing the Holocaust from the children's point of view was different. Although they were able to survive, their lives were still taken away. Their childhood was nonexistent. The children lost all of their families and they were only in their early teen years. How horrible a thought it is. I think what I would do if I were one of them, and I wouldn't be able to live. I don't know what I would do without my family.
>
> The worst part of the movie was when one of the girls was almost forced to live with abusive adults who claimed to be her parents. I was relieved when the girl's memory came back and she was able to stay with the people who loved her most.

Alla writes,

> Today I went to visit my great uncle. Since I am Russian, I'm used to calling him my grandfather. It's very awkward for me to start talking to him about the Holocaust. He was the only survivor out of his family. In his little town, Breshev, in Poland, he lost any trace of family. My grandfather is about 5′5″ and has thick, gray hair coming in from the sides of his shiny bald head. His face is wrinkled, like that of a wise man. The man is eighty-nine years old. His hands tremble and he limps as he walks. When he speaks you can tell that he is an intellectual. He doesn't waste his breath on meaningless things.
>
> My grandfather was only seventeen years old when the Nazis took his family. In his slight Yiddish accent my grandfather told me, "The Germans don't believe it themselves," he paused as he lifted his baby-blue eyes at me, "how is the rest of the world supposed to believe it." At that moment I felt a sharp pain in my chest. I knew exactly how he felt. His family exterminated like insects. I could feel the bottomless rage and discontent he must feel. For eternity. "Remember," he said as he took my hand. "All we can do now is remember." The pain seemed to have lifted from his eyes.

A Field Trip and a Survivor

My class visits the Holocaust Center in West Bloomfield, Michigan. They wander through the subterranean chambers of the museum pausing to read anti-Semitic posters, view displays of life before the war, and watch videos that take them into the camps. They sit in an amphitheatre and watch an eight-minute video in which local survivors describe their experiences. Then, we gather in a windowless classroom to meet and hear Irna Gorman, a survivor who says she speaks out because hatred and prejudice should not be part of our lives.

Gorman tells of hiding in a small barn loft with her family. For entertainment they pushed lice and vermin out of their skin. She learned that different-sized lice have different sounds, and they could make a symphony out of squeezing them. She became mute. She couldn't move. She became a mere shell. The years of hunger destroyed everything in her. Had the farmer who hid them been discovered, he and his children would have been killed and his possessions burned. When liberation came, he had to carry them down the stairs. They had to crawl away on their hands and knees.

Her son, a neurologist, asked, "If we can go to the moon and come back, can't we find the part of our brain that makes us into animals?"

She tells us how after liberation she was teased in school for being Jewish. She tells us that eighty to ninety of her immediate family died. She tells us, "Someone has to speak out."

My students are mesmerized by her presence. They are a rapt audience. No one nods off. Afterward, students gather around Irna Gorman to give her a hug. Al says of his experience, "I couldn't look at her at the end. She was kind of eating through me. We read about these things and we see these things in movies and films. When someone's standing in front of you and making eye contact with you, I could see how much it hurt her, and it also hurt me."

Nick says, "It's like you almost don't want to look at her. There's nothing you can do when she's standing there on the verge of tears. If I looked, I would have wanted to get up and hug her."

And from Kate, who put into a succinct journal entry what all of us felt:

I just wanted to write a quick entry about the speaker at the museum even though I don't need anymore pages in my journal, because the experience was too important to go unmentioned. Firstly, I noticed how she didn't want the door closed and insisted it stay open despite the noise from the group outside. I couldn't help but wonder afterwards if she felt some deepset claustrophobia after spending two whole years in that confined loft with her family. She also said she wanted the light on so she could see our faces, even if it meant putting up with that irritating buzzing noise. I listened to her every word with fascination. It was incredible to me that she had managed to survive such a horrific experience, from the conditions they lived in to watching her own mother die helplessly, to going home after the war and facing the hate and ridicule. It nearly made me cry thinking of this brave woman as the dirty little girl who wet herself before the eyes of her cold tormentors. The way she was able not to hate those children even now, looking back, is incredible. She recognizes that they were just ignorant because of what their parents and other children had told them. I was supposed to leave early to get to work on time, but I couldn't bring myself to stand up while she was still talking. Not only would I feel disrespectful, but I just wanted to hear the rest. Nobody left early. It was just an experience I won't ever forget, it was really just unbelievable.

Field Trips in Cyberspace

For those who do not have a nearby Holocaust museum, there are several websites that provide rather complete tours of current and past exhibitions. With the click of a mouse, students can visit museums in Jerusalem, Washington, D.C., Los Angeles, and Detroit. Each of these websites provides exhibits that once hung on the museum's walls. There are extensive archives and photograph collections to visit. One can "walk the halls" of the museum by clicking into connecting screens and links.

As students visit an Internet site, they might take notes as if they were physically in a museum and comment on what they observe. I ask, "What do you see as you pass through the exhibits? Which sites would you advise others to visit? Why? Why not?"

Another way to see the museums is to read their mission statements. What is their purpose? Do you think they achieve their purpose through their websites?

At the end of the semester as part of my students' final exam, I ask them to assess at least three Holocaust museum websites. What kinds of exhibits are offered? Are these worth visiting? Why? What do we learn from them? I want them to apply what they have learned by evaluating how well others teach about the Holocaust.

Holocaust Websites

Yad VaShem, the Holocaust museum in Israel, offers tours of its sights and a few exhibits. Most noteworthy is *The Auschwitz Album,* a book of photographs taken by SS men during May and June 1944. The photographs show Hungarian Jews arriving at Auschwitz and lining up for delousing or gas. How chilling it is to see these photographs of women and children, exhausted from their train ride, looking like they are merely in transit—and knowing they will be dead within hours (*www.yadvashem.org.il/Auschwitz_Album/*).

At Yad VaShem, *The Sites of Remembrance* may be visited (*www .yadvashem.org.il/remembrance/index.html*). Linked are twenty-three other sites and exhibits at Yad VaShem—including sites about Oskar Schindler, Raoul Wallenberg, and the French of the village of Les Chambon who saved over four hundred Jewish children.

The United States Holocaust Memorial Museum in Washington, D.C., has some wonderful online exhibits (*www.ushmm.org/exhibits/exhibit.htm*). Among them are sites about Jewish displaced persons from 1945–1951; The Holocaust in Greece; The Voyage of the *St. Louis;* The Hidden History of the Kovno Ghetto, Kristallnacht; The Nazi Olympics in Berlin, 1936; The Doctors' Trial (the Nuremberg Code and Human Rights); and "Images of Internment" by Josef Nassy. All have photographs and text to explain and show.

"The Nazi Olympics in Berlin" (*www.ushmm.org/olympics/index.html*) is an incredible site, taking the visitor through not only the history of racist laws in Germany, but also the political implications of Jews and blacks participating in the 1936 Olympics. Many Jews boycotted the Olympics. Many blacks went, hoping to dispel racist stereotypes in both Germany and the United States. Black track star Jesse Owen won a gold metal only to be shunned by Hitler, who refused to shake his hand. The site also has biographies and photographs of many of the Jewish athletes in their prime from across Europe who within the next eight years were themselves victims of Hitler's killing centers.

For a tour of United States Holocaust Memorial Musem's permanent exhibit, "The Holocaust: A Learning Site for Students" presents the history of the Holocaust as it is presented as the Museum's Permanent Exhibition (*www.ushmm.org/outreach/index.html*). The site has five major parts: Nazi Rule, Jews in Prewar Germany, The Final Solution, The Nazi Camp System, and Rescue and Resistance. Time lines, photographs, and historical background are provided.

The Holocaust Center, West Bloomfield, Michigan, (*holocaustcenter .org/exhibit.shtml*) shows some of its exhibits online. Of particular interest may be a game, "You Choose," (*holocaustcenter.org/lifechance.shtml*), in which players are asked to make the kinds of choices a Jew living in Nazi Germany during the 1930s may have had to make.

The Museum of Tolerance and the Simon Wiesenthal Center in Los Angeles (*motlc.wiesenthal.org/exhibits/*) offers archives for research and several virtual exhibits: "Visas for Life," the story of Chiune Sugihara, Japanese rescuer of Jews during the Holocaust; "Dignity and Defiance," which commemorates the Warsaw ghetto uprising in 1943; and "And I Still See Their Faces: Images of Polish Jews," an exhibit of the photographs taken before the war.

Final Assessment

And finally, how to assess the semester of study? A test? A written exam? I chose to assign a final project that I hope will force students to think about what they have learned, to make some sense out of the inordinately huge amount of material they have studied. Therefore, I created a three-part final project. All students have to reassess what they understand about the Holocaust and why they chose to study it.

Surprisingly (or not so surprisingly) the projects students did were enlightening and provocative. I received several art projects: A poster-sized collage from magazines of people suffering from more recent genocides superimposed with images from the Holocaust; an exquisite pencil drawing of an open Bible, an open Torah, a mother holding her child—all with a background of smoke rising from a crematory; a pencil drawing of train tracks leading to Auschwitz—and the entrance to Auschwitz burned and in that yawning expanse, the words, "Never Again"; a water color of four hands—all wearing or passing on the same ring, which was a gift passed from one who did not survive, to her sister—and then to her sister's daughter—and then to her sister's granddaughter, my student.

If what we want from our students is to process and assimilate the information we teach, then what I saw on students' final exams was the synthesis of a semester's learning. Perhaps of all the assessments of our class, the following two pieces describe best what students surmise from a class like ours: Trisha:

> After all of the nightmares, all of the horrors that I have witnessed, until this day I do not know exactly why I took this course. Maybe I took it because I wanted to know the details of what happened, I wanted to be grossed out. Maybe I took it because I wanted a blow-off class or maybe I took it because I needed another English class and this one sounded interesting. I have gone over this question many times before in my mind. I have asked myself when I woke up in a cold sweat, "Why?" I have wondered why I continue trudging through books and seeing the genocide play over and over in my mind. But every time that I ask myself why I am in this class I come up blank. In fact, in some ways I felt that I am not supposed to know why I am in this class, only accept that I am here, and that I may be able to help others understand the Holocaust after I am done. I don't regret my decision to take this course, but it wasn't an easy course to take and it is probably one of the only courses that changed my life forever.
>
> From this course I learned so much about humanity, about human nature, about control, about life and death. I learned of the killing of a whole people and how the killing was organized by merely one single man. Jews'

Holocaust Literature
Final Project—Due your last day of class

Part I. Choose one of the following questions/projects:

1. Assume a semester-long Holocaust Literature class is *not* offered at a given school. Your job is to create a Holocaust Literature unit that could be taught in approximately one- to two-weeks' worth of classes. From the attached list, select one or two films, one book, and one or two shorter pieces. Consider the following questions: Who is your audience? What grade? What class? (American History? European History? English?) What do you want your students to learn during the unit? What are your objectives? What do you hope to accomplish in class discussions? *Explain your rationale for selecting each of the materials you think should be taught.* Create activities that will enhance students' understanding of the materials.

2. Assess the quality of Holocaust sites on the World Wide Web. Examine at least five Holocaust websites. Assume the reader has a minimal Holocaust education. Which sites provide what? Describe the sites. Inform the reader of your essay about which sites to go to and why. What will we find there? Is the information accurate? Are there good visuals? How is it organized? What is the slant or agenda? Who produces the site? Who is the intended audience for this site?

3. Create a Holocaust project you feel is significant. Write a paper, a short story, a series of poems, or create an art project to explore some aspect of the Holocaust that interests and intrigues you.

Part II. Assess this course

What worked for you? What was boring? What do you think is most important to learn about the Holocaust? What books, films, discussions were most effective for you? What about journals? Were they helpful to you in forcing you to think about issues raised, materials read and watched and discussed? If you were to restructure the course, what would you do? What was the most meaningful experience of the course?

Part III. Why you took this class

On the first day of class, I asked, "Why are you taking this course? What do you hope to learn? Discover? Think about? What is the Holocaust?" Now, how would you answer some of our original questions: *Why did you take this course? What did you learn? Discover? Think about? What is the Holocaust? What does it mean?*

Figure 12–1. *"Faith" by Stephen Stakhiv. To me the Holocaust meant physical and mental struggles, some mental punishments being more severe than physical. One of the mental tests that the entire Holocaust population had to go through was a test in faith. As the war continued more and more faith had just disappeared in the ferocious flames, just going up in smoke with the many bodies that followed.*

lives were taken away during the Holocaust. Survivors will never be the same. Some Jews hid during the Holocaust, some were caught and shot to death. Some found kind non-Jews to care for them, while others weren't so lucky. I learned that the Holocaust was not only the killing, but also the dehumanization of an entire people; it was the killing of spirits, of minds, of souls. The Holocaust taught me that everyone is prejudiced, and almost anyone can be manipulated.

NEVER AGAIN

Figure 12–2 *"Never Again" by Scott Ladue. This is a picture of the gates leading to Auschwitz death camp. As we have learned throughout the past four-and-a-half months, some of the worst things man has EVER done were done here. Mass gassings, mass burnings, mass killings . . . all took place through this gate. There was not only one, but three crematories. But enough background information, no need for facts we already know.*

I chose to do this art project rather than an essay, because I thought everyone would be doing the essay and I should do something different. I decided on the scariest vision I could recall from the past semester. The first thing and the last thing to pop into my head was a picture of the gates to Auschwitz. Just the idea that this was the last sight hundreds of thousands of people saw before dying is too powerful to ignore.

I took a lighter to the gate. I think that fire signifies not only the death and the burning, but also a little bit of hope, such as in an eternal flame. Though it does represent the gate to hell in my drawing, it also represents closure . . . that it has been burned down forever.

Most of all from this course I discovered that no one will ever know why this happened. You can analyze it all you want, look at the facts, ask questions, take as many courses as you choose and you will never know why. The scary part about that is not knowing why prevents you from stopping it from happening again. The scary part is in not knowing why, you never really get any answers. In not knowing why, you are studying something that will eventually just put you back where you started again. The Holocaust is a horror, a mass killing of an innocent people, a tragedy, and a wonder. In order to fully learn about the Holocaust, to learn all the facts, soak in all the information, one must go outside one's mind. One must be able to look at the Holocaust and not ask why, because if you ask why, you end up searching for an answer that will never come, and it will haunt you, it will confuse you, it will make you crazy if you let it. The meaning of the Holocaust is different for everyone, and myself, I haven't yet figured out what it means.

Steven:

I took the course because I thought it would reinforce what I already knew about hate and the Holocaust. Instead, I learned something about the nature of man. Man is typically a frail beast, and though we lay a thin coat of paint on top of that bestiality and call it civilization, the beast is always there—whether we wear loin cloths and carry a club or wear a suit and tie with a shoulder holster, it's there. The Holocaust is a recent expression of that. It means that we must add and strengthen the coat of paint.

And from Nick:

The class is over and what should we leave knowing? I've said many times now what I've learned, and that is we can't let bad things keep going. We have to stand up and make a change. I know it sounds corny. It's the truth though. Teaching and standing up for what is right is the only way we can stop another holocaust.

After taking this class, my condolences go out to every survivor and to all that perished. If it means anything. Sometimes I feel guilty being Catholic. But then I think about it. I wasn't there. I didn't accept it. Right now my mind is filled with so much information. Sometimes I want to cry when I really think about what happened. I'll say it again, I can't believe something like this could happen.

From this day on my eyes will never close.

Amen.

Appendix A: Teaching the Holocaust in 90 Minutes

How do you teach events that defy knowledge, experiences that go beyond imagination? How do you tell children, big and small, that society could lose its mind and start murdering its own soul and its own future?

ELIE WIESEL

I have been lucky. I have had a whole semester to teach literature of the Holocaust. This is a luxury—to have time for discussions and videos and readings. But what if you don't have a whole semester?

I asked my students what they would teach if they had only two weeks to teach the Holocaust. I hoped they could tell me what they would want to study if they had time for only one book, one video, one short story, one website. Most could not limit their choices to a single book, video, or website. Blake would teach *Maus, Survival in Auschwitz, The Master Race,* and *Schindler's List.* Gary said he didn't even have to think twice about which book he would have his students read: *Night.* He would also show *Schindler's List.* David would have his class read *Night* and watch *The Diary of Anne Frank;* he would teach Wu Tang's "Never Again" and Primo Levi's poem, "On Trial." Clare would teach *Maus* and *Night* and show *Anne Frank Remembered* and *Schindler's List;* she would also teach Wu Tang's "Never Again." And Justin, who hopes to be make movies and who could not be held to "just two weeks," would have his student's read Yevgeny Yevtushenko's "Babi Yar," Cynthia Ozick's "The Shawl," Levi's *Survival in Auschwitz,* Spiegelman's *Maus,* and he would show *Daring to Resist, Night and Fog,* and *Schindler's List.*

In other words, he would try to cram the work of a whole semester into two to three weeks.

According to Dan whose proposed curriculum is even more extensive,

> It is every human being's duty to invest just a few hours to bear witness, in an attempt to at least acknowledge that which no one will understand. . . . All in all, I would want students to be provoked. I would want them to leave thinking about my class. I would want to know that this material reached them, because this material is too important to be passive about. My goal would be simple. I would want the students to care about what had happened.

To be provoked . . . to care about what had happened. Ideally, that is what we do when we educate. The danger, as my students warn, is using up class time with too much information. We MUST pause to reflect and to discuss—to make sense of the awesome stories and facts. So how do we choose what to leave out? How do we select the best materials and lessons?

If students have never been exposed to Holocaust Literature, I would teach *Night,* by Elie Wiesel. The book, only 109 pages of simple, yet beautiful prose, tells the story of Elie Wiesel's life from when it was normal, just before the German occupation of Hungary, through his internment in Auschwitz with his father, to his liberation. If students have already read *Night,* I would suggest either *Survival in Auschwitz* by Primo Levi (more sophisticated and difficult) or *Maus I* and *Maus II* by Art Spiegelman. As for video, I would show *One Survivor Remembers* or *The Last Days* or *Witness: Voices from the Holocaust* to show historically how the Holocaust developed and so that students may "see" and "hear" a Holocaust survivor speaking of his or her experiences. I might also show *Schindler's List* to show how art reflects history and to look at the various stages of the tightening noose—as portrayed by Spielberg. The United States Holocaust Memorial Museum's website provides historical background to all the major events of the Holocaust, from the coming of the racial laws to the deportations, to the camps.

If Holocaust Literature is to be incorporated into an English curriculum, I would suggest one book each year in conjunction with one or two videos:

Grade 7: *The Diary of Anne Frank*
          The Diary of Anne Frank, Anne Frank Remembered

Grade 8: *I Have Lived a Thousand Years*
          One Survivor Remembers

Grade 9: *Night*
          The Last Days

Grade 10: *Maus I and II*
Witness: Voices of the Holocaust; Schindler's List

Grade 11: *Incident at Vichy*
Assignment: Rescue, America and the Holocaust:
Deceit and Indifference

Grade 12: *Survival in Auschwitz*, "The Shawl"
The Garden of the Finzi-Contini, Hate.org,
The Holocaust on Trial

The literature may also be used when studying and writing the memoir. In particular, *Night* by Elie Wiesel and *The Diary of Anne Frank* lend themselves as models of first person narrative. Other prose to consider are Gerda Weissmann Klein's *All But My Life,* Paul Steinberg's *Speak You Also,* and Tadeusz Borowski's "This Way for the Gas, Ladies and Gentlemen." Each of these pieces, written in vastly different styles, shows students how good writing conveys experience. Each is a model for writing the personal narrative.

I've often used "The Shawl" by Cynthia Ozick in creative writing to teach how an author "makes up" a story. So much of fiction seems semi-autobiographical—the author writes what she knows, writes from experience. But how does one imagine an experience that was not her own? We discuss where the story may have come from—perhaps a story Ozick heard, something she may have read, an image she felt compelled to explore. After reading through the story—usually twice—we go around the room pointing out images and sentences and metaphors. Then I ask students to write a short story from a point of view that is not their own about an experience they never had—except in their imaginations.

If the Holocaust is to be incorporated into an American History curriculum, I would show *Deceit and Indifference: America and the Holocaust* and perhaps the Varian Fry video, *Assignment: Rescue* which portrays the effort of one man to distribute U.S. visas to artists and intellectuals trapped in Camp des Milles, near Marseilles. The exercise/simulation in which students have to decide who is deserving of a visa to the United States forces students to assess what it means to be the "savior" of the world, what it means to be selective about who gets into our country under our immigration policy. As for a book of literature, I might assign *Incident at Vichy* by Arthur Miller to get at the issues of taking a moral stand and being a bystander. I might also teach *The Sunflower,* as it leads to a symposium with many of the world's intellectuals about the nature of forgiveness.

If teaching European History, I would probably show the Abba Eban film, *Heritage of the Jews: The Crucible of Europe* or *The People's Century: The Mas-*

ter Race to illustrate historical anti-Semitism in Europe and the development of racial laws. I would ask students to read *Night* by Elie Wiesel and/or *Survival in Auschwitz* by Primo Levi to understand something about the effect of the German policy of extermination on its human victims. The Holocaust challenges all we know about civilization. To study the Holocaust in this context forces us to examine our precepts and concepts of how Western society has developed and how it has been challenged. You may want to use some of the websites that provide original documents to assign a research paper based on primary documents. Of particular interest are the Nizkor Project (*www.nizkor.org/*), the Auschwitz-Birkenau Memorial and Museum (*www.auschwitz.org.pl/html/eng/start/index.html*), and the Simon Wiesenthal Center (*motlc.wiesenthal.com*).

Another way to present the material, films, and books is chronologically — in the order in which they were produced — to show how the American public gradually became aware. Begin with *Anne Frank* (both the diary and film), *Night and Fog* (1946) and ask what one might assume about the Holocaust based on these works. Consider the Eichmann trial in Jerusalem (1961) as well as *Judgment at Nuremberg* (1961). Consider Arthur Miller's play, *Incident at Vichy,* which opened in 1965. Then look at Elie Wiesel's *Night* which was not widely released in the United States until 1967 when it became a Selection of Commentary Library Book Club. In 1978, perhaps in response to the production of *Roots* which energized the already strong black pride movement, *Holocaust,* a television docu-drama appeared. Following that, a wave of writing and research about the Holocaust began. Survivors' testimonies began to be recorded in earnest and stored by Yale University in its Fortunoff Archive. In the early 1990s, we got Art Spiegelman's "mice" books, *Maus I* and *Maus II,* as well as Steven Spielberg's *Schindler's List.* The Holocaust Museum in Washington, D.C., opened to promote the study of democratic values ("The Museum's primary mission is to advance and disseminate knowledge about this unprecedented tragedy; to preserve the memory of those who suffered; and to encourage its visitors to reflect upon the moral and spiritual questions raised by the events of the Holocaust as well as their own responsibilities as citizens of a democracy" *www.ushmm.org/mission.html*); the Museum of Tolerance opened in Los Angeles to promote tolerance. What do these works and institutions reflect about the America that received them? How do they enhance the study of the Holocaust?

Appendix B: A Compendium of Stories, Poems, Memoirs, and Videos

Stories

Lucien's Story, Kroh, Aleksandra (Chapter 4)
"The Shawl," Cynthia Ozick (Chapter 10)
"A Spring Morning," Ida Fink (Chapter 5)
"This Way for the Gas, Ladies and Gentlemen," Tadeusz Borowski (Chapter 8)
"Three Gifts," I. L. Peretz (Chapter 3)

Poems

"Babi Yar," Yevgeny Yevtushenko (Chapter 5)
"The Colonel," Carolyn Forche (Chapter 2)
"The Dance," Siamanto (Chapter 2)
"The Hangman," Maurice Ogden (Chapter 2)
"The Locket," Willa Schneberg (Chapter 2)
"Never Again," Wu Tang (Chapter 9)
"On Trial," Primo Levi (Chapter 9)
"Shema," Primo Levi (Chapter 9)
"A Song at the End of the World," Czeslaw Milosz (Chapter 5)
"Things That Are Worse Than Death," Sharon Olds (Chapter 2)

Video, Documentary

America and the Holocaust (Chapter 4)
Anne Frank Remembered (Chapter 6)
Assignment: Rescue (Chapter 4)
Daring to Resist (Chapter 6)
Facing Hate (Chapters 2, 7)
Hate.com (Chapter 3)
Holocaust (Chapter 5)
The Holocaust on Trial (Chapter 7)
Into the Arms of Strangers (Chapter 6)
The Long Way Home (Chapter 12)
Kovno Ghetto (Chapter 5)
The Master Race (Chapter 7)
Night and Fog (Chapter 9)
One Survivor Remembers (Chapter 10)
Shoah, excerpts (Chapter 9)
To Speak the Unspeakable: The Message of Elie Wiesel (Chapter 8)
Voices from the Attic (Chapter 6)
The Warsaw Ghetto (Chapter 5)
Witness: Voices from the Holocaust (Chapter 12)

Video, Full-Length Feature

Au Revoir les Enfants (Chapters 4, 6)
Escape from Sobibor (Chapter 6)
Europa, Europa (Chapter 6)
The Diary of Anne Frank (Chapter 6)
The Garden of the Finzi-Continis (Chapter 9)
The Killing Fields (Chapters 2, 3)
Schindler's List (Chapter 7)
The Wannsee Conference (Chapter 7)
Under the Domim Tree (Chapter 12)

Play

Incident at Vichy (Chapter 4)

Memoir

Auschwitz: True Tales from a Grotesque Land, Sara Nomberg-Przytyk (Chapter 10)

The Diary of Anne Frank (Chapter 5)

The Good Old Days, excerpt (Chapter 7)

I Have Lived a Thousand Years, by Livia Bitton-Jackson (Chapter 10)

I was a Doctor in Auschwitz, Dr. Gisella Perl (Chapter 10)

Justyna's Narrative, Gusta Davidson Draenger (Chapter 6)

Martin Luther and the Nuremberg Laws (Chapter 3)

Maus I, Art Spiegelman (Chapters 5, 12)

Maus II, Art Spiegelman (Chapters 8, 12)

Mein Kampf (Chapter 3)

Night, Elie Wiesel (Chapter 8)

The Sunflower, Simon Wiesenthal (Chapter 11)

Survival in Auschwitz, Primo Levi (Chapter 9)

Glossary

Aktion/Action   Soldiers and police sweeping through the ghetto to cull out and arrest Jews.

Anti-Semitism   Hatred for Jews.

Auschwitz   A death camp in Poland where 1.5 million Jews were killed.

Babi Yar   A suburb of Kiev where 33,771 Jews were killed by Einsatzgruppen.

"Canada"   Name given to warehouse at the camps for goods confiscated from arriving prisoners.

Chaldean   A Christian from Iraq.

Einsatzgruppen   German killing squads.

Ghetto   An area of a city where Jews are restricted.

Haftling   A detainee or prisoner.

Holocaust   With a capital "H," Holocaust refers to the German extermination of six million Jews, with a small "h," holocaust means a sacrificial offering consumed by fire.

Jim Crow Laws   Laws in the American South designed to subjugate African Americans.

Jude   German for "Jew."

Judenrat   A Jewish committee in the ghetto.

Judenrein   German for "Jew free."

Lager   German for concentration camp, often referred to in German as KZ, for Konzentrationslager

Midrash   An interpretation of a passage from the Hebrew Scriptures.

Musselman/Muselman/Muslim   A derogatory term for a prisoner who is among the walking dead. The reference to "Muslim" may refer to those who wrapped their heads in bandages which resembled turbans.

Nazi   A member of Hitler's National Socialist German Workers' Party.

Nuremberg Laws   Laws passed in Germany in 1935 and 1938 to subjugate and deprive Jews of the rights of citizenship.

Shoah   Hebrew for Holocaust, conflagration.

Survivor   A Jew who spent the war years in Europe, whether in hiding or in the camps.

Swastika   A symbol with four arms bent at right angles; a symbol of the Third Reich, *also* a Hindu symbol for prosperity and a native American design.

Yiddish   Language of Eastern European Jews written with Hebrew characters.

Zadik   Hebrew for righteous person.

Works Cited

Adalian, Robin. 1991. "Teaching About Genocide," February. Vol. 55, No. 2, *www.hyeetch.nareg.com.au/genocide/story4_p1.html*.

The American Experience: America and the Holocaust: Deceit and Indifference. 1994. PBS.

Anne Frank Remembered. 1996. Columbia TriStar Home Video Entertainment.

Arendt, Hannah. 1963. *Eichmann in Jerusalem: A Report on the Banality of Evil.* New York: Penguin Books.

Assignment: Rescue: The Story of Varian Fry and the Emergency Rescue Committee. 1998. (Black-and-white and color, 26 minutes), (*www.almondseed.com/fry*) New York: Richard Kaplan Productions.

Balakian, Peter. 1998. *Black Dog of Fate: A Memoir.* New York: Broadway Books.

Bartov, Omer. 2000. "Once Again I've Got to Play General to the Jews" from the war diary of Blutordenstrager Felix Landau, *The Holocaust: Origins, Implementation, Aftermath.* New York: Routledge. Originally in Klee, Ernst, Dressen, Willi, and Riess, Volker (eds). 1991. *"The Good Old Days": The Holocaust as Seen by Its Perpetrators and Bystanders.* Burnstone, Deborah, trans. New York: The Free Press.

Bernstein, Richard. 1995. *Review* An Obsession with Anne Frank: Meyer Levin and the Diary. *The New York Times,* September 27.

Bettleheim, Bruno. 1960. *Harpers.* November.

Bitton-Jackson, Livia. 1999. *I Have Lived a Thousand Years.* New York: Aladdin Paperbacks.

Bolkosky, Sid. 2000. Voices Vision: Holocaust Survivor Oral Histories. *http://holocaust.umd.umich.edu/*

Borowski, Tadeusz. 1976. *This Way for the Gas, Ladies and Gentlemen.* New York: Penguin Books.

Cage, Nicholas. 1996. *Eleni.* New York: Ballantine Publishing Group.

Cohen, Roger. April 27, 2001. "Where G.I.'s Were Consumed by the Holocaust's Terror: A Filmmaker Helps Thaw Memories of Wartime Guilt. *The New York Times.*

Daring to Resist: Three Women Face the Holocaust. 2000. PBS/Martha Lubel Productions.

Desowitz, Bill. May 7. 2000. *The New York Times.*

Draenger, Gusta Davidson. 1996. *Justyna's Narrative.* Amherst: The University of Massachusetts Press.

Eban, Abba. 1984. *Heritage: Civilization & the Jews.* New York: Summit Books.

Escape from Sobibor. 1987. Zenith Productions. Avid Home Entertainment.

Facing Hate with Bill Moyers and Elie Wiesel. 1991. New York: Mystic Fire Video.

Fink, Ida. 1987. *A Scrap of Time.* New York: Schocken Books.

Fink, Ida. 1997. *Traces.* New York: Metropolitan Books.

Forche, Carolyn. 1978. "The Colonel," in *The Country Between Us.* New York: Harper Collins.

Fortunoff Video Archive for Holocaust Testimonies, Yale University, tape A-67: testimony of Bessie K.

Frank, Anne. 1991. *The Diary of a Young Girl: The Definitive Edition.* New York: Bantam Books.

Fry, Varian. 1945. *Assignment: Rescue.* New York: Scholastic Inc.

Furman, Harry, ed. *The Holocaust and Genocide: A Search for Conscience: An Anthology for Students.* Online. Educators' Resource Center. *www.holocaustcommission.org/educator_resources/miligram.html 3/12/00.*

Ganor, Solly. 1995. *Light One Candle.* New York: Kodansha Press.

The Garden of the Finzi-Continis. 1971. Vittorio de Sica, director. Foreign Films.

Goldhagen, Daniel J. 1997. *Hitler's Willing Executioners: Ordinary Germans & the Holocaust.* New York: Vintage Books.

Goodrich, Frances and Hackett, Albert. 1995. *The Diary of Anne Frank.* 20th Century Fox Home Entertainment.

Gourevitch, Philip with Terri Gross. National Public Radio interview. Fresh Air, 10/7/98. *whyy.org/cgi-gin/F Ashowretrieve.cgi?2574*

Gourevitch, Philip. 1998. *We Regret to Inform You That Tomorrow We Will Be Killed with Our Families: Stories from Rwanda.* New York: Farrar, Straus & Giroux.

Gutman, Israel. Editor-in-Chief. 1990. *Encyclopedia of the Holocaust, Volume 2.* New York: MacMillan.

Halo, Thea. 2000. *Not Even My Name: From a Death March in Turkey to a New Home in America, a Young Girl's True Story of Genocide & Survival.* New York: Saint Martin's Press.

HATE.COM: Extremists on the Internet. 2000. HBO.

Heger, Heinz. 1994. *The Men with the Pink Triangle.* Los Angeles: Alyson Books.

Heritage: Civilization and the Jews #4: The Crucible of Europe. 1984. Films Incorporated (60 minutes).

Heritage: Civilization and the Jews #8: Out of the Ashes. 1984. Films Incorporated (60 minutes).

Hilberg, Raul. l985. *Destruction of the European Jews,* Student Edition. New York and London: Holmes & Meier.

Hitler, Adolf. trans. Manheim, Ralph. 1943. *Mein Kampf.* New York: Houghton Mifflin.

Holocaust. 1978. Republic Pictures.

The Holy Scriptures: A Jewish Bible According to the Masoretic Text. 1972. "Leviticus," XVI, 21–22. Tel Aviv: Sinai Publishing.

. . . *I Never Saw Another Butterfly* . . . : *Children's Drawings and Poems from Terezin Concentration Camp, 1942–1944.* 1978. New York: Schocken Books.

Judgment at Nuremberg. 1997. MGM.

The Killing Fields. 1996. Warner Home Video.

Klein, Gerda Weissmannn. 1995. *All But My Life.* New York: Hill and Wang.

Kovno Ghetto: A Buried History. 1997. A&E Television Networks, The History Channel, producer/director/writer, Herbert Kronsey, writer/narrator, Sir Martin Gilbert, marketed and distributed in U.S. by New Video Group, 126 Fifth Avenue, NY l00ll. (100 minutes)

Kroh, Aleksandra. Wainhouse, Austryn. 1996. *Lucien's Story.* Evanston, Illinois: Northwestern University Press.

Langer, Lawrence L. 2000. Foreword to *Witness: Voices from the Holocaust.* New York: The Free Press.

The Last Days. 1999. Survivors of the Shoah Visual History Foundation.

Levi, Primo. 1992. *Collected Poems.* New York: Faber & Faber.

Levi, Primo. 1993. *The Reawakening.* New York: Touchstone.

Levi, Primo. 1993. *Survival in Auschwitz: The Nazi Assault on Humanity.* New York: Touchstone.

Life Is Beautiful (subtitled). 2000. Buena Vista Home Video.

Lipstadt, Deborah. 1993. *Denying the Holocaust: The Growing Assault on Truth & Memory.* New York: The Free Press.

The Long Way Home. 1997. Academy award, Best Documentary, Moriah Finis of the Simon Wiesenthal Center and Seventh Art Releasing (120 minutes).

Lustig, Arnost. Nemcova, Jeanne. 1976. *Darkness Casts No Shadows,* in *Truth and Lamentation: Stories and Poems on the Holocaust.* Urbana, Illinois: The University of Chicago Press.

Malle, Louis. 1987. *Au Revoir les Enfants.* Orion Home Video.

Miller, Arthur. 2000. "Guilt and *Incident at Vichy.*" In *Echoes Down the Corridor: Collected Essays, 1944–2000.* New York: Viking.

Miller, Arthur. 1965. *Incident at Vichy.* New York: Penguin Books.

Miller, Judith. 1990. *One by One by One: Facing the Holocaust.* New York: Simon and Schuster.

Night and Fog (subtitled). 1955. France: Video Yesteryear.

Nomberg-Przytyk, Sara. Translated by Roslyn Hirsch. Edited by Eli Pfefferkorn and David Hirsch. 1985. *Auschwitz: True Tales from a Grotesque Land.* Chapel Hill: The University of North Carolina Press.

Nova: Holocaust on Trial. 2000. PBS.

Novick, Peter. 1999. *The Holocaust in American Life.* Boston: Houghton Mifflin Company.

Obedience: The Milgram Experiment. 1965. Film, 16 mm, 44 minutes. New Haven: Yale University.

Olds, Sharon. 1989. "Things That Are Worse Than Death." In *The Dead and the Living,* New York: Knopf.

One Survivor Remembers. 1995. Direct Cinema Limited.

Ozick, Cynthia. October 6. 1997. "Who Owns Anne Frank?" *The New Yorker.*

Ozick, Cynthia. 1990. *The Shawl.* New York: Vintage Books.

Paxton, Robert O. October 16. 1997. "Vichy on Trial," *The New York Times,* (*search.nytimes.com/search/daily/bin/fastweb?getdoc+site+17268+4++*)

The People's Century, 1900–1999: The Master Race. 1997. PBS Video, WBGH Boston and BBC. (Color and black-and-white, running time: 60 minutes)

Peretz, Isaac L. 1996. "Three Gifts." In *The I. L. Peretz Reader,* New York: Random House Value Publishing, Incorporated.

Peretz, Isaac L. 1995. "Three Gifts," read by Joanna Gleason, Tape 3, in *Jewish Short Stories from Eastern Europe and Beyond.* National Yiddish Book Center and KCRW. (to order: 800-973-7437)

Perl, Gisella. 1948. *I Was a Doctor in Auschwitz.* North Stratford, NH: Ayer Company.

Piercy, Marge. 1994. "The Housing Project at Drancy." In *Truth and Lamentation: Stories and Poems on the Holocaust.* University of Illinois Press: Urbana and Chicago.

Porton, Gary G. 1999. "Scapegoat." In *The World Book Encyclopedia.* Online. Chicago.

The Producers. 1999. Avco Embassy.

Sachs, Nelly. 1967. "O, the Chimneys," in *O, the Chimneys: Selected Poems, Including the Verse Play, Eli.* New York: Farrar, Straus & Giroux.

Schneberg, Willa. 2000. "The Locket," in *American Poetry Review.* January/February.

Schindler's List. 1993. Los Angeles: Universal Studios Home Video.

Schwarz, Daniel R. 1999. *Imagining the Holocaust.* New York: St. Martin's Press.

Shoah. 1985. New Yorker Video.

Shoah: An Oral History of the Holocaust. 1985. New York: Pantheon Books.

Siamanto. 1915. *www.hyeetch.nareg.com.au/genocide/story4_p1.html.*

The Sorrow and the Pity. 2000. Image Entertainment.

Spiegelman, Art. 1986. *Maus I: My Father Bleeds History.* New York: Pantheon Books.

Spiegelman, Art. 1991. *Maus II: A Survivors Tale: And Here My Troubles Began.* New York: Random House.

Spiegelman, Art. 1994. *The Complete Maus.* CD-ROM: Voyager. (to order: *www.earth-resources.net/p246.htm*)

State of Florida Commissioner's Task Force on Holocaust Education Website, "Mission Statement." *holocaust.fiu.edu/* 2/10/00.

Steinberg, Paul. 2000. *Speak You Also: A Survivor's Reckoning.* New York: Metropolitan Books.

Stout, David. 2000. "No Place for John Wayne at Indian Bureau," *The New York Times,* September 22, A12.

There Once Was a Town. 2000. Washington, D.C.: WETA (124 minutes).

"36 Questions About the Holocaust." Museum of Tolerance Online Multimedia Learning Center. *motlc.Wiesenthal.com/resources/questions/index.html.*

Under the Domim Tree. 1995. Israel: Screen Entertainment Ltd.

United States Holocaust Memorial Museum. *www.ushmm.org/education/guidelines.html.*

United States Holocaust Memorial Museum Guidelines for Teaching About the Holocaust. *www.ushmm.org/education/guidelines.html.*

Voices from the Attic. 1993. Santa Monica, CA: Direct Cinema Limited (57 minutes).

Wannsee Conference. 1987. Directed by Heinz Schirk. Prism Entertainment.

The Warsaw Ghetto. 1969. London: BBC (51 minutes).

Weitzman, Mark. 1988. "Coming to Grips with teaching the Holocaust." In *Momentum: Journal of the National Catholic Educational Association,* Museum of Tolerance, Online Multimedia Learning Center, *motlc .weisenthal.com/resources/education/teacherintro/index.html*

"Why Teach the Holocaust?" Holocaust Memorial Center, West Bloomfield, Michigan, *holocaustcenter.org/*

Wiesel, Elie. 1976. *Messengers of God: Biblical Portraits and Legends,* New York: Simon and Schuster

Wiesel, Elie. 1999. "The Question of Genocide." *Newsweek,* April 12.

Wiesel, Elie. l990. "The Nobel Address and The Nobel Lecture." In *From the Kingdom of Memory*. New York: Schocken Books.

Wiesel, Elie. 1990. "Bitburg," in *From the Kingdom of Memory: Reminiscences*. New York: Schocken Books.

Wiesel, Elie. 1967. *Night*. New York: Bantam Books.

Wiesel, Elie. 1978. "Then and Now: the Experiences of a Teacher." *Social Education* 42: 266–71.

Wiesenthal, Simon. 1997. *The Sunflower: On the Possibilities and Limits of Forgiveness*. New York: Schocken Books.

Winter, Miriam. 1997. *Trains*. Jackson, Michigan: Kelton Press.

Witness: Voices from the Holocaust. 1999. Joshua Greene Productions, Inc.

Wu-Tang. 1998. "Never Again," on the *Killa Bees* CD. Los Angeles: Priority Records.

Index

All But My Life, 139
Allen, Woody, 43
America and the Holocaust: Deceit and Indifference, 50, 175
American Civil Liberties Union, 35–36
American GIs, 111
Amnesty International, 24
Anne Frank Remembered, 74, 80, 174
Annie Hall, 43
Anti-defamation League, 35–36
Arendt, Hannah, 4, 49–50, 63–64, 94, 116, 135
Armenian genocide, 7, 8–9, 23
Arnost, Lustig, 144
Asner, Ed, 29
Assignment: Rescue, 44, 46–47, 175
Au Revoir les Enfants, 41–42
The Auschwitz Album, 109, 166
Auschwitz/Birkenau, xvi, xix, 28, 50, 54, 56–57, 73, 74, 77, 80, 81, 88, 98, 101, 102, 107, 108, 109–10, 112–25, 134, 135–36, 140–46, 156, 159, 166
Auschwitz: True Tales from a Grotesque Land, 141–42, 156

Babi Yar, 41, 70
Babi Yar, 70, 72
Bartov, Omer, 86
Beethoven, Ludwig Van, 103–4
Begnini, Roberto, 131
Beloved, 10
Berg, Mary, 67
Berga, 111

Bergen-Belson, 77
Bergman, Rabbi Aaron, 116
Bernstein, Michael Andre, 118
Bettleheim, Bruno, 78
Bitton-Jackson, Livia, 134–36, 139–40
Bolkosky, Sid, 161–62
Bomba, Abraham, 128–29
Borowski, Tadeusz, 109–10
Brandes, Philip, 48
Brecht, Bertolt, 44
Breton, Jaqueline and André, 44
Brooks, Mel, 130
Burke, Edmund, 38
Burnfes, Alexander 63, 64, 67

Cambodia, xx, 12–13, 22, 25
"Canada," 109–10
Canto of Ulysses, 117
Chagall, Marc, 44, 146
Chelmno, 56, 128
Childbirth in Camp C, 140
Children:
    French, 38, 43, 167
    hidden, 74–84, 163, 165–66
Chiles, Governor Lawton, xvii
Churchill, Winston, 37, 41, 50
The Colonel, 7, 11–13, 40
Columbine High School, 4, 16, 52, 139
Concentration camps:
    Auschwitz, xvi, xix, 28, 50, 54, 56–57, 73, 74, 77, 80, 81, 88, 98, 102, 107, 108, 109–10, 112–25, 134, 135–36, 140–46, 156, 159, 166
    Berga, 111

Concentration camps (*cont.*)
  Bergen-Belson, 77
  Chelmno, 56, 128
  Maidanek, 56
The Crucible, 47

Dalai Lama, 153
The Dance, 7, 8–10, 40
Dante, xix, xxiii, 21, 112, 117
Daring to Resist, 75, 84–85, 173
de Sica, Vittorio, 113
de Beauvoir, Simone, 127
Deuteronomy, 114
Denying the Holocaust, 98
The Diary of a Young Girl, xi, xv–xvi, xxii,
    51, 74–81, 86, 174–6
Didactic poetry, 40
Draenger, Gusta Davidson, 75, 84
Drancy, 43

Eban, Abba, 26, 28, 33–34, 175
Eichman Trial, 98
Eichmann in Jerusalem, 4, 49–50, 63–64,
    94, 116, 135
Einsatzgruppen, 29, 92, 95–98
Eisenhower, Dwight D., xi, 163
Eishyshok, 29
El Salvador, 11
Elek, Judit, 107
Eliach, Yaffa, 29
Eliot, T. S., 70–71
Escape from Sobibor, 75, 85
Europa, Europa, 75, 83
Euthanasia, 34, 108

*Facing Hate with Elie Wiesel and Bill
    Moyers*, 37, 50, 107
Faulkner, William, 143
Final Solution, 54, 73
Fink, Ida, 53, 68–70
Florida, Holocaust education,
    xviii–xix
Forché, Carolyn, 7, 11–13, 40
Found poem, 106
Frank, Anne, xi, xv–xvi, xxii, 51, 70, 74–
    81, 86, 174–76
France:
  children, 38, 43

collaboration, 43
  Vichy government, 43, 44, 47
Fry, Varian, 44, 46–47

Ganor, Solly, 71, 97
The Garden of the Finzi-Continis, 113, 175
Gilbert, Martin, 108–9
Gilligan, Carol, 142–43
Goeth, Amon, 87–88
Goldhagen, Daniel Jonah, 4, 92
The Good Old Days, 92
Goodrich, Francis, 78
Goodstein, Debbie, 81
Gorman, Irna, 162, 165–66
Gourevitch, Philip, xx
Green, Gerald, 63, 66–67, 86
Guernica, 55
Guggenheim, Charles, 111
Gypsies, 27, 49, 74, 108, 141

Habe, Jose, 153
Hackett, Albert, 78
Handicapped, 108
The Hangman, 40
Harrison, Earl G., 163
Hate sites, 35–37
Hate.com, 37, 99, 175
Heger, Heinz, 109–11
*Heritage: Civilization and the Jews: Out of
    the Ashes*, 33–34
*Heritage: Civilization and the Jews:
    The Crucible of Europe*, 26–
    28, 175
Heschel, Abraham Joshua, 153
Hidden children, 74–84, 163, 165–66
Hilberg, Raul, 27
Hillel, 42
Hirsch, David, 84
Hirsch, Roslyn, 84
History Place, 95, 119
Hitler, 23, 32–33, 41, 46, 47, 49, 56, 64–
    65, 83, 123, 130, 155
Hitler's Willing Executioners, 4, 92
Holocaust, 63, 66–67, 86, 176
Holocaust education (Florida), xiii–xix
Holocaust Memorial Center, West
    Bloomfield, 39, 164–65
Holocaust on Trial, 98–99, 175

Homosexuals, 36, 74, 108, 109–11
The Housing Project at Drancy, 43

I Have Lived a Thousand Years, 134–36, 139–40, 174
I Never Saw Another Butterfly . . ., 148–49
I Was a Doctor in Auschwitz, 140–42, 144
Iliad, 100–1
Incident at Vichy, xi, 47–50, 175
Into the Arms of Strangers, 81
Irving, David, 98

Jim Crow Laws, 26
Job, 24, 49, 101, 122, 134, 147–48
Judenrat, 63–64, 66, 74
Justyna's Narrative, 75, 84

Keneally, Thomas, 87
Kiev, 70
Killa Bees, 132–33
The Killing Fields, 25
Kindertransport, 81
Klarsfeld, Serge, 43
Klein, Gerda Weissman, ix–xi, 96–97, 135, 137–39, 146, 174–75
Klein, Kurt, ix–xi, 138
Kohlberg, Laurence, 93–94, 142
Kosovo, 39
Kovno Ghetto, 54, 63, 65–67, 167
Krakow, 84
Krakow Ghetto, 54
Kristallnacht, 21, 34, 112, 167
Kroh, Alexsandra, 42

Ladue, Scott, 171
Landau, Felix, 92
Langer, Lawrence, 158
Lanzmann, Claude, 85, 127–30
The Last Days, 107–8, 162, 174
Le Chambon, 38, 167
The Lemon, 144
Levi, Primo, xi, xxi, 8, 54, 112–18, 125–27, 136, 113–16, 135–36, 141, 144, 153, 160, 174, 176
Levin, Meyer, 78–9
Leviticus, 3–4
The Life and Lie of Franco, 55
Life is Beautiful, 131–32

Light One Candle, 71, 97
Lipstadt, Deborah, 98
A Living Torch, 141–42, 156
The Long Way Home, 163
The Locket, 7, 12–13, 25, 40
Lost Children of Berlin, 162
Lucien's Story, 42
Luther, Martin, 25–26

Maidanek, 56
Malle, Louis, 41–42
Mann, Heinrich, 44
Masson, André, 44
The Master Race, 33–34, 175–76
Maus, xi, xxi, xxii, 54–62, 74, 108, 158–60, 173–76
Mein Kampf, 32–33
The Men With the Pink Triangle, 109–11
Mengele, Dr. Josef, 46, 141, 143,
Mentally ill, 108
Milgram, Stanley, 4, 97–98
Miller, Arthur, xi, xxii, 47–50
Miller, Judith, ii, 48
Milosz, Czeslaw, 70–71
Morrison, Toni, 10
Moyers, Bill, 37
Museum of Tolerance, 22, 21, 167
Mussolini, Benito, 113

Nanes, Laura, 18
Never Again, 132–33, 173
Niemoller, Reverend Martin, 39–40
Night, xi, xvi, xxii, 8, 57, 11–19, 100–9, 112, 117, 122, 139, 158, 173–76
Night and Fog, 123–25, 173, 176
Nomberg-Prytyk, Sara, 141–42, 156
Novick, Robert, xviii, 28
Nuremberg Laws, 26, 28, 34, 54, 57, 125, 127
Nuremburg Trials, 34, 98, 123, 124, 125, 127, 150

O, The Chimneys, 147–48
Ogden, Maurice, 40
Olds, Sharon, 7, 9–10, 40, 70
Olère, David, 118
Olympics—Berlin, 167
On Trial, 125–27

One Survivor Remembers, 137–39, 146, 174
Ophuls, Marcel, 43
Ozick, Cynthia, 75, 77, 79, 80–81, 144–47, 173, 175

Papon, Maurice, 43
Paragraph 111, 175
Partisans, 73, 74, 85
Pasternak, Abraham, 161–62
Patton, General George S., 163
Paxton, Robert O., 43
Perelman, Solly, 83
Peretz, I. L., 28–29
Perl, Gisella, 140–42, 144
Picasso, Pablo, 55
Piercy, Marge, 43
Plowzov Ghetto, 54
Poems:
  found, 106
  observation, 146
  persona, 147
  witness, 7–20
Political prisoners, 108–9
Prince, Jen, 18–19
The Producers, 130–31
Putnick, Bethany, 119–20

Rap music, 132–33
The Reawakening, 160
Renais, Alain, 123–25
Rise and Fall of the Third Reich, xvi
Rollo, Katie, 19
Roosevelt, Franklin, 37, 41, 50
Rosa, 144, 146
Rwanda, xx, 39

Sachs, Nelly, 147–48
Sagon, Ginetta, 24
St. Louis (ship), 51
Scapegoating, 3–4
Schindler, Oskar, x, 42, 87, 90
Schindler's List, 42, 54, 78, 86–91, 107–8, 147, 162, 174–76
Schneberg, Willa, 7, 12–13, 25, 40
Schwarz, Daniel, xviii, xxi, 75
A Scrap of Time, 68
Second generation, xvi, 3, 30, 54, 58, 59, 157, 158–60

Shapero, William, 111
The Shawl, 144–47, 173, 175
Shema, 113–16
Shepherd, Matthew, 4
Shirer, William, xvi
Shoah, 85, 127–30
Siamanto, 7, 8–10, 40, 146
Simon Wiesenthal Center, 30, 62, 70, 167, 176
Simulations, 44–6
Sobibor, 56, 73, 75, 85
A Song at the End of the World, 70–71
Sonderkommandos, 118
The Sorrow and the Pity, 43
The Sound and the Fury, 143
Soviet prisoners of war, 108, 110
Speak You Also: A Survivor's Reckoning, 118, 157–58
Spiegelman, Art, xi, xxi, xxii, 54–62, 74, 108, 158–60, 173–76
Spielberg, Steven, 42, 54, 86–91, 107–8, 147, 162, 174
A Spring Morning, 68–70
Srebnik, Simon, 128
Stakhiv, Stephen, 170
Steinberg, Paul, 118, 157–58
Sugihara, Chiune, 71, 167
The Sunflower: On the Possibilities and Limits of Forgiveness, xi, xxii, 151–56
Survival in Auschwitz, 8, 54, 112–18, 122, 135–36, 173–76
Survivors of the Holocaust, 162
Survivors of the Shoah Visual History Foundation, 86, 107–8, 162
Survivors: Testimonies of the Holocaust, 162
Swastika, 30–32, 56–7, 60, 61, 62

Talmud, 89
There Once Was a Town, 29
Things Worse Than Death, 7, 9–10, 40, 70
This Way for the Gas, Ladies and Gentlemen, 109–10
To Speak the Unspeakable: The Message of Elie Wiesel, 107
Traces, 68
Trains, 75
Treblinka, 56, 73, 128

The Three Gifts, 28–29
Thureau, Becky, 17

Under the Domim Tree, 163–64
United States Holocaust Memorial Museum, xi, xxi, 21, 29, 34–35, 39, 44, 62, 65, 67, 83, 91, 119, 123, 167, 174

The Value of a Piece of String, 142
VanHelden, Julie, 120–21
Vichy, France, 43, 44, 47
Violin Concerto in D, Opus 61, 103–4
Voices from the Attic, 75, 81–82

Wannsee Conference, 73, 91–92
Warsaw, 71
Warsaw Ghetto, 54, 62–65, 67, 71, 74, 167

The Warsaw Ghetto, 63–64, 67, 74, 127, 167
Weitzman, Mark, 22
Who Owns Anne Frank?, 75, 79
Wiesel, Elie, xi, xvi, xxii, 5, 8, 22, 24, 37, 38, 41, 50–51, 57, 100–9, 112, 122, 117, 139, 158, 160, 173–76
Wiesenthal, Simon, xi, xxii, 151–56
Winter, Miriam, 75, 82
Witness: Voices from the Holocaust, 158, 162, 175
Wu Tang, 132–33, 173

Yad Vashem, 82, 107, 119, 166–67
Yevtushenko, Yevgeny, 70, 72, 173

Zuckerman, Itzhak, 127
Zyclon-B, 98, 109

Please remember that this is a library book,
and that it belongs only temporarily to each
person who uses it. Be considerate. Do
not write in this, or any, library book.

DATE DUE

SE 18 '0?			
NO 14 '03			